THE *M*USIC ADDRESS BOOK

W9-CFO-436

THE
*M*USIC
ADDRESS
BOOK

HOW TO REACH

ANYONE

WHO'S ANYONE

IN MUSIC

MICHAEL LEVINE

PERENNIAL LIBRARY

HARPER & ROW, PUBLISHERS, New York
Grand Rapids, Philadelphia, St. Louis, San Francisco
London, Singapore, Sydney, Tokyo, Toronto

THE MUSIC ADDRESS BOOK. Copyright © 1989 by Michael Levine. All rights reserved. Printed in the United States of America. No part of this book may be used or repro- duced in any manner whatsoever without written permission except in the case of brief quotations embodied in critical articles and reviews. For information address Harper & Row, Publishers, Inc., 10 East 53rd Street, New York, N.Y. 10022.

FIRST EDITION

Designed by Abigail Sturges

Library of Congress Cataloging-in-Publication Data

Levine, Michael.
    The music address book : how to reach anyone who's anyone in
music / by Michael Levine. — 1st ed.
        p.   cm.
    ISBN 0-06-096383-2
    1. Popular music—Directories.   I. Title.
ML17.L4   1989
781.64'025—dc20   89-45102

89 90 91 92 93 CC/RRD 10 9 8 7 6 5 4 3 2 1

Without music, life would be a mistake.

—Friedrich Nietzsche

*After silence, that which comes nearest
to expressing the inexpressible is music.*

*To all those who give us the music that begins
where words leave off . . . this book is dedicated.*

—Michael Levine

CONTENTS

ACKNOWLEDGMENTS

Writing, or in my case compiling, a book is a unique experience. It's a little like putting a special message into a bottle and releasing it into the sea. You are never quite sure who it will reach or when.

I owe much to the following people for helping me launch this book:

My new literary agent and friend, Alice Martell.

A friend who guided me through the music industry maze and helped make this project possible, Sal Manna.

My family: Arthur, Marilyn, and Patty Levine.

My office family: Kim Akhtar, Mark Armstrong, Sue Bennett, Marla Capra, June Anne Chalfant, Tracy Flores, Stephanie Kavoulakos, Monique Moss, Marc Powell, Marcee Rondan, Mitchell Schneider, Laura Sterrett, Jeff Wagner, Mike Webb, and Leah Marie West.

My special friends: Rana Bendixen, Betsy Borns, Ken Bostic, Bill Calkins, Susan Gauthier, Richard Imprescia, Bette Jackson, Richard Lawson, Karen L'Heureux, Nancy Mager, John McKillop, Ruth Opolion, Dennis Prager, Heidi Rotbart, and Erline White.

My business associates: Lloyd Braun, Beth Cadman, John Colter, Dick DeBlois, Marc Graboff, Wayne Mejia, Renie Millman, and Diana Reisdorf.

HOW TO USE THIS BOOK

The world of popular music is an enormously large one. There are artists in rock, country, jazz, R&B, pop, blues, gospel, ethnic, big band, middle-of-the-road, and folk, plus newer genres such as rap, heavy metal, adult contemporary, and new age. Behind the scenes are record producers, songwriters, record company executives, journalists, disc jockeys, music video directors, and on and on. I have attempted to include as many of the most important people as possible, ranging over as many musical styles as there are, all in this one volume.

It was often difficult deciding whether someone should be included. To those inadvertently left out, my apologies. To those who were considered but did not make the final cut, maybe you will next time.

For fans, here's your opportunity to write to your favorite artists. For musicians, here are the people who can help you get ahead in the music industry. For both, remember that as in any entertainment field people tend to move and change addresses frequently—as do agents, managers, record companies, and so on. I have included the latest and most reliable addresses anywhere. Even if a person is no longer there by the time you mail a letter, it's a start in tracking that person to his or her current business address. I strongly urge you not to show up in person to those included here, but rather to send a letter. It's professional and it's courteous.

For behind-the-scenes talent, I've identified what they're largely known for, such as record production or songwriting. However, I haven't separated or identified performers with a particular musical style. The way I look at it, music is *music,* not *labels.* Diversity and new horizons are what music is about—and, in its own way, what this book is about too. Enjoy!

IF YOU ARE A MUSICIAN . . .
GETTING YOUR MUSIC HEARD

Everyone in the music business is looking for that tremendously talented artist and that Number One hit. But no record company executive, music publisher, agent, manager, or producer knows who that artist is or what that song sounds like—until he or she hears it. That's why they are on a never-ending talent search. But while some may attend live performances, most spend the majority of their time listening to demo tapes. Each and every day they listen to dozens of tapes, trying to find an undiscovered but gifted songwriter or musician.

Many of these tapes reach them via mail or are delivered to their offices. Some come recommended, others are unsolicited. If yours is in the latter category, being heard, and heard promptly, will be tougher but by no means impossible. If your song is good, it doesn't make any difference who you are. They will want you.

So, how do you get your music heard? You've already taken an important step by having this book in your hands. You now have the names and direct addresses of many of the people who can help you with your career. Write or call them and ask if they are accepting new material. Never send a demo to the A&R (Artist & Repertoire) department of a record company without specifying an individual's name. If you do, your music may end up in the circular file.

The following are some of the most commonly asked questions about breaking into the music business and hopefully some helpful answers:

Q. What is a demo?
A. In the music business, people want to hear your work, not read it. Sometimes you'll get the chance to play it for a producer or record company executive in person. But more often than not, you'll need to deliver your work to them, and that's done in the form of an audio tape. A demonstration tape, or demo, is a simply but professionally produced four-song audio cassette, engineered in a recording studio.

Q. *How do I mail or deliver my demo?*

A. Use a padded envelope or small box to present your demo. If it's coming "over the transom" (i.e., you're sending it to a stranger), give it the best chance for success by using a printed or typed return address on the envelope, preferably using a business name. Sloppily-written and illegible addressing will hardly show a stranger that you're a serious, professional artist. You can send your demo first-class, but if you're doing a mass mailing and need to save money, there is also a less expensive class of mail specifically for audio record-ings. Tell the counter person at your local post office that enclosed is an audio cassette. If there is also a letter enclosed, tell the postal employee that too. You'll be charged the going rate for a first-class letter, but the rest of the weight will be at the lower fee.

Q. *What do I say in the cover letter?*

A. Every demo should include a cover letter. If not, it will be tossed away. If you have an agent, manager, otherwise-important-person, or friend of the addressee who can make sure that you'll be paid attention to, have them write the letter, on their letterhead.

In the cover letter, briefly explain who you are (a photo might be useful, too). Ask for the addressee's comments, suggestions, etc. Be friendly and creative but also get to the point. There's no need to go on about how "this is the next Number One record." Music industry professionals know it's not that easy. It will signal to them that you're new to the business, and that means more work for them.

Q. *What else should I include in the envelope?*

A. Make certain your name, address, and telephone number are written on the tape. Also, include a list of the songs in the order they're heard on the tape and a typed lyric sheet for each song, again with your name, address, telephone number, and the copyright no-tice on each. Just as important (if you want a response or want the tape returned) include a self-addressed, stamped envelope.

Q. *I'm worried about someone stealing my song. How can I protect my rights when I send a tape of my music?*

A. Once you write a song, it's yours, you own it. But it's best if you *register* that copyright with the government. Registration makes it much easier in a court of law if there is ever a problem. You can do this by registering your copyright with the U.S. Library of Con-gress Copyright Office. You will need either Form PA (for music sheets or song lyrics) or Form SR (for sound recordings). Form SR covers the recording itself as well as the music and lyrics that have been recorded. So if you use Form SR, you don't need to use Form PA. You can get the necessary forms by writing the Copyright Office, Library of Congress, Washington, D.C. 20559; or calling the 24-hour hotline number (202) 287-9100 and telling the message machine which forms you need. You can also pick up forms at any U.S. Government Printing Office.

When you complete and return the forms, you will also need to include one non-returnable copy of the work, whether a song or lyric sheet, or a tape cassette. Copyright registration costs $10 for each separate work. However, if you are registering many songs and want to save a few dollars, simply send all your songs on one cassette. For the $10 fee, they will all be copyrighted at once, provided you give the collection a single title. Even something as simple as "The Works of Jane Smith" will do. If you want the individual titles listed too, file Form CA with another $10 fee.

After filing, you will receive a certification. You may then print a copyright notice on your work. The notice should read: Copyright (Year) by (Your Name). Copyright protection lasts for 50 years after the death of the last surviving writer of the song.

If you need further information, call the Copyright Office at (202) 287-8700, or write to the Information and Publications Section, LM-455, Copyright Office, Library of Congress, Washington, D.C. 20559.

AVOIDING RIPOFFS

Here are some professional tips (from interviews with leaders within the music industry) for avoiding ripoffs.

• Never pay a company to connect you with a collaborator. If you need a collaborator, try searching for organizations that offer collaboration services to their members.

• Don't pay to have your lyrics or poems set to music. For a fee, "music mills" might use the same tune for hundreds of lyrics and poems, whether it sounds good or not. Publishers will identify one of these melodies as soon as they hear it.

• Don't pay to have your songs published. An established company interested in your songs will assume the responsibility *and* the cost of promoting your work. That company invests in your song because it anticipates a profit once the song is recorded and released.

• Never sell your songs unconditionally. It's dishonest for anyone to offer you such a deal.

• Don't pay to have your material "reviewed" by a company that may be interested in recording, producing, or publishing it. Distinguished companies review material free of charge as a means of searching for hits for their artists or recording projects. Of course, consultation and critique by another songwriter, or by someone not in search of original material, is a different matter.

• Read all contracts carefully before signing. Never sign any contract you're in doubt about or don't understand. Never assume that any contract is better than no contract at all. Remember it's well worth paying an attorney to review a contract before you sign it, thus avoiding a bad situation later that may cost you thousands of dollars in royalties if your song becomes a hit.

ARE YOU ANYONE?

The Music Address Book is updated regularly, and you can play an active role in this procedure. If you are notable in any field (or know someone who is), send your name, mailing address, and some documentation of your notability (newspaper clippings are effective) for possible inclusion in our next edition.

Also, we are very interested in learning of any success stories that may have resulted from *The Music Address Book.*

Write to:

Michael Levine, Author
The Music Address Book
8730 Sunset Blvd., Sixth Floor
Los Angeles, CA 90069

If you have found *The Music Address Book: How to Reach Anyone Who's Anyone in Music* to be useful, you may also find its predecessors, *The Address Book: How to Reach Anyone Who's Anyone* and *The Corporate Address Book: How to Reach the 1,000 Most Important Companies in America* (Perigee), of assistance. In *The Corporate Address Book,* we present, in an easy-to-use format, the direct addresses and phone numbers of the thousand most important companies in America, companies that affect each of our lives.

WRITE TO ME

*Whatever happens to us in our lives, we find questions con-
stantly recurring that we would like to discuss with some friend. Yet
it is hard to find just the right friend that we should talk to. Often
it is easier to write to someone whom we do not ever expect to
see . . .*

—Eleanor Roosevelt

During the last few years, I have received tens of thousands of
letters, ranging from loving to vituperative, from owners of *The
Address Book* and *The Corporate Address Book*. Despite the over-
whelming task of answering this mail, I rather enjoy the letters.

It takes a little getting used to, receiving letters from people you
don't know, but I have, and it's actually a joy.

Please, a couple of rules if you write:

• Remember to include a self-addressed, stamped envelope. For
reasons of both time and expense, this is the only way that I can
respond to mail. Unfortunately, I've had to draw the line: no SASE,
no reply.

• I need your comments. While I confess that I'm partial to
success stories, all comments from purchasers of the book have
helped me a great deal with future editions, so fire away. As Colonel
Oliver North said, "The good, the bad, and the ugly."

• Many people have written to request addresses of people not
listed in the book. As much as I would like to, I simply can't open up
this can of worms. Requests for additional addresses are carefully
noted and considered for inclusion in future editions.

• Receiving a photo from someone who writes adds an entirely
new dimension to the letter, so feel free. After all, from the photo on
the back cover, you know what I look like, and I'm rather anxious to
see you.

Keep those cards and letters coming.

Michael Levine
8730 Sunset Blvd.
Sixth Floor
Los Angeles, CA 90069

THE ADDRESSES

The A Strings
P.O. Box 120897
Nashville, TN 37212

A&M Recording
1416 N. La Brea Ave.
Hollywood, CA 90028
Recording studio

ABC
9200 Sunset Blvd. (PH 15)
Los Angeles, CA 90069

AC/DC
11 Leominster Rd.
Morden, Surrey SM4, England

ASCAP (American Society of Composers, Authors and Publishers)
One Lincoln Plaza
New York, NY 10023
Performing rights organization

AWGO Prods.
16–18 Beak St.
London W1R 3HA, England
Music video producers/directors

a-ha
P.O. Box 203
Watford WD1 3YA, England

Aaberg, Philip
P.O. Box 227
Bloomington, IN 47402

Abba
P.O. Box 2072 S-100 41
Stockholm, Sweden

Abbado, Claudio
c/o CAMI
165 W. 57th St.
New York, NY
Classical conductor

Abbey Road Studios
3 Abbey Rd.
St. John's Wood
London NW8 9AY, England

Abbott, Elliott
21241 Ventura Blvd. (#251)
Woodland Hills, CA 91364
Personal manager

Abbott, Gregory
P.O. Box 68
Bergenfield, NJ 07621-0068

Abdul, Paula
151 El Camino Dr.
Beverly Hills, CA 90212

Abercrombie, John
234 Cabot St. (#6)
Beverly, MA 01915

Abrams, Lee
6500 River Chase Circle E.
Atlanta, GA 30328
Radio programming consultant

Academy of Country Music
6255 Sunset Blvd. (#915)
Hollywood, CA 90028

Accept
Am Angelsdorn 47
D-5024 Pulheim, West Germany

The Accused
c/o Combat Records
187-07 Henderson Ave.
Hollis, NY 11423

Ackerman, Will
c/o Windham Hill Records
247 High St.
Palo Alto, CA 94305
Record company executive

Acuff, Roy
2510 Franklin Rd.
Nashville, TN 37204

Acuff-Rose-Opryland Music
2510 Franklin Rd.
Nashville, TN 37204
Music publisher

Adams, Bryan
406–68 Water St.
Vancouver, BC V6B 1A4, Canada

Adams, Gayle
2 Professional Dr. (#240)
Gaithersburg, MD 20879

Adams, George
P.O. Box 201
Wageningen, Holland

Adams, Johnny
c/o Rounder Records
1 Camp St.
Cambridge, MA 02140

Adams, Pepper
c/o Uptown
276 Pearl St.
Kingston, NY 12401

Addison, John
3815 W. Olive Ave. (#202)
Burbank, CA 91505
Film composer

Adler, Lou
c/o A&M Records
1416 N. La Brea Ave.
Hollywood, CA 90028
Record producer

The Adventures
Unit 32, Ransomes Docks
35–37 Parkgate Rd.
London SW11 4NP, England

Aerosmith
P.O. Box 4668
San Francisco, CA 94101
Fan club

Affirmation
c/o Passport Jazz
3619 Kennedy Rd.
S. Plainfield, NJ 07080

Age of Chance
c/o Virgin Records
9247 Alden Dr.
Beverly Hills, CA 90210

The Agency
41 Britain St. (#200)
Toronto, ON M5A 1R7, Canada
Booking agent

Agency for the Performing Arts
9000 Sunset Blvd. (#1200)
Los Angeles, CA 90069
Booking agent

Agent
c/o S.L. Feldman
1534 W. 2nd Ave.
Vancouver, BC V6J 1H2, Canada

Air Supply
c/o Arista Records
6 W. 57th St.
New York, NY 10019

Akiyoshi, Toshiko
5820 Wilshire Blvd. (#301)
Los Angeles, CA 90036

Alabama
c/o Dale Morris
818 19th Ave. S.
Nashville, TN 37203

Alago, Michael
c/o Elektra Records
75 Rockefeller Plaza
New York, NY 10019
A&R executive

• **The Alarm**
3 E. 54th St. (#1400)
New York, NY 10022

Albert, Christine
c/o CBS Records
34 Music Square E.
Nashville, TN 37203

Albright, Gerald
10100 Santa Monica Blvd. (#1600)
Los Angeles, CA 90067

The Album Network
120 N. Victory Blvd.
Burbank, CA 91502
Radio and record tip sheet

Alden, Rick
c/o Elektra Records
75 Rockefeller Plaza
New York, NY 10019
Record company executive

Aldo Nova
c/o Pearlman
228 W. 55th St.
New York, NY 10019

Aldrich, Jeff
c/o Chrysalis Records
645 Madison Ave.
New York, NY 10022
Record company executive

Alice
A + B Mgmt.
Via Lusardi, 5
Milan 20100, Italy

Alisha
1168 E. 73rd St.
Brooklyn, NY 11234

Allem
c/o Dick Scott
159 W. 53rd St.
New York, NY 10019

Allen, Andy
c/o Island Records
14 E. 4th St.
New York, NY 10012
Record company executive

Allen, Debbie
8730 Sunset Blvd. (PH W)
Los Angeles, CA 90069

Allen, Deborah
10100 Santa Monica Blvd. (#1600)
Los Angeles, CA 90067

Allen, Donna
10100 Santa Monica Blvd. (#1600)
Los Angeles, CA 90067

Allen, Peter
6 W. 77th St.
New York, NY 10023

Allen, Rex Jr.
900 19th Ave. S. (#201)
Nashville, TN 37212

Allen, Steve
15201 Burbank Blvd.
Van Nuys, CA 91411

Allison, Jerry
Route #1 (#222)
Lyles, TN 37098

Allison, Mose
P.O. Box 210103
San Francisco, CA 94121

Allman, Gregg
P.O. Box 4331
Marietta, GA 30061

Almeida, Laurindo
P.O. Box 1987
Studio City, CA 91604

Almo Irving Music
1358 N. La Brea Ave.
Hollywood, CA 90028
Music publisher

Almond, Marc
c/o Capitol Records
1750 N. Vine St.
Hollywood, CA 90028

Almost Brothers
c/o Sandy Neese
21 Music Square E.
Nashville, TN 37203

Alonso, Maria Conchita
8899 Beverly Blvd.
Los Angeles, CA 90048

Alpert, Herb
1416 N. La Brea Ave.
Hollywood, CA 90028

Alphaville
Ruedigerstr 95
5000 Koein 91, West Germany

Alston, Gerald
c/o Motown Records
6255 Sunset Blvd.
Los Angeles, CA 90028

Altschuler, Bob
c/o CBS Records
51 W. 52nd St.
New York, NY 10019
Record company executive

Alvin, Dave
c/o Vision Mgmt.
2112 N. Cahuenga Blvd.
Los Angeles, CA 90068

Alvin, Phil
c/o Vision Mgmt.
2112 N. Cahuenga Blvd.
Los Angeles, CA 90068

Alvin and the Chipmunks
4400 Coldwater Canyon (#300)
Studio City, CA 91604

Always, Billy
c/o Mitchell
1320 S. Lauderdale
Memphis, TN 38106

The Amazing Rhythm Aces
2980 Beverly Glen Circle (#302)
Los Angeles, CA 90077

America
8730 Sunset Blvd. (PH W)
Los Angeles, CA 90069

America's Top Ten
1037 N. Cole Ave.
Los Angeles, CA 90038
Music television series

American Famous Talent
816 W. Evergreen
Chicago, IL 60622
Booking agent

American Federation of Musicians
1501 Broadway (#600)
New York, NY 10019
Union

American Management
17530 Ventura Blvd. (#108)
Encino, CA 91316

American Music Awards
c/o Dick Clark Productions
3003 West Olive Ave.
Burbank, CA 91505

Ames, Durelle
c/o Our Gang
1012 16th Ave. S.
Nashville, TN 37212

Ames, Ed
c/o Robert Gewald
58 W. 58th St.
New York, NY 10019

Ampex Corp.
401 Broadway
Redwood City, CA 94063-3199
Audio equipment manufacturer

Amram, David
461 Sixth Ave.
New York, NY 10011

Amusement Business
49 Music Square W.
Nashville, TN 37203
Industry magazine

Ana
c/o E/P/A Records
51 W. 52nd St.
New York, NY 10019

Anderle, David
c/o A&M Records
1416 N. La Brea Ave.
Hollywood, CA 90028
A&R executive

Anderson, Ernestine
P.O. Box 845
Concord, CA 94522

Anderson, John
c/o MCA Records
1701 West End Ave.
Nashville, TN 37203

Anderson, Jon
c/o Arista Records
6 W. 57th St.
New York, NY 10019

Anderson, Laurie
c/o Gail Turner
530 Canal St.
New York, NY 10013

Anderson, Lynn
818 18th Ave. S.
Nashville, TN 37203-3219

Anderson, Ray
c/o E/P/A Records
51 W. 52nd St.
New York, NY 10019
Record company executive

Anderson, Tony
c/o Arista Records
6 W. 57th St.
New York, NY 10019
Record company executive

Andrews, Julie (Julia Wells)
c/o Triad
10100 Santa Monica Blvd.
16th Floor
Los Angeles, CA 90067

Andrews, Maxene
31308 Via Colinas (#109)
Westlake Village, CA 91362

Andrews, Patti
P.O. Box 1793
Encino, CA 91316

Angel
c/o ATI
888 Seventh Ave.
New York, NY 10019

Angel City
10100 Santa Monica Blvd. (#1600)
Los Angeles, CA 90067

Angelle, Lisa
c/o Capitol Records
1111 16th Ave. S.
Nashville, TN 37212

The Angels
141 Dunbar Ave.
Fords, NJ 08863

Angelus, Pete
c/o Diamond Dave Ent., Inc.
3960 Laurel Canyon Blvd.
Studio City, CA 91604
Personal manager

Animotion
P.O. Box 67037
Los Angeles, CA 90067

Anka, Paul
P.O. Box 100
Carmel, CA 93921

Ann, Sue
c/o MCA Records
70 Universal City Plaza
Universal City, CA 91608

Ann-Margret (Olsson)
1888 Century Park E. (#1400)
Los Angeles, CA 90067

Ant, Adam (Stuart Goddard)
45/53 Sinclair Rd.
London W14, England

Anthony, Christina
c/o Geffen Records
9130 Sunset Blvd.
Los Angeles, CA 90069
Record company executive

Anthony, Ken
c/o KSJO
1420 Koll Circle
San Jose, CA 95112
Program director/disc jockey

Anthony, Polly
c/o E/P/A Records
1801 Century Park W.
Los Angeles, CA 90067
Record company executive

Anthrax
P.O. Box 968
Old Bridge, NJ 08857

Anton, Susan
151 El Camino Dr.
Beverly Hills, CA 90212

Anvil
18653 Ventura Blvd. (#311)
Tarzana, CA 91356

Any Day Now
29 Lynton Rd.
Queenspark, London NW6,
England

Apollonia (Patty Kotero)
9000 Sunset Blvd. (#1200)
Los Angeles, CA 90069

April Wine
354 Youville St.
Montreal PQ H2Y 2C3, Canada

Arata, Tony
P.O. Box 5493
Hilton Head, SC 29938

Ardent Recording
2000 Madison Ave.
Memphis, TN 38111
Recording studio

Arkush, Allan
151 El Camino Dr.
Beverly Hills, CA 90212
Music video director

Armatrading, Joan
27 Queensdale Pl.
London W11, England

Armored Saint
P.O. Box 295
Temple City, CA 91780

Armoury Show
P.O. Box 3070 Uptown
Hoboken, NJ 07030

Armstrong, Frankie
c/o Folklore
1671 Appian Way
Santa Monica, CA 90401

Armstrong, Vanessa Bell
c/o The Covenant
8508 Wyngate St.
Sunland, CA 91040

Arnold, Eddy
P.O. Box 97
Brentwood, TN 37027

Arp Instruments
45 Hartwell Ave.
Lexington, MA 02173
Synthesizer manufacturer

Arrington, Steve
c/o General Talent
1700 Broadway
New York, NY 10019

The Art Of Noise
P.O. Box 119
London W11 4AN, England

ArtRock
225 E. Liberty Plaza
Ann Arbor, MI 48104
Rock poster art

Asher, Dick
c/o PolyGram Records
810 Seventh Ave.
New York, NY 10019
Record company executive

Asher, Peter
644 N. Doheny Dr.
Los Angeles, CA 90069
Producer/personal manager

**Ashford and Simpson
(Nickolas and Valerie)**
c/o Radio City Music Hall Prods.
1260 Ave. of the Americas
New York, NY 10020

Ashkenazy, Vladimir
c/o ICM
40 W. 57th St.
New York, NY 10019

Asia
c/o Sun Artists
9 Hillgate St.
London W8 7SP, England

Aslan
1888 Century Park E. (#1400)
Los Angeles, CA 90067

Asleep At The Wheel
6060 N. Central Expressway
(#428)
Dallas, TX 75205

Associated Booking Corp.
1995 Broadway
New York, NY 10023
Booking agent

The Association
9000 Sunset Blvd. (#1200)
Los Angeles, CA 90069

Astley, John
c/o Atlantic Records
75 Rockefeller Plaza
New York, NY 10019

Astley, Rick
c/o David Anthony Prods.
649 Knutsford Rd.
Latchford, Warrington
Cheshire WA4 1JJ, England

Aswad
c/o Wasted Talent
321 Fulham Rd.
London SW10 9QL, England

Atkins, Chet
806 17th Ave. S.
Nashville, TN 37203

Atkinson, Paul
c/o RCA Records
6363 Sunset Blvd.
Los Angeles, CA 90028
A&R executive

Atlanta Rhythm Section
727 Huston Rd.
Lawrenceville, GA 30245

Atlantic Starr
7080 Hollywood Blvd. (#602)
Los Angeles, CA 90028

Atlantic Studios
1841 Broadway
New York, NY 10023
Recording studio

Augustin, Nat
c/o In Time
11 Bellfield Ave.
Harrow Weald, Middlesex,
England

Austin, Chris
P.O. Box 120897
Nashville, TN 37212

Austin, Patti
10100 Santa Monica Blvd. (#1600)
Los Angeles, CA 90067

Autograph
17530 Ventura Blvd. (#105)
Encino, CA 91316

Autry, Gene
P.O. Box 710
Los Angeles, CA 90078

• **Autumn**
P.O. Box 252
Hollywood, CA 90078

Avalon, Frankie (Avallone)
230 W. 55th St. (#17D)
New York, NY 10019

Avalon Attractions
17835 Ventura Blvd. (#201)
Encino, CA 91316
Concert promoters

Avant, Clarence
c/o Tabu Prods.
9229 Sunset Blvd. (#311)
Los Angeles, CA 90069
Personal manager

The Average White Band
3 E. 54th St. (#1400)
New York, NY 10022

Avis, Meiert
19 W. 21st St. (#703)
New York, NY 10024
Music video director

Axe, Lillian
P.O. Box 93789
Los Angeles, CA 90093-0789

Axton, Hoyt
3135 Cedarwood Dr. (#614)
Tahoe City, CA 95730

Axton, Mae B.
P.O. Box 1077
Hendersonville, TN 37075
Songwriter

Ayeroff, Jeff
c/o Virgin Records
9247 Alden Dr.
Beverly Hills, CA 90210
Record company executive

Ayers, Roy
1860 Broadway (#1518)
New York, NY 10023

Aykroyd, Dan
9200 Sunset Blvd. (#428)
Los Angeles, CA 90069

Aznavour, Charles
(Varenagh Aznourian)
4 Rue de Lieules
78 Galluis, France

Azoff, Irving
c/o MCA Records
70 Universal City Plaza
Universal City, CA 91608
Record company executive

Aztec Camera
10100 Santa Monica Blvd.
(#1600)
Los Angeles, CA 90067

Azymuth
P.O. Box 1040
Nitreroi 24000, Brazil

The B 52's
c/o Direct Mgmt.
945A N. La Cienega Blvd.
Los Angeles, CA 90069

BAM
5951 Canning St.
Oakland, CA 94609
Fan magazine

BB&Q
233 W. 26th St. (#1W)
New York, NY 10001

Blvd.
c/o MCA Records
70 Universal City Plaza
Universal City, CA 91608

BMG Music
1133 Ave. of the Americas
New York, NY 10036
Music publisher

BMI (Broadcast Music, Inc.)
8730 Sunset Blvd.
Los Angeles, CA 90069
Performing rights group

Babineau, Marko
c/o Geffen Records
9130 Sunset Blvd.
Los Angeles, CA 90069
Record company executive

Babylon
c/o Arista Records
6 W. 57th St.
New York, NY 10019

Bacharach, Burt
10100 Santa Monica Blvd.
16th Floor
Los Angeles, CA 90067
Songwriter

Bachman-Turner Overdrive
c/o S.L. Feldman
1534 W. 2nd Ave.
Vancouver, BC V6J 1H2, Canada

The Back Door
P.O. Box 410
Utica, NY 13503
The Doors tribute act

Backer, Steve
c/o E/P/A Records
51 W. 52nd St.
New York, NY 10019
Music video executive

Backstage
5150 Wilshire Blvd. (#302)
Los Angeles, CA 90036
Industry magazine

Bad Company
1790 Broadway (PH)
New York, NY 10019

Baez, Joan
P.O. Box 1026
Menlo Park, CA 94025

Bailey, Pearl
P.O. Box L
Lake Havasu City, AZ 86403

Bailey, Philip
28405 Sand Canyon Rd. (#A)
Canyon Country, CA 91351

Bailey, Razzy
P.O. Box 2977
Hendersonville, TN 37077

Baillie and the Boys
P.O. Box 40661
Nashville, TN 37204

Baker, Anita
c/o BNB
9545 Wilshire Blvd.
Beverly Hills, CA 90212

Baker, Butch
c/o Gayle Ents.
51 Music Sq. E.
Nashville, TN 37203

Baker, Cary
c/o IRS Records
100 Universal City Plaza
(Bldg. 422)
Universal City, CA 91608
Publicity executive

Baker, Dave
15123 Sherman Way (#202)
Van Nuys, CA 91405

Baker, Jay
c/o WFBQ
6161 Fall Creek Rd.
Indianapolis, IN 46220
Disc jockey

Baker, Linda
c/o Reprise Records
3300 Warner Blvd.
Burbank, CA 91510
Record company executive

Balaam and the Angel
c/o Chapter 22
6 New St.
Warwick CV34 4RX, England

The Balancing Act
100 Universal City Plaza
(Bldg. 422)
Universal City, CA 91608

Baldry, Long John
41 Britain St. (#200)
Toronto, ON M5A 1R7, Canada

Baldwin Piano and Organ
1801 Gilbert Ave.
Cincinnati, OH 45202
Instrument manufacturer

Balin, Marty
10 Waterville St.
San Francisco, CA 94124

Balis, Rick
c/o KSHE
700 Union Station Annex
St. Louis, MO 63103
Radio station program director

Ball, David
c/o RCA Records
30 Music Square W.
Nashville, TN 37203

Ball, Marcia
8306 Appalachian Dr.
Austin, TX 78759

Ball, Patrick
c/o Nancy Carlin
1930 Cameron Ct.
Concord, CA 94518

Ballard, Hank (and the Midnighters)
c/o T. MacNeil Mgmt.
11457 Harrisburg Rd.
Los Alamitos, CA 90720

The Bama Band
c/o Entertainment Artists
819 18th Ave. S.
Nashville, TN 37203

Bambaataa, Afrika
200 W. 51st St. (#1410)
New York, NY 10021

Bambi Slam
c/o Warner Bros. Records
3300 Warner Blvd.
Burbank, CA 91510

Bananarama
40 Weymouth St.
London W1, England

Bandy, Moe
1609 Hawkins St.
Nashville, TN 37203

The Bangles
4455 Torrance Blvd.
Suite 4455
Torrance, CA 90503
Fan club

Banks, Tony
25 Ives St.
London SW3, England

Bannon, R.C.
P.O. Box 23110
Nashville, TN 37202

Barackman, Michael
c/o EMI-Manhattan Records
1370 Ave. of the Americas
New York, NY 10019
A&R executive

Barber, George
25 Juniper Lane
Riverside, CT 06878
Big Band expert

Barbieri, Gato
200 W. 51st St. (#1410)
New York, NY 10019

Barbis, Dino
c/o Warner Bros. Records
3300 Warner Blvd.
Burbank, CA 91510
Record company executive

Barbutti, Pete
P.O. Box 3819
La Mesa, CA 92044

Bardeaux
611 Palm St. (#F)
La Habra, CA 90631

Bardens, Pete
P.O. Box 775
Bryn Mawr, PA 19010

Bare, Bobby
59 Music Square W.
Nashville, TN 37203

Bar-Kays
c/o PolyGram Records
810 Seventh Ave.
New York, NY 10019

Barlow, Barriemore
c/o De Novo
18808 Topanga Beach Rd.
Malibu, CA 90265

Barnes, Jimmy
P.O. Box 314, Vaucluse
Sydney, NSW, Australia

Baron, Peter
c/o Geffen Records
9130 Sunset Blvd.
Los Angeles, CA 90069
Music video executive

Barren Cross
1252 Aviation Blvd. (#A-133)
Redondo Beach, CA 90278

Barris, Chuck
1990 S. Bundy Dr. (PH)
Los Angeles, CA 90025
Creator of Gong Show

Barron, Steve
49 W. 27th St. (#903)
New York, NY 10001
Music video director

Barry, Jeff
9100 Sunset Blvd. (#200)
Los Angeles, CA 90069
Record producer

Barry, John
c/o BMI
8730 Sunset Blvd.
Los Angeles, CA 90069
Film composer

Barsalona, Frank
c/o Premier Talent Agency
3 E. 54th St.
New York, NY 10022
Booking agent

Bart-Milander Associates
4146 Lankershim Blvd. (#300)
N. Hollywood, CA 91602
Agent for film/TV composers

Basia
c/o Epic Records
51 W. 52nd St.
New York, NY 10019

Count Basie Orchestra
111 Eighth Ave. (#1501A)
New York, NY 10011

Basil, Toni
9595 Wilshire Blvd. (#505)
Los Angeles, CA 90212
Choreographer/singer

Bass Desires
P.O. Box 396
Beverly, MA 01915

Bassey, Shirley
Villa Capricorn
55 Via Campione
6816 Bissone, Switzerland

Bates, Peg Leg
Kerhonkson, NY 12446

Bauman, Jon "Bowzer"
3168 Oakshire Dr.
Los Angeles, CA 90068

Baumgartner, Burt
c/o CBS Records
51 W. 52nd St.
New York, NY 10019
Record company executive

Baumstein, Ken
c/o EMI-Manhattan Records
1370 Ave. of the Americas
New York, NY 10019
Record company executive

Bay City Rollers
27 Preston Grange Rd.
Preston Pans, E.
Lothian, Scotland

Beach Boys
101 Mesa Lane
Santa Barbara, CA 93109

Bearsville Recording Studio
Speare Rd.
Bearsville, NY 12409

Beastie Boys
298 Elizabeth St.
New York, NY 10012

The Beat
P.O. Box 29820
Los Angeles, CA 90029
Third World music magazine

The Beat Farmers
c/o Denny Bruce
2667 N. Beverly Glen Blvd.
Bel Air, CA 90077

Beat Rodeo
434-A E. 89th St. (#122)
New York, NY 10128

> Beatle Fan
P.O. Box 33515
Decatur, GA 30033
Fan magazine

> Beatlemania
8665 Wilshire Blvd. (#208)
Beverly Hills, CA 90211
Tribute act

The Beau Brummels
17620 Sherman Way (#8)
Van Nuys, CA 91406

Beau Nasty
c/o WTG Records
1801 Century Park W.
Los Angeles, CA 90067

Beausoleil
c/o Folklore
1671 Appian Way
Santa Monica, CA 90401

Beauvoir, Jean
c/o Overland
1775 Broadway
New York, NY 10019

Beck, Curtis
c/o Enigma Records
1750 E. Holly Ave.
El Segundo, CA 90245
Record company executive

Beck, Jeff
c/o Ernest Chapman
11 Old Lincoln's Inn
London WC2, England

Beckett, Barry
1609 Roy Acuff Pl.
Nashville, TN 37203

The Bee Gees
(Barry, Maurice, and Robin Gibb)
P.O. Box 8179
Miami Beach, FL 33139-0179

Beefheart, Captain
(Don Van Vliet)
P.O. Box 1897
San Francisco, CA 94101

Beggars Banquet
P.O. Box 6152
New York, NY 10128
Rolling Stones fan newsletter

> Belafonte, Harry
P.O. Box 1700
Ansonia Station
New York, NY 10023

Bell, Archie
1780 Century Circle (#4)
Atlanta, GA 30345

Bellamy Brothers
P.O. Box 3153
Winter Haven, FL 33880

Belle, Regina
c/o Worldwide
641 Lexington Ave.
New York, NY 10022

Bellson, Louie
P.O. Box L
Lake Havasu City, AZ 86403

The Belmonts
c/o Mars Talent
168 Orchid Dr.
Pearl River, NY 10965

Below Zero
c/o EMI-Manhattan Records
1370 Ave. of the Americas
New York, NY 10019

Benatar, Pat (Andrejewski)
c/o New Star
60 W. 70th St.
New York, NY 10023

Bendett, David
2431 Briarcrest Rd.
Beverly Hills, CA 90210
Booking agent

Benedetti, Robert
Sunset Strip Tattoo
8418 Sunset Blvd.
Los Angeles, CA 90069
Rock 'n' roll tattoo artist

Benesch, Marc
c/o CBS Records
51 W. 52nd St.
New York, NY 10019
Record company executive

Bennett, Alex
c/o KITS
1355 Market St. (#152)
San Francisco, CA 94103
Disc jockey

Bennett, Bill
c/o MCA Records
70 Universal City Plaza
Universal City, CA 91608
Record company executive

Bennett, Tony
101 W. 5th St.
New York, NY 10019

Benoit, David
555 W. 57th St. (#1228)
New York, NY 10019

Benson, George
c/o Ken Fritz
444 S. San Vicente Blvd.
Los Angeles, CA 90048

Bentall, Barney
151 John St. (#301)
Toronto, ON N5V 2T2, Canada

Benton, Barbi
8425 W. Third St. (#307)
Los Angeles, CA 90048

Berger, Bill
c/o Island Records
14 E. 4th St.
New York, NY 10012
Record company executive

Berger, Larry
c/o WPLJ
1330 Ave. of the Americas
New York, NY 10019
Radio station program director

Bergman, Alan and Marilyn
c/o Freedman, Kinzelberg &
Broder
1801 Ave. of the Stars
Los Angeles, CA 90067
Songwriters

Bergman, Jo
c/o Warner Bros. Records
3300 Warner Blvd.
Burbank, CA 91510
Music video executive

Berlin, Irving (Israel Baline)
1290 Sixth Ave.
New York, NY 10019

Berman, David
c/o Capitol Records
1750 N. Vine St.
Hollywood, CA 90028
Record company executive

Bernardo, Mike
c/o CBS Records
51 W. 52nd St.
New York, NY 10019
Record company executive

Bernsen, Randy
15123 Sherman Way (#202)
Van Nuys, CA 91405

Bernstein, Adam
49 W. 27th St. (#903)
New York, NY 10001
Music video director

Bernstein, Elmer
1801 Ave. of the Stars (#911)
Los Angeles, CA 90067
Film composer

Bernstein, Leonard
24 W. 57th St.
New York, NY 10019
Classical composer/conductor

Bernstein, Peter
c/o Neal Levin
9595 Wilshire Blvd. (#505)
Beverly Hills, CA 90212
Film composer

Berry, Chuck (Charles Berry)
Berry Park, Buckner Rd.
Wentzville, MO 63385

Betancourt, John
c/o PolyGram Records
810 Seventh Ave.
New York, NY 10019
Record company executive

Bettman, Gil
10000 Santa Monica Blvd. (#305)
Los Angeles, CA 90067
Music video director

Betts, Dickie
40 W. 57th St.
New York, NY 10019

Between The 222
Bilderdijkpark 4A
Amsterdam 1052 RZ,
The Netherlands

Beug, John
c/o Warner Bros. Records
3300 Warner Blvd.
Burbank, CA 91510
Record company executive

Bhatia, Amin
P.O. Box 775
Bryn Mawr, PA 19010

Biafra, Jello
150 Fifth Ave. (#1002)
New York, NY 10011

Bicknell, Ed
c/o Damage Mgmt., Ltd.
10 Southwick Mews
London WZ 1JG, England
Personal manager

Big Audio Dynamite
c/o Overland
1775 Broadway
New York, NY 10019

Big Country
c/o ATI
888 Seventh Ave.
New York, NY 10106

Big Heat
Rondor House
10A Parsons Green
London SW6 4TW, England

Big Mouth
2980 Beverly Glen Circle (#302)
Los Angeles, CA 90077

Big Pig
P.O. Box 276
Albert Park, VIC 3206, Australia

Big Twist and the Mellow Fellows
c/o American Famous
816 W. Evergreen
Chicago, IL 60622

Biggs, Bob
c/o Slash Records
7381 Beverly Blvd.
Los Angeles, CA 90036
Record company executive

Bikel, Theodore
Money Hill Rd.
Georgetown, CT 06829

Billboard
1515 Broadway
New York, NY 10036
Industry magazine

Billy & The Beaters
1015 N. Fairfax Ave.
Los Angeles, CA 90046

Bingenheimer, Rodney
c/o KROQ
3500 W. Olive Ave.
Burbank, CA 91505
Disc jockey

Bisceglia, Rick
c/o Arista Records
6 W. 57th St.
New York, NY 10019
Record company executive

Bishop, Elvin
338 Village Lane
Los Gatos, CA 95030

Bishop, Stephen
c/o MCA
70 Universal Plaza
Universal City, CA 91608

Bitch
c/o Good Sport
4547 Kraft Ave.
N. Hollywood, CA 91302

BizRap
c/o Choices
Brotman Medical Center
3828 Delmas Terrace
Culver City, CA 90230
Musicians' drug/alcohol treatment

Black
c/o A&M Records
1416 N. La Brea Ave.
Hollywood, CA 90028

Black, Clint
c/o RCA Records
30 Music Square W.
Nashville, TN 37203

Black Entertainment Television
4217 Wheeler Ave.
Alexandria, VA 22304

Black Flag
P.O. Box 1
Lawndale, CA 90260

Black Music Association
1500 Locust St.
Philadelphia, PA 19102

Black 'N Blue
P.O. Box 6709
Portland, OR 97228-6709

Black Oak Arkansas
487 Red Fox Run
Lilburn, GA 30247-2473

Blacker, Ira
c/o Mr. I. Mouse, Ltd.
920 Dickson St.
Marina del Rey, CA 90292
Personal manager

Blackwell, Chris
c/o Island Records
14 E. 4th St.
New York, NY 10012
Record company executive

Blackwood, James
5180 Park Ave.
Memphis, TN 38117

Blackwood, Nina
c/o Entertainment Tonight
5555 Melrose Ave.
Los Angeles, CA 90038
Music reporter

Blackwood Singers
P.O. Box 17272
Memphis, TN 38187

Blade, Richard
c/o KROQ
3500 W. Olive Ave.
Burbank, CA 91505
Disc jockey

Blades, Ruben
1674 Broadway (#703)
New York, NY 10019

Blake, Norman and Nancy
P.O. Box 9188
Colorado Springs, CO 80932

Blakeley, Peter
c/o Capitol Records
1750 N. Vine St.
Hollywood, CA 90028

Blakely, Ronee
400 S. Beverly Dr. (#216)
Los Angeles, CA 90212

Blakey, Art
c/o Bridge
106 Fort Green Place
Brooklyn, NY 11217

Bland, Bobby Blue
3500 W. Olive Ave. (#740)
Burbank, CA 91505-4628

Blast!
19431 Business Center Dr.
Northridge, CA 91324
Fan magazine

The Blasters
2667 N. Beverly Glen
Los Angeles, CA 90077

Bley, Paul
P.O. Box 225, Village Station
New York, NY 10014

Block, Rory
c/o Concerted Efforts
110 Madison Ave.
Newtonville, MA 02160

Blood Brothers
c/o Zomba
1348 Lexington Ave.
New York, NY 10128

Blood, Sweat & Tears
8665 Wilshire Blvd. (#208)
Los Angeles, CA 90211

Bloodgood
P.O. Box 6023
Bellevue, WA 98008

Bloom, Ritch
c/o Capitol Records
1750 N. Vine St.
Hollywood, CA 90028
Record company executive

Blow, Kurtis (Walker)
c/o General Talent
1700 Broadway
New York, NY 10019

Blow Monkeys
c/o RCA Records
1133 Ave. of the Americas
New York, NY 10036

Blu, Peggi
P.O. Box 279
Hopkins, MN 55343

Blue Mercedes
c/o MCA Records
70 Universal City Plaza
Universal City, CA 91608

Blue Murder
c/o Geffen Records
9130 Sunset Blvd.
Los Angeles, CA 90069

Blue Nile
c/o Linn Records
235 Drakemire Dr.
Glasgow G45 952, Scotland, UK

Blue Oyster Cult
c/o Pearlman
228 W. 55th St.
New York, NY 10019

Blue Riddim Band
4901 Main (#218)
Kansas City, MO 64112

Blue Rodeo
c/o Atlantic Records
75 Rockefeller Plaza
New York, NY 10019

Bluegrass Music Association
P.O. Box 16
Elm Spring, AR 72728

Bobb, Merlin
c/o Atlantic Records
75 Rockefeller Plaza
New York, NY 10019
A&R executive

Boberg, Jay
c/o I.R.S. Records
100 Universal City Plaza
(Bldg. 422)
Universal City, CA 91608
Record company executive

Bobo, Willie
9220 Sunset Blvd. (#212)
Los Angeles, CA 90069

The Bobs
859 O'Farrell St.
San Francisco, CA 94109

BoDeans
c/o Reprise Records
3300 Warner Blvd.
Burbank, CA 91510

Bofill, Angela
c/o Moress-Nanas
2128 Pico Blvd.
Santa Monica, CA 90405

Bogguss, Suzy
c/o Capitol Records
1111 16th Ave. S.
Nashville, TN 37212

Bohannon, Bill
P.O. Box 18284
Shreveport, LA 71138

Bolling, Claude
155 W. 72nd St. (#706)
New York, NY 10023

Bolton, Michael
c/o Contemporary
Communications
155 E. 55th St.
New York, NY 10022

Bon Jovi
P.O. Box 4843
San Francisco, CA 94101
Fan club

Bonds, Gary "U.S." (Anderson)
141 Dunbar Ave.
Fords, NJ 08863

Bone, Mike
c/o Chrysalis Records
645 Madison Ave.
New York, NY 10022
Record company executive

Bonedaddys
143 S. Cedros Ave.
Solana Beach, CA 92075

Bonfire
4250 S. Olive St. (#115)
Denver, CO 80237
Fan club

Bono, Sonny (Salvatore)
1700 N. Indian Ave.
Palm Springs, CA 92262

The Boogie Boys
c/o Hush Prods.
231 W. 58th St.
New York, NY 10019

Boogie Down Productions
c/o General Talent
1700 Broadway
New York, NY 10019

Book of Love
c/o William Morris
1350 Ave. of the Americas
New York, NY 10019

Booker T. and the MGs
c/o Concerted Efforts
110 Madison Ave.
Newtonville, MA 02160

Boom Boom Boom
c/o New Thunder
8 Carnaby St.
London W1V 1PG, England

Boom Crash Opera
The Village Centre (#27A)
Kings Cross
Sydney, NSW 2011, Australia

The Boomtown Rats
44 Seymour
London W1, England

Boone, Debby
15315 Magnolia Blvd. (#208)
Sherman Oaks, CA 91403

Boone, Larry
604 Hill Rd.
Brentwood, TN 37027

Boone, Pat (Charles)
9255 Sunset Blvd. (#519)
Los Angeles, CA 90069

Bop
P.O. Box 2592
Hollywood, CA 90078
Teen magazine

Borge, Victor
Fieldpoint Park
Greenwich, CT 06830

Boston
1560 Trapelo Rd.
Waltham, MA 02154

Boston Pops Orchestra
301 Massachusetts Ave.
Boston, MA 02115

Bottom Line
15 W. 4th St.
New York, NY 10012
Nightclub

Botwin, Will
c/o Side One Mgmt.
1775 Broadway
New York, NY 10019
Personal manager

Boulez, Pierre
Postfach 22
Baden Baden,
West Germany
Classical composer/conductor

Bourgeois Tagg
P.O. Box 1994
San Francisco, CA 94101

Bowen, Jimmy
c/o Universal Records
1701 West End Ave.
Nashville, TN 37203
Producer/record company
executive

Bowers, Bryan
P.O. Box 9188
Colorado Springs, CO 80932

Bowie, David (Jones)
641 Fifth Ave. (#22Q)
New York, NY 10022

Box of Frogs
c/o Ernest Chapman
11 Old Lincoln's Inn
London WC2, England

Boxcar Willie
1300 Division St. (#103)
Nashville, TN 37203

Boxoffice
1800 N. Highland Ave. (#710)
Hollywood, CA 90028
Trade magazine

The Boxtops
2011 Ferry Ave. (#U-19)
Camden, NJ 08104

Boy George (O'Dowd)
153 George St.
London W1, England

Boy Meets Girl
c/o Direct Mgmt.
945A N. La Cienega Blvd.
Los Angeles, CA 90069

Boyce, Kim
P.O. Box 1889
Brentwood, TN 37027

Boyd, Liona
7060 Hollywood Blvd. (#1212)
Los Angeles, CA 90028

Boyd, Ray
c/o WVEE
120 Ralph McGill Blvd.
Atlanta, GA 30365
Radio station program director

Boylan, John
1801 Century Park W.
Los Angeles, CA 90067
Record producer

The Boys
c/o Motown Records
6255 Sunset Blvd.
Los Angeles, CA 90028

Boys Club
P.O. Box 1116
Minneapolis, MN 55458-1116
Fan club

Boys of the Lough
P.O. Box 7138
Berkeley, CA 94707

Brack, Steve
c/o WTG Records
1801 Century Park W.
Los Angeles, CA 90067
Record company executive

Brady, Paul
c/o Damage Mgmt.
10 Southwick Mews
London WZ 1JG, England

Bragg, Billy
35 Bravington Road
London W9 3AB, England

Brandmeier, Jonathan
875 N. Michigan Ave. (#3742)
Chicago, IL 60611
Disc jockey

Branigan, Billy
c/o DAS
83 Riverside Dr.
New York, NY 10024

Branigan, Laura
c/o General Talent
1700 Broadway
New York, NY 10019

Branson, Richard
c/o Virgin Ltd.
95 Ladbroke Grove
London W11, England
Record company executive

Breakfast Club
c/o Patrick Rains
8752 Holloway Dr.
Los Angeles, CA 90069

Breathe
c/o A&M Records Ltd.
136–140 New Kings Rd.
London SW6 4LZ, England

Brecker, Michael and Randy
234 Cabot St. (#6)
Beverly, MA 01915

Brendel, Alfred
c/o Colbeat
111 W. 57th St.
New York, NY 10019

Brenner, J.B.
c/o A&M Records
1416 N. La Brea Ave.
Hollywood, CA 90028
Record company executive

Breslauer, Jacobson, Rutman & Sherman
10880 Wilshire Blvd.
Los Angeles, CA 90024
Business managers

Brewer & Shipley (Mike and Tom)
c/o David Bendett
2431 Briarcrest Rd.
Beverly Hills, CA 90210

Brickell, Edie (and New Bohemians)
c/o Geffen Records
9130 Sunset Blvd.
Los Angeles, CA 90069

Bricklin
c/o Golden Guru
119 Cuthbert St.
Philadelphia, PA 19106

Bridenthal, Bryn
c/o Geffen Records
9130 Sunset Blvd.
Los Angeles, CA 90069
Publicity executive

Bridgewater, Dee Dee
P.O. Box 5617
Beverly Hills, CA 90210

Brighton Rock
P.O. Box 719, Station C
Queen St. W.
Toronto, ON M6J 3S, Canada

Briley, Martin
P.O. Box 7451
New York, NY 10022

Brill, Billy
c/o MCA Records
70 Universal City Plaza
Universal City, CA 91608
Record company executive

Britny Fox
P.O. Box 9
Audubon, NJ 08106

Britannia Row
35 Britannia Row
Islington, London N1 8QH,
England
Recording studio

Broadcasters
c/o Enigma Records
1750 E. Holly Ave.
El Segundo, CA 90245

Brodey, John
c/o Polydor Records
3800 Alameda Ave. (#1500)
Burbank, CA 91505
Record company executive

Brodey, Mavis
c/o MCA Records
70 Universal City Plaza
Universal City, CA 91608
Record company executive

Brody, Lane (and Tom Bresh)
P.O. Box 24775
Nashville, TN 37202

Broken Homes
c/o MCA Records
70 Universal City Plaza
Universal City, CA 91608

Bromberg, David
P.O. Box 9109
San Rafael, CA 94912

Bronski Beat
134 Wigmore St.
London W1, England

Bronson, Harold
c/o Rhino Records
2225 Colorado Ave.
Santa Monica, CA 90404
Record company executive

Brookins, Robert
c/o MCA Records
70 Universal City Plaza
Universal City, CA 91608

Brooklyn Bridge
141 Dunbar Ave.
Fords, NJ 08863

Brooklyn Dreams
1224 N. Vine St.
Los Angeles, CA 90038

Brooks, Elkie
c/o 8 Ball
134 Lots Rd.
London SW10, England

Brooks, Garth
c/o Capitol Records
1111 16th Ave. S.
Nashville, TN 37212

Brooks, Kix
c/o Capitol Records
1111 16th Ave. S.
Nashville, TN 37212

Brooks, Lonnie
P.O. Box 60234
Chicago, IL 60660

Bros
P.O. Box 276
London E27 BW, England

The Brothers Four
P.O. Box 135
Vashon, WA 98070

**Brothers Johnson
(George and Louis)**
c/o John McClain
1416 N. La Brea Ave.
Hollywood, CA 90028

Brothers Management
141 Dunbar Ave.
Fords, NJ 08863
Personal manager/booking agent

Broughton, Bruce
3815 W. Olive Ave. (#202)
Burbank, CA 91505
Film/TV composer

Brown, Bobby
18653 Ventura Blvd.
Suite 707
Tarzana, CA 91356
Fan club

Brown, Clarence "Gatemouth"
P.O. Box 958
Bogalusa, LA 70427

Brown, Dave
c/o WWDC
1150 Connecticut Ave.
Washington, DC 20036
Program director/disc jockey

Brown, James
218 W. 57th St. (#3A)
New York, NY 10019

Brown, Jay
6311 Romaine St. (#7311)
Los Angeles, CA 90038
Music video director

Brown, Jim Ed
P.O. Box 121089
Nashville, TN 37212

Brown, Jocelyn
200 W. 51st St. (#1410)
New York, NY 10019

Brown, Julie
c/o Sire Records
75 Rockefeller Plaza
New York, NY 10019

Brown, Julie
c/o MTV
1775 Broadway
New York, NY 10019
Veejay

Les Brown and His Band of Renown
P.O. Box 3996
Westlake Village, CA 91361

Brown, T. Graham
(Anthony Graham Brown)
c/o Starbound
128 Volunteer Dr.
Hendersonville, TN 37075

Brown, Tony
c/o MCA Records
1701 West End Ave.
Nashville, TN 37203
A&R executive

Browne, Jackson
1888 Century Park E. (#1400)
Los Angeles, CA 90028

Brownmark
c/o Motown Records
6255 Sunset Blvd.
Los Angeles, CA 90028

Brozman, Bob
c/o Rounder Records
1 Camp St.
Cambridge, MA 02140

Brubeck, Dave
601 Montgomery St.
San Francisco, CA 94111

Bruce, Ed
P.O. Box 120428
Nashville, TN 37212

Bruford, Bill
c/o EG Mgmt.
63A Kings Rd.
London SW3 4NT, England

Brunette
7095 Hollywood Blvd. (#104-348)
Hollywood, CA 90028
Fan club

Brunman, Glen
c/o E/P/A Records
1801 Century Park W.
Los Angeles, CA 90067
Publicity executive

Brusco, Charlie
1593 Monroe Dr.
Atlanta, GA 30324
Personal manager

Bryant, Anita
P.O. Box 899
Selma, AL 36701

Bryson, Peabo (Pepo)
c/o David Franklin
1290 S. Omni International
Atlanta, GA 30303

Buch, Danny
c/o Atlantic Records
75 Rockefeller Plaza
New York, NY 10019
Record company executive

Buckaroos
c/o OMAC
237 W. Yosemite Ave.
Manteca, CA 95336

Buckingham, Lindsay
c/o Warner Bros. Records
3300 Warner Blvd.
Burbank, CA 91510
Attn: Elaine Gellar

The Buckinghams
P.O. Box 82
Great Neck, NY 11021

Buckwheat Zydeco
227 E. 25th St. (#A)
New York, NY 10010

Buffalo, Norton
P.O. Box 2489
San Rafael, CA 94901

Buffalo Springfield Revisited
c/o Village Producers
1616 Butler Ave.
Los Angeles, CA 90025

Buffet, Jimmy
P.O. Box 480
Snowmass, CO 81654

The Buggles
22 St. Peters Sq.
London W69 NW, England

Buie, Buddy
3864 Oakcliff Court
Doraville, GA 30340
Record producer

Buie, Kim
c/o Island Records
6526 Sunset Blvd.
Los Angeles, CA 90028
A&R executive

Bulletboys
c/o Warner Bros. Records
3300 Warner Blvd.
Burbank, CA 91510

Bulley, Terence
23 Ramillies Place
London W1, England
Music video director

The Burch Sisters
c/o Mercury Records
10 Music Square S.
Nashville, TN 37203

Burdon, Eric
611 Broadway (#822)
New York, NY 10012

**Burkhart, Abrams, Douglas,
Elliot & Assoc.**
6500 Riverchase Circle E.
Atlanta, GA 30328
Radio programming consultants

Burks, Bill
c/o Capitol Records
1750 N. Vine St.
Hollywood, CA 90028
Record company executive

Burnett, T-Bone (J. Henry Burnett)
6255 Sunset Blvd. (#1214)
Hollywood, CA 90028

Burnette, Billy
10100 Santa Monica Blvd. (#1600)
Los Angeles, CA 90067

Burning Spear
c/o Fast Lane Prods.
4590 MacArthur Blvd., NW
Washington, DC 20007

Burns, Ralph
3815 W. Olive Ave. (#202)
Burbank, CA 91505
TV/film/theatre composer

Burnstein, Cliff
P.O. Box 3070 Uptown
Hoboken, NJ 07030
Personal manager

Burrell, Kenny
c/o Helen Keane
49 E. 96th St.
New York, NY 10128

Burtnik, Glen
1790 Broadway (PH)
New York, NY 10019

Burton, Gary
c/o Ted Kurland
173 Brighton Ave.
Boston, MA 02134

The Busboys
8833 Sunset Blvd. (PH W)
Los Angeles, CA 90069

Busby, Jheryl
c/o Motown Records
6255 Sunset Blvd.
Los Angeles, CA 90028
Record company executive

Busey, Gary
c/o Moress-Nanas Mgmt.
2128 Pico Blvd.
Santa Monica, CA 90405

Bush, Kate
c/o EMI-Manhattan
1370 Ave. of the Americas
New York, NY 10019

Bush, Stan
c/o ICM
40 W. 57th St.
New York, NY 10019

Butcher, Jon
c/o Pasha Music
5615 Melrose Ave.
Hollywood, CA 90038

Butler, George
c/o CBS Records
51 W. 52nd St.
New York, NY 10019
A&R executive

Butler, Henry
211 Thompson St. (#1D)
New York, NY 10012

Butler, Jay
c/o WQBH
2056 Penobscot Bldg.
Detroit, MI 48226
Disc jockey

Butler, Jerry "Ice Man"
c/o ECI
200 Inwood Dr.
Wheeling, IL 60090

Butler, Jonathan
c/o Zomba
1348 Lexington Ave.
New York, NY 10128

Butler, Larry
P.O. Box 120485
Nashville, TN 37212

Buziak, Bob
c/o RCA Records
1133 Ave. of the Americas
New York, NY 10036
Record company executive

By All Means
c/o Island Records
14 E. 4th St.
New York, NY 10012

Byrd, Donald
10100 Santa Monica Blvd. (#1600)
Los Angeles, CA 90067

The Byrds
c/o Scott Dean
428 Hill St.
Reno, NV 89501

Byrne, David
1775 Broadway (#700)
New York, NY 10019

Byrnes, Peter
c/o Complete Circuit
17 Cadman Plaza W.
Brooklyn, NY 11201

Bywater, Geoff
c/o MCA Records
1755 Broadway
New York, NY 10019
Record company executive

CBGB & OMFUG
315 Bowery
New York, NY 10003
Seminal punk nightclub

CBS Songs
51 W. 52nd St.
New York, NY 10019
Music publisher

CBS Studios
49 E. 52nd St.
New York, NY 10022
Recording studio

CMJ (College Music Journal)
830 Willis Ave.
Albertson, NY 11507
Industry newsletter on new music

The CS Angels
c/o Swingbest
60 Weston St.
London SE1 3QJ, England

CVC Report
648 Broadway
New York, NY 10012
Music video programming guide

Cabaret Voltaire
c/o EMI-Manhattan Records
1370 Ave. of the Americas
New York, NY 10019

Cabo Frio
P.O. Box 396
Beverly, MA 01915

Caesar, Shirley
P.O. Box 1790
Waco, TX 76796

Cafaro, Al
c/o A&M Records
1416 N. La Brea Ave.
Hollywood, CA 90028
Record company executive

Cafferty, John
(and the Beaver Brown Band)
c/o QBQ
48 E. 50th St.
New York, NY 10022

Cage, John
101 W. 18th St.
New York, NY 10011
Avant-garde composer

Cahn, Sammy
2049 Century Park E. (#2500)
Los Angeles, CA 90067
Songwriter

Cain, Jackie (and Roy Kral)
c/o Hartstein
8822 Evanview Dr.
Los Angeles, CA 90069

Cain, Tane
16530 Ventura Blvd. (#201)
Encino, CA 91436

Caine, Andrew
c/o Big Time
10 Inchmery Rd.
London SE6 2NA, England

Cale, J.J.
P.O. Box 210103
San Francisco, CA 94121

The California Raisins
c/o Will Vinton
1400 NW 22nd Ave.
Portland, OR 97210

The Call
c/o Heaton
6858 Los Altos Pl.
Hollywood, CA 90068

Callner, Marty
1242 Lago Vista
Beverly Hills, CA 90210
Music video director

Calloway, Cab
1040 Knollwood Rd.
White Plains, NY 10603

Camelot Enterprises
8000 Freedom Ave. NW
N. Canton, OH 44720
Retail music chain

Cameo
1422 Peachtree St., NW (#816)
Atlanta, GA 30309

Cameron, Doug
41 Britain St. (#200)
Toronto, ON M5A 1R7, Canada

Cameron, Scott
822 Hillgrove Ave.
Western Springs, IL 60558
Personal manager

Camilo, Michel
c/o Portrait Records
51 W. 52nd St.
New York, NY 10019

Camouflage
c/o Atlantic Records
75 Rockefeller Plaza
New York, NY 10019

Camp, Steve
P.O. Box 1606
Franklin, TN 37065

Campbell, Glen
9200 Sunset Blvd. (#823)
Los Angeles, CA 90069

Camper Van Beethoven
10100 Santa Monica Blvd. (#1600)
Los Angeles, CA 90067

Candi
100 Universal City Plaza
(Bldg. 422)
Universal City, CA 91608

Candy
c/o Howard Marks
655 Madison Ave.
New York, NY 10021

Cannata
c/o E/P/A Records
51 W. 52nd St.
New York, NY 10019

Canned Heat
17337 Ventura Blvd. (#300C)
Encino, CA 91316

The Cannons
c/o Mandrell Mgmt.
713 W. Main St.
Hendersonville, TN 37075

Canyon
P.O. Box 1373
Lewisville, TX 75067

Capaldi, Jim
P.O. Box 272
London N20 0BY, England

Caparro, Jim
c/o E/P/A Records
51 W. 52nd St.
New York, NY 10019
Record company executive

Capitol Studios
1750 N. Vine St.
Hollywood, CA 90028
Recording studio

Caplan, Michael
c/o E/P/A Records
51 W. 52nd St.
New York, NY 10019
Record company executive

Captain and Tennille
(Daryl Dragon and Toni Tennille)
P.O. Box 262
Glenbrook, NV 89413-0262

Captain Sensible
c/o Andy McQueen
22 Denmark St.
London WC2, England

Cara, Irene
8033 Sunset Blvd. (#735)
Los Angeles, CA 90046-2427

Carey, Kathleen
c/o Unicity Music
90 Universal City Plaza
Universal City, CA 91608
Music publisher

Carey, Tony
340 W. 28th St. (#13G)
New York, NY 10001

Caribou Ranch Recording Studio
P.O. Box 310
Nederland, CO 80466

Carl, Max
c/o Bill Siddons
1588 Crossroads of the World
Hollywood, CA 90028

Carlisle, Belinda
11500 San Vicente Blvd.
Los Angeles, CA 90049

Carlton, Larry
3208 Cahenga Blvd. (#42)
Los Angeles, CA 90069

Carlton, Ray
c/o Elektra Records
75 Rockefeller Plaza
New York, NY 10019
Record company executive

Carmen, Eric
c/o John Baruck
1046 Carol Dr.
Los Angeles, CA 90069

Carmen, Pauli
c/o Alive Ent.
1775 Broadway
New York, NY 10019

Carne, Jean
P.O. Box 27641
Philadelphia, PA 27641

Carnegie Hall
881 Seventh Ave.
New York, NY 10019

Carnes, Kim
1112 N. Sherbourne Dr.
Los Angeles, CA 90069

Carolan, Drew
900 Broadway (#604)
New York, NY 10003
Music video director

Carpenter, Mary Chapin
c/o CBS Records
34 Music Square E.
Nashville, TN 37203

Carpenter, Richard
P.O. Box 1084
Downey, CA 90240

Carr, Allan
439 N. Bedford Dr. (#1000)
Beverly Hills, CA 91210
Musical film/theatre producer

Carr, Tim
c/o Capitol Records
1370 Ave. of the Americas
New York, NY 10019
A&R executive

Carr, Vikki (Florence Cardona)
c/o VI-CAR Enterprises
8961 Sunset Blvd.
Los Angeles, CA 90069

Carrack, Paul
Western House, Harlequin Ave.
Great West Rd.
Brentford, Middlesex, England

Carrasco, Joe "King" (Teutsch)
P.O. Box 12333
Austin, TX 78711

Carriere, Glory-Anne
c/o Prestige
117 W. 7th Ave.
Vancouver, BC V5Y 1K5, Canada

Carson, Lori
c/o Geffen Records
9130 Sunset Blvd.
Los Angeles, CA 90069

Carson, Phil
17 Berrets Rd.
London, England
Personal manager

Carter, Betty
(Lillie Mae Jones)
117 St. Felix St.
Brooklyn, NY 11217

Carter, John
c/o Atlantic Records
9229 Sunset Blvd. (#710)
Los Angeles, CA 90069
A&R executive

Carter, Nell
10100 Santa Monica Blvd. (#1600)
Los Angeles, CA 90067

Carter, Ron
c/o Bridge
106 Fort Greene Pl.
Brooklyn, NY 11217

Carter Family
P.O. Box 508
Hendersonville, TN 37075

Cartwright, Lionel
c/o MCA Records
1701 West End Ave.
Nashville, TN 37203

Case, Keith
1016 16th Ave. S.
Nashville, TN 37212
Booking agent/personal manager

Case, Peter
10100 Santa Monica Blvd. (#1600)
Los Angeles, CA 90067

Casey, Joe
c/o CBS Records
34 Music Square E.
Nashville, TN 37203
Record company executive

Cash, Andrew
25 Bay Mills Blvd. (#502)
Agincourt, ON M1T 3P4, Canada

Cash, Johnny
9000 Sunset Blvd. (#1200)
Los Angeles, CA 90069

Cash, June Carter
c/o CBS Records
51 W. 52nd St.
New York, NY 10019

Cash, Rosanne
c/o Side One Mgmt.
1775 Broadway
New York, NY 10019

Cash Box
330 W. 58th St.
New York, NY 10019
Industry magazine

Cashflow
1422 W. Peachtree St., NW (#816)
Atlanta, GA 30309

Cashman, Terry
c/o Lifesong
94 Grand Ave.
Englewood, NJ 07631
Songwriter

Cassidy, Thomas
417 Marawood Dr.
Woodstock, IL 60098
Booking agent/personal manager

Castor, Jimmy
845 Third Ave.
New York, NY 10022

Catania, Bob
c/o Island Records
14 E. 4th St.
New York, NY 10012
Record company executive

• **Caterwaul**
100 Universal City Plaza
(Bldg. 422)
Universal City, CA 91608

₊The Cats
3 E. 54th St. (#1400)
New York, NY 10022

₊ **Cats Can Fly**
41 Britain St. (#200)
Toronto, ON M5A 1R7, Canada

Caufield, Tom
c/o PolyGram Records
810 Seventh Ave.
New York, NY 10019

Causey, Buddy
1545 Kennesaw Trace
Kennesaw, GA 30144

Cavallo, Ruffalo & Fargnoli
(Bob, Joe and Steve)
11355 W. Olympic Blvd. (#555)
Los Angeles, CA 90064
Personal manager

Caviano, Bob
254 W. 51st St.
New York, NY 10019
Booking agent/personal manager

Cecilio & Kapono
(Cecilio Rodriguez &
Henry Kaaihue)
P.O. Box 88172
Honolulu, HI 96830

Cetera, Peter
c/o Tom Ross
1888 Century Park E.
14th Floor
Los Angeles, CA 90067

Chacon, Iris
c/o Spotlite
221 W. 57th St.
New York, NY 10019

Chad and Jeremy (Stuart and
Clyde)
9000 Sunset Blvd. (#1200)
Los Angeles, CA 90069

Chairman of the Board
2300 E. Independence Blvd.
Charlotte, NC 28205

Chaltas, George
c/o CBS Records
1801 Century Park W.
Los Angeles, CA 90067
Record company executive

The Chambers Brothers
5218 Almont St.
Los Angeles, CA 90032

The Champs
5218 Almont St.
Los Angeles, CA 90032

Chandler, Gene
c/o Associated Booking
1955 Broadway
New York, NY 10023

Channel 2
c/o Borrow-Hunter
33 Borough Rd., Middlesex
Cleveland TS1 5DP, England

Channing, Carol
151 El Camino Dr.
Beverly Hills, CA 90212

The Chantels
5218 Almont St.
Los Angeles, CA 90032

Chapin, Tom
c/o Complete Circuit
17 Cadman Plaza W.
Brooklyn, NY 11201

Chapman, Beth Nielsen
P.O. Box 120897
Nashville, TN 37212

Chapman, Gary
c/o RCA Records
30 Music Square W.
Nashville, TN 37203

Chapman, Mike
c/o Dreamland
8920 W. Olympic Blvd.
Beverly Hills, CA 90211
Record producer/songwriter

Chapman, Roger
c/o Summerhaze
9 Downs Rd., GB-Beckenham
Kent BR3 2IY, England

Chapman, Tracy
c/o Lookout
506 Santa Monica Blvd.
Santa Monica, CA 90401

Chapter 8
c/o Capitol Records
1750 N. Vine St.
Hollywood, CA 90028

Charles, Ray (Ray Robinson)
c/o Joe Adam
CBS Records
1801 Century Park W.
Los Angeles, CA 90067

Charles, Suzette
P.O. Box 69180
Los Angeles, CA 90069

Charo
9107 Wilshire Blvd. (#500)
Beverly Hills, CA 90210-5526

Cheap Trick
520 University Ave.
Madison, WI 53703

Checker, Chubby (Ernest Evans)
1650 Broadway (#1011)
New York, NY 10019

The Checkmates
c/o Associated Booking
1995 Broadway
New York, NY 10023

Cher (Cherilyn Sarkasian)
9200 Sunset Blvd. (#1001)
Los Angeles, CA 90069

Cherokee Recording Studios
751 N. Fairfax Ave.
Hollywood, CA 90046

Cherrelle
9229 Sunset Blvd. (#311)
Los Angeles, CA 90069

Cherry, Ava
c/o Pasha Music
5615 Melrose Ave.
Hollywood, CA 90038

Chess Records
2120 S. Michigan Ave.
Chicago, IL
Former studio of blues greats

Chester, Johnny
49 Malabar Crescent (#307)
Eltham, VIC 3095, Australia

The Chevalier Brothers
c/o The Key Code
245 Dawes Rd.
London SW6 7RE, England

The Chi-Lites
250 W. 57th St. (#330)
New York, NY 10107

Chianda, Sheila
c/o CBS Records
51 W. 52nd St.
New York, NY 10019
Record company executive

Chic
250 W. 57th St. (#330)
New York, NY 10107

Chicago
2029 Century Park E. (#450)
Los Angeles, CA 90067

The Chiffons
c/o Knight
185 Clinton Ave.
Staten Island, NY 10301

Child, Desmond
1780 Broadway (#1208)
New York, NY 10019
Songwriter

Childress, Lisa
120 N. Springfield
Bolivar, MO 65613

Childs, Harold
c/o Warner Bros. Records
3300 Warner Blvd.
Burbank, CA 91510
Record company executive

Childs, Toni
c/o MFC Mgmt.
1428 S. Sherbourne Dr.
Los Angeles, CA 90035

Chilton, Alex
611 Broadway (#526)
New York, NY 10012

Chin, Brian
c/o Profile Records
740 Broadway
New York, NY 10003
A&R executive

China Crisis
63 Frederick St.
Edinburgh EH2 1LH, Scotland,
UK

Chinnock, Billy
274 Madison Ave. (#301)
New York, NY 10016

Choirboys
P.O. Box 442
Kings Cross, NSW 2011, Australia

Chong, Thomas
11661 San Vicente Blvd. (#1010)
Los Angeles, CA 90049

Christian, Meg
c/o Olivia Records
4400 Market St.
Oakland, CA 94608

The Christians
c/o Island Records
14 E. 4th St.
New York, NY 10012

Christie, Lou (Lugee Geno Sacco)
1645 E. 50th St. (#10-H)
Chicago, IL 60615

Christmas
100 Universal City Plaza
(Bldg. 422)
Universal City, CA 91608

Christopher, Gavin
9200 Sunset Blvd. (#915)
Los Angeles, CA 90069

Christopher, Johnny
P.O. Box 120485
Nashville, TN 37212

Chrome, Molly
100 Universal City Plaza
(Bldg. 422)
Universal City, CA 91608

Chrysalis Music Group
9255 Sunset Blvd.
Los Angeles, CA 90069
Music publisher

• **The Church**
10100 Santa Monica Blvd. (#1600)
Los Angeles, CA 90067

Ciani, Suzanne
c/o MCEG
11355 Olympic Blvd.
Los Angeles, CA 90064

Cinderella
P.O. Box 543
Drexel Hill, PA 19026
Fan club

Cinema
c/o Mid-Coast
5249 Rice Rd.
Antioch, TN 37013

Cinquemani, Vinny
c/o The Agency
41 Britain St. (#200)
Toronto, ON M5A 1RZ, Canada
Booking agent

• **Circle Jerks**
c/o Frontier
1776 Broadway
New York, NY 10019

Circus
3 W. 18th St.
New York, NY 10011
Fan magazine

Circus of Power
c/o RCA Records
1133 Ave. of the Americas
New York, NY 10036

Cities
18653 Ventura Blvd. (#311)
Tarzana, CA 91356

Clannad
c/o RCA Records
1133 Ave. of the Americas
New York, NY 10036

Clapton, Eric
1888 Century Park E. (#1400)
Los Angeles, CA 90067

Clark, Anne
9 Eccleston St., Belgravia
London SW1 W9LX, England

Clark, Dick
3003 W. Olive Ave.
Burbank, CA 91505

Clark, Linda
P.O. Box 1304
Burbank, CA 91507
Personal manager

Clark, Petula
410 Park Ave. (10th Floor)
New York, NY 10022

Clark, Roy
c/o Jim Halsey Co.
3225 S. Norwood Ave.
Tulsa, OK 74135

Clarke, Stanley
P.O. Box 25863
Los Angeles, CA 90025

The Clash
268 Camden Rd.
London NW1, England

The Classics IV
P.O. Box 68045
Indianapolis, IN 46268

Clayderman, Richard
10100 Santa Monica Blvd. (#1600)
Los Angeles, CA 90067

Clayton, Merry
c/o RCA Records
6363 Sunset Blvd.
Los Angeles, CA 90028

Clearmountain, Bob
441 W. 53rd St.
New York, NY 10019
Record producer

Clearwater, Eddy
c/o Concerted Efforts
110 Madison Ave.
Newtonville, MA 02160

Cleary, Dan
720 Holmby Ave.
Los Angeles, CA 90024
Personal manager

Clegg, Johnny (and Savuka)
c/o Alive Ent.
8271 Melrose Ave.
Los Angeles, CA 90046

Clements, Vassar
P.O. Box 170
Hermitage, TN 37076

Clemons, Clarence
c/o ICM
40 W. 57th St.
New York, NY 10019

Cleveland, Rev. James
P.O. Box 4632
Detroit, MI 48243

Cliff, Jimmy
c/o Victor Chambers
51 Lady Musgrave Rd.
Kingston, Jamaica

Clifford, Patrick
c/o A&M Records
595 Madison Ave.
New York, NY 10022
Record company executive

Climax Blues Band
3 E. 54th St. (#1400)
New York, NY 10022

Climie Fisher (Simon and Rob)
c/o EMI Records
20 Manchester Square
London W1A 1ES, England

Clinton, George
2418 W. Thoreau St.
Inglewood, CA 90303

Clooney, Rosemary
650 N. Bronson (#148)
Los Angeles, CA 90004

The Clovers
1650 Broadway (#611)
New York, NY 10019

Club Nouveau
c/o Jay King
414 12th St.
Sacramento, CA 95814

Coakley, Sean
c/o Arista Records
6 W. 57th St.
New York, NY 10019
Record company executive

The Coasters
4484 Pennwood (#233)
Las Vegas, NV 89102

Cobham, Billy
P.O. Box 514
Marietta, GA 30061

Coburn, Bob
c/o KLOS
3321 S. La Cienega Blvd.
Los Angeles, CA 90016
Disc jockey

Cochran, Hank (Garland Cochran)
P.O. Box 120537
Nashville, TN 37212

Cochran, Wayne
13719 Ventura Blvd. (#H)
Sherman Oaks, CA 91423

Cochrane, Tom
41 Britain St. (#400)
Toronto, ON M5A 1R7, Canada

Cock Robin
P.O. Box 357
Beverly Hills, CA 90213

Cockburn, Bruce
c/o Joanne Smale
686 Main Level, Richmond St. W.
Toronto, ON M6J 1C3, Canada

Cocker, Joe (John)
c/o QBQ
48 E. 50th St.
New York, NY 10022

Cocks, Jay
c/o Time
Time & Life Building
Rockefeller Center
New York, NY 10020
Music critic

Cocteau Twins
c/o Capitol Records
1750 N. Vine St.
Hollywood, CA 90028

Cody, Commander (George Frayne)
2980 Beverly Glen Circle (#302)
Los Angeles, CA 90077

Coe, David Allan
Route #3 (#549)
Dickson, TN 37055

Cohen, Leonard (Norman Cohen)
c/o CBS Records
1801 Century Park W.
Los Angeles, CA 90067

Cohen, Mitchell
c/o Arista Records
6 W. 57th St.
New York, NY 10019
A&R executive

Cohen, Steve
9200 Sunset Blvd. (#1220)
Los Angeles, CA 90069
Personal manager

Cohen, Stu
c/o Warner Bros. Records
3300 Warner Blvd.
Burbank, CA 91510
Record company executive

Cole, Natalie
c/o Dan Cleary Mgmt.
720 Holmby Ave.
Los Angeles, CA 90024

Coleman, Desiree
526 S. 3rd St.
Philadelphia, PA 19147

Coleman, Durell
c/o BNB
9545 Wilshire Blvd.
Beverly Hills, CA 90212

Coleman, Ornette
P.O. Box 106
New York, NY 10013

Coley, John Ford
10100 Santa Monica Blvd. (#1095)
Los Angeles, CA 90067

Collins, Albert
P.O. Box 578190
Chicago, IL 60657-8190

Collins, Bootsy (William)
414 E. Walnut St. (#920)
Cincinnati, OH 45202

Collins, Judy
P.O. Box 1296
Cathedral Station
New York, NY 10025

Collins, Phil
Shalford
Surrey, England

Collins, Tim
215 1st St.
Cambridge, MA 02142
Personal manager

Collins, Willie
c/o Hush Prods.
231 W. 58th St.
New York, NY 10019

Colombier, Michel
P.O. Box 779
Mill Valley, CA 94942

Colon, Willie
c/o Third World
200 Varick St.
New York, NY 10014

Colonel Abrams
c/o AMI
1776 Broadway
New York, NY 10019

Colour Box
10100 Santa Monica Blvd. (#1600)
Los Angeles, CA 90067

The Colourfield
c/o Pete Hadfield
132 Liverpool Rd.
London N1 1LA, England

Colson, Gail
25 Ives St.
London SW3, England
Personal manager

Colter, Jessi (Miriam Johnson)
1117 17th Ave. S
Nashville, TN 37203

Comden, Betty (and Adolph Green)
c/o ICM
40 W. 57th St.
New York, NY 10019
Songwriters

⌄Commodores
3151 Cahuenga Blvd. W. (#235)
Los Angeles, CA 90068

⬩Communards
151 El Camino Dr.
Beverly Hills, CA 90212

Como, Perry
c/o RCA Records
1133 Ave. of the Americas
New York, NY 10036

Company B
c/o Atlantic Records
75 Rockefeller Plaza
New York, NY 10019

Con Funk Shun
200 W. 51st St. (#1410)
New York, NY 10019

Concerted Efforts
110 Madison Ave.
Newtonville, MA 02160
Booking agent

Concrete Blonde
100 Universal City Plaza
(Bldg. 422)
Universal City, CA 91608

Conlee, John
38 Music Square E. (#300)
Nashville, TN 37203

Conley, Earl Thomas
63 Music Square W.
Nashville, TN 37203

Conniff, Ray
c/o CBS Records
51 W. 52nd St.
New York, NY 10019

Connors, Norman
c/o Capitol Records
1750 N. Vine St.
Hollywood, CA 90028

Consolo, Tom
1046 Carol Dr.
W. Hollywood, CA 90069
Personal manager

Conte, Patti
c/o EMI-Manhattan Records
1370 Ave. of the Americas
New York, NY 10019
Publicity executive

Conti, Bill
4146 Lankershim Blvd. (#300)
N. Hollywood, CA 91602
Film composer

The Contours
218 W. 57th St. (#3A)
New York, NY 10019

The Controllers
400A 56th St.
Fairfield, AL 35064

Conwell, Tommy
c/o Cornerstone Mgmt.
23 E. Lancaster Ave.
Ardmore, PA 19003

Cooder, Ry
c/o Warner Bros. Records
3300 Warner Blvd.
Burbank, CA 91510

Cook, Jeff
c/o Elektra Records
75 Rockefeller Plaza
New York, NY 10019
Record company executive

Coolidge, Rita
c/o Jim McCue
8899 Beverly Blvd.
Suite 612
Los Angeles, CA 90048

Cooper, Alice (Vincent Furnier)
8033 Sunset Blvd. (#745)
Los Angeles, CA 90046

Cooper, Bernadette
c/o MCA Records
70 Universal City Plaza
Universal City, CA 91608

Cooper, Michael
c/o General Talent
1700 Broadway
New York, NY 10019

Cooper, Epstein, and Hurewitz
9465 Wilshire Blvd.
Beverly Hills, CA 90212
Music attorneys

Cope, Julian
c/o Outlaw
36–38 West St.
London WC2, England

Copeland, Ian
c/o Frontier Booking Int.
1776 Broadway
New York, NY 10019
Booking agent

Copeland, Miles
c/o Firstar Mgmt.
194 Kensington Park Rd.
London W11, England
Manager/record company
executive

Copeland, Stewart
c/o Firstar Mgmt.
194 Kensington Park Rd.
London W11, England

Copland, Aaron
c/o Boosey and Hawkes
24 W. 57th St.
New York, NY 10019

Cording, Tom
c/o Enigma Records
1750 E. Holly Ave.
El Segundo, CA 90245
Publicity executive

Core, Margot
c/o E/P/A Records
51 W. 52nd St.
New York, NY 10019
Record company executive

Corea, Chick (Armando Corea)
2635 Griffith Park Blvd.
Los Angeles, CA 90039

Cornelius, Don
9255 Sunset Blvd. (#420)
Los Angeles, CA 90069
Creator/host of Soul Train

Cornelius, Helen
P.O. Box 12321
Nashville, TN 37212

**Cornelius Brothers and Sister Rose
(Edward, Carter, and Rose
Cornelius)**
c/o Carolina Attractions
203 Culver Ave.
Charleston, SC 29407

Cossu, Scott
P.O. Box 9388
Stanford, CA 94305

Costello, Elvis (Declan McManus)
Western House, Harlequin Ave.
Great West Road, Brentford
Middlesex TW8 9EW, England

Cotillion Music
75 Rockefeller Plaza
New York, NY 10019
Music publisher

Cottle, Redd
c/o David Franklin
1290 S. Omni International
Atlanta, GA 30303

Cotton, James
11541 S. Hale Ave.
Chicago, IL 60643

Country Music
149 Fifth Ave.
New York, NY 10010
Fan magazine

Country Music Association
P.O. Box 22299
Nashville, TN 37202

Country Music Foundation
4 Music Square E.
Nashville, TN 37203

Courage, John
8306 Wilshire Blvd. (#1008)
Beverly Hills, CA 90211
Personal manager

Coury, Al
c/o Geffen Records
9130 Sunset Blvd.
Los Angeles, CA 90069
Record company executive

The Cover Girls
P.O. Box Q
Bronx, NY 10452

Warren Covington Orchestra
c/o Abby Hoffer
233½ E. 48th St.
New York, NY 10022

Cowboy Jazz
c/o Lone Star Talent
2138 Flag Marsh Rd.
Mount Airy, MD 21771

Cowboy Junkies
c/o RCA Records
1133 Ave. of the Americas
New York, NY 10036

Craaft
c/o Mainhattan Music
Obertshaeuserstr 70
Müehlheim, West Germany

Craddock, Billy "Crash"
P.O. Box 6798
Greensboro, NC 27405

Craigo, Jack
c/o Chrysalis Music
9255 Sunset Blvd.
Los Angeles, CA 90069
Music publishing executive

Cramer, Floyd
c/o Sutton
119 W. 57th St.
New York, NY 10019

The Cramps
c/o Frontier
1776 Broadway
New York, NY 10019

Crawford, Randy
c/o Ken Fritz
648 N. Robertson Blvd.
Los Angeles, CA 90069

Cray, Robert
P.O. Box 210103
San Francisco, CA 94121

Crazy House
c/o Chrysalis Records
645 Madison Ave.
New York, NY 10022

Creach, Papa John
c/o Sylvakian Music
1122 La Jolla Ave.
Los Angeles, CA 90035

Creative Artists Agency
1888 Century Park E. (#1400)
Los Angeles, CA 90067

Creem
7715 Sunset Blvd. (#204)
Los Angeles, CA 90046
Fan magazine

Crenshaw, Marshall
200 W. 57th St. (#1403)
New York, NY 10019

The Crew Cuts
29 Cedar St.
Creskill, NJ 07626

The Crickets
Rt. 1 (#222)
Lyles, TN 37098

Cries
c/o Complete Circuit
17 Cadman Plaza W.
Brooklyn, NY 11201

Criss, Peter
c/o Aucoin Mgmt.
645 Madison Ave.
New York, NY 10022

Criteria Recording Studios
1755 NE 153rd St.
N. Miami Beach, FL 33181

Crosby, David
c/o Bill Siddons
1588 Crossroads of the World
Los Angeles, CA 90028

Cross
c/o Virgin Records
9247 Alden Dr.
Beverly Hills, CA 90210

Cross, Christopher (Geppert)
114 W. 7th St. (#717)
Austin, TX 78701

Crouch, Andrae
1821 Wilshire Blvd. (#200)
Santa Monica, CA 90403

Crowded House
P.O. Box 333
Prahran, VIC 3181, Australia

Crowe, J.D.
P.O. Box 1210
Hamilton, OH 45012

Crowell, Rodney
60 W. 70th St. (#1)
New York, NY 10023

The Crusaders
8467 Beverly Blvd. (#100)
Los Angeles, CA 90048

Cruzados
P.O. Box 2426
Hollywood, CA 90078

Cry Before Dawn
c/o Epic Records
51 W. 52nd St.
New York, NY 10019

The Crystals
5218 Almont St.
Los Angeles, CA 90032

Cugat, Xavier
Ritz Hotel
Barcelona, Spain

The Cult
30 Pridstow Pl.
London W2 5AE, England

Culture Club
34A Green Lane
Northwood, Middlesex, England

Cummings, Burton
c/o Marty Kraemer
8300 Cambie Rd.
Richmond, BC V64 1J9, Canada

Curb, Mike
c/o Curb Records
3907 W. Alameda Ave.
Burbank, CA 91505
Record company executive

Curbishley, Bill
c/o Left Field Services
157 W. 57th St.
New York, NY 10019
Personal manager

The Cure
200 W. 57th St. (#1403)
New York, NY 10019

Curiosity Killed The Cat
1888 Century Park E. (#1400)
Los Angeles, CA 90067

Currie, Cherie and Marie
151 El Camino Dr.
Beverly Hills, CA 90212

Curry, Adam
c/o MTV
1775 Broadway
New York, NY 10019
Veejay

Curtis, Sonny
Route #2 (#61)
Dickson, TN 37055

The Cutting Edge
8335 Sunset Blvd.
W. Hollywood, CA 90069
Music television series

Cutting Crew
P.O. Box 1994
San Francisco, CA 94101

Cymone, Andre
715 Florida Ave. S. (#410)
Minneapolis, MN 55426

D.C. La Croix
P.O. Box 5657
Sherman Oaks, CA 91413

DJ Jazzy Jeff and the Fresh Prince
c/o Jive Records
1348 Lexington Ave.
New York, NY 10128

• **DNA**
6311 Romaine St. (#7015)
Los Angeles, CA 90038
Music video producers/directors

D.O.A.
c/o Profile Records
740 Broadway
New York, NY 10003

Dailey, Robert
6209 Oakbank Dr. (#56)
Azusa, CA 91702
Surf music expert

Daily, E.G.
c/o MFC
1428 S. Sherbourne Dr.
Los Angeles, CA 90035

Daily Variety
1400 N. Cahuenga Blvd.
Hollywood, CA 90028
Trade magazine

da' Krash
c/o Capitol Records
1750 N. Vine St.
Hollywood, CA 90028

Dale
c/o Warner Bros. Records
3300 Warner Blvd.
Burbank, CA 91510

Dale, Dick
909 Parkview Ave.
Lodi, CA 95240

Dalglish, Malcolm
P.O. Box 277
Bloomington, IN 47402

Dalton, Lacy J.
c/o Ten Ten Mgmt.
1010 16th Ave. S.
Nashville, TN 37212

Daltrey, Roger
c/o Left Services
157 W. 57th St.
New York, NY 10019

Damian, Michael
9000 Sunset Blvd. (#1200)
Los Angeles, CA 90069

The Damned
c/o Independent Ent.
509 Madison Ave.
New York, NY 10022

Damone, Vic (Vito Farinola)
9046 Sunset Blvd. (#208)
Los Angeles, CA 90069

Dane, Dana
c/o Hurby Azor
27-11 Humphrey St. E.
Queens, NY 11369

Daniel, Doug
c/o Arista Records
6 W. 57th St.
New York, NY 10019
Record company executive

Daniels, Charlie
210 25th Ave. N. (#N-101)
Nashville, TN 37203

Daniels, Eddie
9000 Sunset Blvd. (#1200)
Los Angeles, CA 90069

Daniels, Sky
c/o KFOG
55 Green St.
San Francisco, CA 94111
Disc jockey

Danko, Rick
c/o Skyline
85 Fairhaven Lane
Marstons Mills, MA 02648

Danny and the Juniors
168 Orchid Dr.
Pearl River, NY 10965

Danse Society
c/o Nomis Mgmt.
17 Gosfield St.
London W1 7PH, England

Danzig
c/o Def American Records
9157 Sunset Blvd.
Los Angeles, CA 90069

D'Arby, Terence Trent
P.O. Box 910 L
London NW1 9AQ, England

Dark Angel
c/o Combat Records
187-07 Henderson Ave.
Hollis, NY 11423

Darren, James (Ercolani)
P.O. Box 1088
Beverly Hills, CA 90213

D'Arrietta, Stewart
P.O. Box 319, Cammeray
Sydney, NSW 2062, Australia

Dash, Sarah
200 W. 57th St. (#907)
New York, NY 10019

Dave (Rowland) and Sugar
P.O. Box 121089
Nashville, TN 37212

David and David
c/o MFC Mgmt.
1428 Sherbourne Dr.
Los Angeles, CA 90035

David, Hal
15 W. 53rd St.
New York, NY 10019
Songwriter

Davidson, John
190 N. Canon Dr.
Beverly Hills, CA 90210

Davies, Gail
c/o MCA Records
1701 West End Ave.
Nashville, TN 37203

Davies, Roger
3575 Cahuenga Blvd. W.
Los Angeles, CA 90068
Personal manager

Davis, Billy, Jr.
31308 Via Colinas (#109)
Westlake Village, CA 91362

Davis, Billy Newton
c/o Worldwide Ent.
641 Lexington Ave.
New York, NY 10022

Davis, Clive
c/o Arista Records
6 W. 57th St.
New York, NY 10019
Record company executive

Davis, Danny (and Nashville Brass)
P.O. Box 1546
Nashville, TN 37202

Davis, Delisa
P.O. Box 252
Hollywood, CA 90078

Davis, Jimmy (and Junction)
3 E. 54th St. (#1400)
New York, NY 10022

Davis, Larry
c/o E/P/A Records
51 W. 52nd St.
New York, NY 10019
Record company executive

Davis, Linda
c/o Erv Woolsey
1000 18th Ave. S.
Nashville, TN 37212

Davis, Mac
151 El Camino Dr.
Beverly Hills, CA 90212

Davis, Mavis Vegas
c/o Johnathan Scott Bogner
4141 Crisp Canyon Rd.
Sherman Oaks, CA 91403

Davis, Miles
c/o Ted Kurland
173 Brighton Ave.
Boston, MA 02134

Davis, Sammy, Jr.
400 S. Beverly Dr. (#410)
Beverly Hills, CA 90212

Davis, Spencer
12457 Ventura Blvd. (#103)
Studio City, CA 91604

Davy D
298 Elizabeth St.
New York, NY 10012

Dax, Danielle
c/o Falcon Stuart
59 Moore Park Rd.
London SW6 2HH, England

Day, Doris (Kappelhoff)
P.O. Box 223163
Carmel, CA 93921

Day, Morris
3580 Wilshire Blvd. (#184)
Los Angeles, CA 90010

Day, Otis (and The Knights)
c/o American Enterprises
239 W. Olive Ave.
Burbank, CA 91502

Dayne, Taylor
c/o Arista Records
6 W. 57th St.
New York, NY 10019

Dazz Band
2519 Carmen Crest Dr.
Los Angeles, CA 90068

The Dead Milkmen
P.O. Box 42684
Philadelphia, PA 19101

Dead or Alive
10100 Santa Monica Blvd. (#1600)
Los Angeles, CA 90067

Dean, Hazell
c/o Capitol Records
1750 N. Vine St.
Hollywood, CA 90028

Dean, Jimmy (Seth Ward)
1341 W. Mockingbird Lane
Dallas, TX 75249

Dean, Joanna
c/o PolyGram Records
810 Seventh Ave.
New York, NY 10019

Dean, Paul
c/o CBS Records
51 W. 52nd St.
New York, NY 10019

Death Angel
P.O. Box 170545
San Francisco, CA 94117

DeBarge, Chico
c/o Motown Records
6255 Sunset Blvd.
Los Angeles, CA 90028

DeBarge, El
c/o Tony Jones Mgmt.
6255 Sunset Blvd.
Los Angeles, CA 90028

deBurgh, Chris
Bargy Castle, Tonhaggard
Wexford, Ireland

Dee, Joey (Joseph DiNicola)
141 Dunbar Ave.
Fords, NJ 08863

The Deele
9229 Sunset Blvd. (#320)
Los Angeles, CA 90069

Deep Purple
P.O. Box 254
Sheffield S6 1DF, England

Dees, Rick
c/o KIIS-FM
6255 Sunset Blvd.
Los Angeles, CA 90028
Radio and TV personality

⊛ **Def Leppard**
P.O. Box 670
Old Chelsea Station
New York, NY 10113
Fan club

DeFranco, Buddy
c/o Willard Alexander
660 Madison Ave.
New York, NY 10021

DeGarmo & Key
1105 16th Ave. (#C)
Nashville, TN 37212

De Grassi, Alex
P.O. Box 9188
Colorado Springs, CO 80932

Deja
c/o Virgin Records
9247 Alden Dr.
Beverly Hills, CA 90210

De Johnette, Jack
Silver Hollow Rd.
Willow, NY 11201

DeJoy, Ed
23241 Ventura Blvd. (#100)
Woodland Hills, CA 91364
Personal manager

Delatte, Mel
c/o I.R.S. Records
100 Universal City Plaza
(Bldg. 422)
Universal City, CA 91608
Record company executive

Del Baizo, Jim
c/o CBS Records
51 W. 52nd St.
New York, NY 10019
Record company executive

DeLeon, Lupe
4031 Panama Ct.
Piedmont, CA 94611
Booking agent

Delerue, Georges
54 Rue de Tocqueville
Paris 75017, France

The Delfonics
2011 Ferry Ave. (#U-19)
Camden, NJ 08104

● Del Fuegos
7381 Beverly Blvd.
Los Angeles, CA 90036

The Del-Lords
188 First Ave. (#6)
New York, NY 10009

Delsener, Ron
27 E. 67th St.
Second Floor
New York, NY 10021
Concert promoter

De Lucia, Paco
c/o Ted Kurland
173 Brighton Ave.
Boston, MA 02134

The Del-Vikings
P.O. Box 70218
Fort Lauderdale, FL 33307

DeMann, Freddie
9000 Sunset Blvd. (#915)
Los Angeles, CA 90069
Personal manager

The Demento Society
P.O. Box 884
Culver City, CA 90203
Dr. Demento fan club

Demme, Jonathan
330 W. 42nd St. (#2410)
New York, NY 10036
Film/music video director

DeNigris, Don
c/o E/P/A Records
51 W. 52nd St.
New York, NY 10019
Record company executive

Denver, John
(Henry Deutschendorf, Jr.)
P.O. Box 1587
Aspen, CO 81612

⟩Depeche Mode
200 W. 57th St. (#1403)
New York, NY 10019

Derek B
c/o Profile Records
740 Broadway
New York, NY 10003

Derringer, Rick (Zehringer)
c/o West Coast Prods.
6222 W. 6th Ave.
Los Angeles, CA 90048

Des Barres, Michael
P.O. Box 4160
Hollywood, CA 90078

Des Barres, Pamela
3575 Cahuenga Blvd. (#470)
Los Angeles, CA 90068
Famous ex-groupie

Desert Rose Band
P.O. Box 8305
Harwin, TX 77036

De Shannon, Jackie
c/o Stone
1052 N. Carol Dr.
Los Angeles, CA 90069

Devine, Tim
c/o Capitol Records
1750 N. Vine St.
Hollywood, CA 90028
A&R executive

DeVito, Karla
c/o Panacea
2705 Glendower Ave.
Los Angeles, CA 90027

Devo
P.O. Box 6868
Burbank, CA 91510

Dewitt, Lew
c/o Our Gang
1012 16th Ave. S.
Nashville, TN 37212

De Young, Dennis
c/o Gold Starship
3575 Cahuenga Blvd. W.
Los Angeles, CA 90068

Diamond, Jim
44 Queen's Square
Strathbungo
Glasgow G41 2AZ, Scotland, UK

Diamond, Marty
c/o Arista Records
6 W. 57th St.
New York, NY 10019
Record company executive

Diamond, Neil
P.O. Box 3357
Hollywood, CA 90028

The Diamonds
9560 Wilshire Blvd. (PH)
Los Angeles, CA 90212

Paul Di'Anno's Battlezone
405 Beach, 146th St.
Neponsit, NY 11694

Dick, Nigel
c/o Propaganda Films
413 S. La Brea Ave.
Los Angeles, CA 90036
Music video director

Dickens, Little Jimmy
P.O. Box 1932
Brentwood, TN 37027

The Dickies
P.O. Box 651
La Mirada, CA 90637

Dickinson, Bruce
c/o EMI-Manhattan Records
1370 Ave. of the Americas
New York, NY 10019
A&R executive

Diddley, Bo
(Ellas McDaniel)
P.O. Box 659
Hawthorne, FL 32640

Dillard, Doug
c/o Keith Case
1016 16th Ave. S.
Nashville, TN 37212

Dillon, Dean
c/o Capitol Records
1111 16th Ave. S.
Nashville, TN 37212

DiMeola, Al
c/o Ted Kurland
173 Brighton Ave.
Boston, MA 02134

Dimples
c/o CBS Records
51 W. 52nd St.
New York, NY 10019

Dino
P.O. Box 2437
Hendersonville, TN 37077

Dio, Ronnie James (Padovana)
18653 Ventura Blvd. (#307)
Tarzana, CA 91356

Dion (DiMucci)
c/o Arista Records
6 W. 57th St.
New York, NY 10019

Dire Straits
10 Southwick Mews
London W2, England

The Dirt Band
P.O. Box 1915
Aspen, CO 81611

Dirty Looks
Rd. 5 (#53)
Selinsgrove, PA 17870

Divinyls
The Watertower (#104)
Rosehill St.
Sydney, NSW 2016, Australia

The Dixie Dregs
5775 Peachtree St.
Atlanta, GA 30342

Dixon, Don
P.O. Box 237
Carrboro, NC 27510
Record producer

Dixon, Jessy
P.O. Box 50358
Nashville, TN 37205

Dixon, Mason
c/o WRBQ
5510 Gray St.
Tampa, FL 33609
Disc jockey

Dixon, Willie
822 Milgrove Ave.
Western Springs, IL 60558

D'Molls
1888 Century Park E. (#1400)
Los Angeles, CA 90067

Dobbis, Rick
c/o E/P/A Records
1801 Century Park W.
Los Angeles, CA 90067
Record company executive

Doctor & The Medics
53 Greek St.
London W1, England

Dr. Demento (Barry Hansen)
925 Westmount Ave.
Los Angeles, CA 90043

Dr. Hook
P.O. Box 121017
Nashville, TN 37212

The Doctors Children
c/o Enigma Records
1750 E. Holly Ave.
El Segundo, CA 90245

Doe, John
c/o Geffen Records
9130 Sunset Blvd.
Los Angeles, CA 90069

Dokken, Don
P.O. Box 67487
Los Angeles, CA 90067

Dolby, Thomas
c/o EMI-Manhattan Records
1370 Ave. of the Americas
New York, NY 10019

Dolby, Ray
100 Potrero Ave.
San Francisco, CA 94103-4813
Creator of Dolby stereo

Doldinger, Klaus
P.O. Box 2230
Reitgasse 10
D-3550 Marburgil, West Germany

Dolenz, Mickey
c/o Leading Artists
445 N. Bedford Dr.
Beverly Hills, CA 90210

Domingo, Placido
c/o Eric Semon
111 W. 57th St.
New York, NY 10019

Domino, Fats (Antoine)
1770 Tchoupatoulas
New Orleans, LA 70130

Donovan (Leitch)
P.O. Box 472
London SW7 2QB, England

Doobie Brothers
370 West Napa
Sonoma, CA 95476

Doppelganger
c/o USA Musico
34 Hemlock Shore Dr.
Atkinson, NH 03811

Do-Re-Mi
The Village Centre (#27A)
Kings Cross
Sydney, NSW 2011, Australia

Dorff, Steve
3815 W. Olive Ave. (#202)
Burbank, CA 91505
Songwriter/record producer

Dorfman, Stanley
c/o Nick Ben-Meir
644 N. Doheny Dr.
Los Angeles, CA 90069
Music television director

Dorian
P.O. Box 8305
Houston, TX 77288

Dornemann, Michael
c/o RCA Records
1133 Ave. of the Americas
New York, NY 10036
Record company executive

Dorsey Then and Now
P.O. Box 414314
Miami Beach, FL 33141

Tommy Dorsey Orchestra
c/o Willard Alexander
660 Madison Ave.
New York, NY 10021

Double
c/o The Swiss Connection
Carmenstr, 12
Zurich CH-8030, Switzerland

Doug and the Slugs
c/o S.L. Feldman
1534 W. 2nd Ave.
Vancouver, BC V6J 1H2, Canada

Douglas, Jerry
c/o Keith Case
1016 16th Ave. S.
Nashville, TN 37212

Douglas, Larry
c/o E/P/A Records
1801 Century Park W.
Los Angeles, CA 90067
Record company executive

Down Avenue
c/o Second Vision
5 Grosby St.
New York, NY 10013

down beat
222 W. Adams St.
Chicago, IL 60606
Jazz/R&B magazine

Downes and Price
33 Music Square W. (#100)
Nashville, TN 37203

Drake, Pete
809 18th Ave. S.
Nashville, TN 37203

Dramarama
10966 Le Conte Ave. (#A)
Los Angeles, CA 90024

The Dramatics
P.O. Box 82
Great Neck, NY 11021

Dream Academy
c/o Warner Bros. Records
3300 Warner Blvd.
Burbank, CA 91510

Dream Syndicate
3 E. 54th St. (#1400)
New York, NY 10022

Dreams So Real
P.O. Box 8061
Athens, GA 30603

The Drifters
4905 S. Atlantic Ave.
Daytona Beach, FL 32019

D'Rivera, Paquito
c/o Helen Keane
49 E. 96th St.
New York, NY 10128

Droz, Henry
c/o WEA
3300 Warner Blvd.
Burbank, CA 91510
Record company executive

Drums and Drumming
20085 Stevens Creek Blvd.
Cupertino, CA 95014
Musicians' magazine

Duchin, Peter
60 E. 42nd St.
New York, NY 10165

Dudek, Les
c/o Falk & Morrow
143 S. Cedros Ave.
Solana Beach, CA 92075

Duke, George
6430 Sunset Blvd. (#1500)
Hollywood, CA 90028

Duke Jupiter
c/o Pelican
A1 Country Club Rd. E.
Rochester, NY 14445

The Dukes of Dixieland
c/o Kevin Bradshaw
309 Rue Bourbon
New Orleans, LA 70130

Duncan, Darryl
c/o Motown Records
6255 Sunset Blvd.
Los Angeles, CA 90028

Duncan, Johnny
Route #2 (#356)
Stephenville, TX 76401

Dunn, Holly
c/o Ten Ten
1010 16th Ave. S.
Nashville, TN 37212

The Duprees
c/o John Salvato
111 W. 6th St.
Bayonne, NJ 07002

Duran Duran
273 Broad St.
Birmingham B12 DS, England

Dury, Ian
c/o Wasted Talent
321 Fulham Rd.
London SW10 9QL, England

Dyer, Ada
c/o Motown Records
6255 Sunset Blvd.
Los Angeles, CA 90028

Dylan, Bob (Zimmerman)
P.O. Box 264
Cooper Station
New York, NY 10003

The Dynatones
P.O. Box 22372
San Francisco, CA 94122

E.I.E.I.O.
c/o Frontier
1776 Broadway
New York, NY 10019

E.P.M.D.
c/o General Talent
1700 Broadway
New York, NY 10019

E.U.
c/o EMI-Manhattan Records
1370 Ave. of the Americas
New York, NY 10019

E-Z-O
c/o Amuse America
407 Park Ave. S.
New York, NY 10016

Earle, Steve
c/o Side One Mgmt.
1775 Broadway
New York, NY 10019

Earth, Wind, and Fire
4323 W. Verdugo Ave.
Burbank, CA 91505

Eason, Don
c/o E/P/A Records
51 W. 52nd St.
New York, NY 10019
Record company executive

Easterhouse
c/o CBS Records
51 W. 52nd St.
New York, NY 10019

Easton, Elliott
c/o Lookout
506 Santa Monica Blvd.
Santa Monica, CA 90401

Easton, Sheena
151 El Camino Dr.
Beverly Hills, CA 90212

Eaton, Anthony
830 Las Casas Ave. (#C)
Pacific Palisades, CA 90272
Music television producer/director

Eazy-E
6430 Sunset Blvd. (#321)
Hollywood, CA 90028

Echo and the Bunnymen
c/o Mike Hancock
36 Clarence St.
Liverpool L35 TN, England

Eckstine, Billy
1061 E. Flamingo Rd. (#7)
Las Vegas, NV 89109

Eckstine, Eddie
c/o Wing/PolyGram Records
810 Seventh Ave.
New York, NY 10019
Record company executive

Eddie, John
130 W. 57th St. (#2A)
New York, NY 10019

Eddy, Duane
P.O. Box 10771
Zephyr Cove, NV 89448

Edmunds, Dave
c/o Polar Union
119–121 Freston Rd.
London W11 4DB, England

Edwards, John
c/o KBPI
1200 17th St. (#2300)
Denver, CO 80202
Disc jockey

Edwards, Jonathan
c/o Keith Case
1016 16th Ave. S.
Nashville, TN 37212

Edwards, Kenny "Babyface"
9229 Sunset Blvd. (#311)
Los Angeles, CA 90069
Record producer

Edwards, Wayne
c/o Capitol Records
1750 N. Vine St.
Hollywood, CA 90028
A&R executive

Egan, Mark
P.O. Box 9188
Colorado Springs, CO 80932

Eichner, Mickey
c/o CBS Records
51 W. 52nd St.
New York, NY 10019
A&R executive

Eight Seconds
c/o S.L. Feldman
1534 W. 2nd Ave.
Vancouver, BC V6J 1H2, Canada

Eighth Wonder
c/o WTG Records
1801 Century Park W.
Los Angeles, CA 90067

Electric Lady Studios
52 W. 8th St.
New York, NY 10011
Recording studio

Electric Light Orchestra
113–117 Wardour St.
London W1, England

Electronic Musician
400 Hollis St. (#12)
Emeryville, CA 94608
Musicians' magazine

11 Bloody Men
2054 University Ave. (#400)
Berkeley, CA 94704

Elgart, Larry
55 E. 74th St.
New York, NY 10021

Elias, Eliane
234 Cabot St. (#6)
Beverly, MA 01915

Ellington, Mercer
c/o Doctor Jazz
1414 Ave. of the Americas
New York, NY 10019

Elliott, Jack
3815 W. Olive Ave. (#202)
Burbank, CA 91505
TV music composer

Elliott, Ramblin' Jack
(Elliott Adnopoz)
c/o Day Prods.
300 W. 55th St.
New York, NY 10019

Ellis, Herb
c/o Lambros
582 Spa Creek Landing
Annapolis, MD 21403

Elson, Bob
c/o ICM
40 W. 57th St.
New York, NY 10019

Elson, Kevin
P.O. Box 5952
San Francisco, CA 94101
Record producer

The Elvis Brothers
c/o Ken Adamany
315 W. Gorham
Madison, WI 53703

Ely, Joe
P.O. Box 160668
Austin, TX 78716

Emerson, Keith
c/o MCEG
11355 Olympic Blvd.
Los Angeles, CA 90064

Emery, Ralph
c/o The Nashville Network
2806 Opryland Dr.
Nashville, TN 37214
Country music disc jockey

Emmanuel
1406 Georgette St.
Santurce, Puerto Rico 00910

Emmons, Bobby
Route #2, Johnson Chapel Rd.
Brentwood, TN 37027

The Emotions
168 Orchid Dr.
Pearl River, NY 19685

English, Jon
P.O. Box 144
Milsons Point
NSW 2061, Australia

Ennis, Tom
c/o Arista Records
6 W. 57th St.
New York, NY 10019
Record company executive

Eno, Brian
c/o Opal
330 Harrow Rd.
London W9 2HP, England

Entertainers Against Hunger
P.O. Box 150934
Nashville, TN 37215-0934

Entwhistle, John
c/o QBQ
48 E. 50th St.
New York, NY 10022

Enya (Eithne Ni Bhroanain)
c/o Geffen Records
9130 Sunset Blvd.
Los Angeles, CA 90069

Erasure
c/o Sire Records
3300 Warner Blvd.
Burbank, CA 91510

Eric B. and Rakim
298 Elizabeth St.
New York, NY 10012

Ertegun, Ahmet
c/o Atlantic Records
75 Rockefeller Plaza
New York, NY 10019
Record company executive

The Escape Club
c/o Atlantic Records
75 Rockefeller Plaza
New York, NY 10019

Eshuys, Margriet
c/o Rock In Waterland
Bilderdijkpark 4A
Amsterdam 1052 RZ
The Netherlands

Esquire
c/o Summa
8507 Sunset Blvd.
Los Angeles, CA 90069

Essex, David (Cook).
109 Eastbourne Mews
London W2, England

Estefan, Gloria
8390 S.W. 4th Street
Miami, FL 33144

Estes, Deon
c/o Negus-Fancey
66 Blenheim Crescent
London W11 1NZ, England

Ethel and the Shameless Hussies
c/o MCA Records
1701 West End Ave.
Nashville, TN 37203

Etheridge, Melissa
c/o Island Records
14 E. 4th St.
New York, NY 10012

Eubanks, Kevin
c/o Abby Hoffer
223½ E. 48th St.
New York, NY 10017

Eurogliders
c/o Sweet Conspiracy
500 Oxford St., Bondi Junction
Sydney, NSW 2022, Australia

Europe
P.O. Box 5080
San Francisco, CA 94101

Eurythmics
(Annie Lennox and Dave Stewart)
P.O. Box 245
London N8 90G, England

Everette, Leon
5325 S. Orange Blossom Trail
Orlando, FL 32809

Everly Brothers (Phil and Don)
2510 Franklin Rd.
Nashville, TN 37204

Everything But The Girl
c/o Basement Music
6 Pembridge Rd.
London W11 3HL, England

Evigan, Greg
c/o Joe Gottfried
15456 Cabrito Rd.
Van Nuys, CA 91406

Ewing, Skip
2980 Beverly Glen Circle (#302)
Los Angeles, CA 90077

Exciter
P.O. Box 6010
Sherman Oaks, CA 91413

Exile
510 W. Short
Lexington, KY 40507

Exodus
c/o Capitol Records
1750 N. Vine St.
Hollywood, CA 90028

Exotic Storm
701 4th Ave. S. (#500)
Minneapolis, MN 55415

Exposé
14352 SW 142nd Ave.
Miami, FL 33186

4 By Four
8899 Beverly Blvd.
Los Angeles, CA 90048

54-40
c/o Warner Bros. Records
3300 Warner Blvd.
Burbank, CA 91510

Fabian (Forte)
6671 Sunset Blvd. (#1502)
Hollywood, CA 90028

The Fabulous 50's
Formula Impressions
9500 Lackland Road
St. Louis, MO 63114
Official newsletter for Greasers &
Kool Kats

The Fabulous Thunderbirds
3001 Lake Austin Blvd.
Austin, TX 78703

Face to Face
c/o PolyGram Records
810 Seventh Ave.
New York, NY 10019

Fachin, Eria
3447 Kennedy Rd., Unit 4
Scarborough, ON M1V 3S1,
Canada

Factor, Andy
c/o Virgin Records
9247 Alden Dr.
Beverly Hills, CA 90210
A&R executive

Fagot, John
c/o Capitol Records
1750 N. Vine St.
Hollywood, CA 90028
Record company executive

Fahey, John
c/o Producers, Inc.
5109 Oak Haven Lane
Tampa, FL 33617

Fairbairn, Bruce
2744 W. 33rd Ave.
Vancouver, BC V6N 2G1, Canada
Record producer

Fairbanks Films
141 Fifth Ave.
New York, NY 10010
Music video producers/directors

Fairchild, Barbara
c/o Hallmark
15 Music Sq.
Nashville, TN 37203

Fairground Attraction
c/o RCA Records
1133 Ave. of the Americas
New York, NY 10036

Fairlight
1610 Butler Ave.
Los Angeles, CA 90025
Synthesizer manufacturer

Fairport Convention
P.O. Box 37
Banbury, Oxon, England

Faith No More
P.O. Box 988
San Francisco, CA 94101

Faithfull, Marianne
Yew Tree Cottage
Aldworth, Berkshire, England

Falana, Lola
10100 Santa Monica Blvd. (#1600)
Los Angeles, CA 90067

Falco
Mohlstrasse 16
D-8000 Munich 80, West Germany

The Fall
10100 Santa Monica Blvd. (#1600)
Los Angeles, CA 90067

Faltermeyer, Harold
1888 Century Park E. (#1400)
Los Angeles, CA 90067
Film composer

The Family Brown
71 Birchview Rd.
Nepean, ON K2G 3G3, Canada

Famous Music Corp.
1 Gulf & Western Plaza
New York, NY 10023
Music publisher

Fania All-Stars
c/o Third World
200 Varick St.
New York, NY 10014

Faraci, Vic
c/o Warner Bros. Records
P.O. Box 120897
Nashville, TN 37212
Record company executive

Faraci, Vince
c/o Atlantic Records
75 Rockefeller Plaza
New York, NY 10019
Record company executive

Farfisa
135 W. Foster Ave.
Bensenville, IL 60106
Organ manufacturer

Fargo, Donna
P.O. Box 15743
Nashville, TN 37215

Farina, Mimi
c/o Bread & Roses
78 Throckmorton Ave.
Mill Valley, CA 94941

Farmer, Art
c/o DeLeon
4031 Panama Ct.
Piedmont, CA 94611

Farner, Mark
P.O. Box 2977
Hendersonville, TN 37077

Farnham, John
c/o Wheatley
49 Bank St., South Melbourne
VIC 3205, Australia

Faster Pussycat
9000 Sunset Blvd. (#405)
Los Angeles, CA 90069

The Fat Boys
250 W. 57th St. (#1723)
New York, NY 10107

Fate
c/o Rock On International
Radhusstraede 4A
1466 Copenhagen K, Denmark

Fates Warning
P.O. Box 31190
Hartford, CT 06103

Feather, Leonard
c/o Los Angeles Times
Times Mirror Square
Los Angeles, CA 90053
Jazz critic

Feehan, Tim
c/o S.L. Feldman
1534 W. 2nd Ave.
Vancouver, BC V6J 1H2, Canada

The Feelies
c/o Ballfield Prods.
9 Bernard Ave.
Haledin, NJ 07508

Feiden, Bob
c/o RCA Records
1133 Ave. of the Americas
New York, NY 10036
A&R executive

Feineigle, Bob
c/o E/P/A Records
51 W. 52nd St.
New York, NY 10019
A&R executive

Feinstein, Michael
c/o Winston Simone
1780 Broadway
New York, NY 10019

Feldman, Sam L.
1534 W. 2nd Ave.
Vancouver, BC V6J 1H2, Canada
Booking agent/personal manager

Feliciano, Jose
8961 Sunset Blvd. (#2B)
Los Angeles, CA 90069

Femme Fatale
c/o MCA Records
445 Park Ave.
New York, NY 10022

Fender
c/o CBS Musical Instruments
1300 E. Valencia Dr.
Fullerton, CA 92634
Guitar manufacturer

Fender, Freddy
(Baldemar Huerta)
P.O. Box 4003
Beverly Hills, CA 90213

Fenster, Jeff
c/o Geffen Records
9130 Sunset Blvd.
Los Angeles, CA 90069
A&R executive

Ferguson, Jay
P.O. Box U
Tarzana, CA 91356

Ferguson, Maynard
P.O. Box 716
Ojai, CA 93023

Ferrante and Teicher
(Arthur and Louis)
P.O. Box 12403, NS Station
Atlanta, GA 30355

Ferry, Bryan
10 Southwick Mews
London SW2, England

Fetchin Bones
P.O. Box 33128
Charlotte, NC 28233

Fey, Barry
2175 S. Cherry
Denver, CO 80222
Personal manager/concert
promoter

Fialka, Karel
100 Universal City Plaza
(Bldg. 422)
Universal City, CA 91608

Fidell, Glenn
c/o Relativity/Combat Records
187-07 Henderson Ave.
Hollis, NY 11423
Record company executive

Fifth Angel
c/o Epic Records
51 W. 52nd St.
New York, NY 10019

The Fifth Dimension
c/o Marc Gordon
1022 N. Palm Ave.
Los Angeles, CA 9009

Fincher, David
c/o Propaganda Films
413 S. La Brea Ave.
Los Angeles, CA 90036
Music video director

Fine Young Cannibals
c/o AGM Mgmt.
1312 N. La Brea Ave.
Hollywood, CA 90028

Fink, Cathy
P.O. Box 5778
Takoma Park, MD 20912

Finn, Tim
c/o Ideal
138 Nelson Rd. S.
Melbourne, VIC 3205, Australia

Fiona
10100 Santa Monica Blvd. (#1600)
Los Angeles, CA 90067

Fiorillo, Elisa
8730 Sunset Blvd. (PH W)
Los Angeles, CA 90069

Firefall
c/o Fantasma
2000 S. Dixie Hwy.
West Palm Beach, FL 33401

Firefox
9200 Sunset Blvd. (#1220)
Los Angeles, CA 90069

Firetown
1888 Century Park E. (#1400)
Los Angeles, CA 90067

Fishbone
3935 Zinland (#8)
Studio City, CA 91604

Fisher, Eddie
c/o Charles Rapp
150 Broadway
New York, NY 10019

Fishof, David
888 Seventh Ave.
New York, NY 10019
Personal manager/concert
promoter

The Fit
c/o A&M Records
1416 N. La Brea Ave.
Hollywood, CA 90028

Fitzgerald, Ella
c/o Norman Granz
451 N. Canon Dr.
Beverly Hills, CA 90210

Fitzgerald, Kit
24 Fifth Ave.
New York, NY 10011
Music video director

Fitzgerald, Rich
c/o Reprise Records
3300 Warner Blvd.
Burbank, CA 91510
Record company executive

Fitzgerald-Hartley
(Larry and Mark)
7250 Beverly Blvd. (#200)
Los Angeles, CA 90036
Personal managers

Five Star
P.O. Box 29, Romford
Essex RM7 OST, England

The Fixx
P.O. Box 4XN
London W1A 4XN, England

Flack, Roberta
c/o Atlantic Records
75 Rockefeller Plaza
New York, NY 10019

The Flamingos
25 High St.
Southboro, MS 10772

Flash Cadillac
P.O. Box 6588
San Antonio, TX 78209

Fleetwood Mac
(also **Mick Fleetwood**)
c/o Warner Bros. Records
3300 Warner Blvd.
Burbank, CA 91510

Fleischman, David
c/o Atlantic Records
75 Rockefeller Plaza
New York, NY 10019
Record company executive

Flesh For Lulu
c/o Hughes Music
76 Hillfield Rd.
London NW6 1QA, England

The Flirts
1776 Broadway (#1801)
New York, NY 10019

Flo and Eddie
(**Mark Volman and Howard
Kaylan**)
c/o Cohen Mgmt.
5831 Sunset Blvd.
Los Angeles, CA 90028

Flock of Seagulls
526 Nicollett Mall
Minneapolis, MN 55402

Florida Custom Coach West
4230 Whitsett Ave. (#4)
Studio City, CA 91604
Creates band tour buses

Flotsam and Jetsam
P.O. Box 2739
Phoenix, AZ 85061

The Flying Pickets
c/o Judy Totten
28 Alexander St.
London W2 5NU, England

Fogelberg, Dan
Mountain Bird Ranch
P.O. Box 824
Pagosa Springs, CO 81147

Fogelsong, Jim
c/o Capitol Records
1111 16th Ave. S.
Nashville, TN 37212
Record company executive

Fogerty, John
P.O. Box 9245
Berkeley, CA 94709

Foghat
1783 Massachusetts
Cambridge, MA 02140

Folks, Scott
c/o EMI-Manhattan Records
1370 Ave. of the Americas
New York, NY 10019
A&R executive

Foos, Richard
c/o Rhino Records
2225 Colorado Ave.
Santa Monica, CA 90404
Record company executive

Forbert, Steve
1700 Hayes St. (#301)
Nashville, TN 37203

Force MDs
c/o General Talent
1700 Broadway
New York, NY 10019

Ford, Lita
8383 Wilshire Blvd. (#546)
Beverly Hills, CA 90211

Ford, Robben
c/o Warner Bros. Records
3300 Warner Blvd.
Burbank, CA 91510

Ford, Tennessee Ernie
P.O. Box 31-552
San Francisco, CA 94131

Fordham, Julia
c/o Virgin Records
9247 Alden Dr.
Beverly Hills, CA 90210

Foreigner
1790 Broadway (PH)
New York, NY 10019

Forester Sisters
128 Volunteer Dr.
Hendersonville, TN 37075
Fan club

Forman, Lynn
c/o E/P/A Records
1801 Century Park W.
Los Angeles, CA 90067
Record company executive

Foster, David
2434 Main St. (#202)
Santa Monica, CA 90405

Foster, Ian
c/o Manna
9 Carnaby St.
London W1V 1PG, England

Foster, Jim
41 Britain St. (#200)
Toronto, ON M5A 1R7, Canada

Foster, Lloyd David
P.O. Box 121656
Nashville, TN 37212

Fountain, Pete
2 Poldras St.
New Orleans, LA 70140

The Four Aces
12 Marshall St. (#8Q)
Irvington, NJ 07111

The Four Freshmen
601 S. Rancho Dr. (#C18)
Las Vegas, NV 89106

The Four Guys
c/o Audiograph
20 Music Square E.
Nashville, TN 37203

The Four Lads
32500 Concord Dr. (#221)
Madison Heights, MI 49071

The Four Seasons
168 Orchid Dr
Pearl River, NY 10965

The Four Tops
200 W. 51st St (#1410)
New York, NY 10019

Fowler, Fred
c/o Chrysalis Records
645 Madison Ave.
New York, NY 10022

Fowley, Kim
c/o Music Connection
6640 Sunset Blvd.
Hollywood, CA 90028
Record producer

Fox, George
P.O. Box 120897
Nashville, TN 37212

Fox, Samantha
P.O. Box 159
Colchester CO3 5RD, England

Frampton, Peter
25 Ives St.
London SW3, England

Franklin, Aretha
8450 Linwood St.
Detroit, MI 48206

Franklin, David
1290 S. Omni International
Atlanta, GA 30303
Personal manager

Franklin, Rodney
c/o CBS Records
51 W. 52nd St.
New York, NY 10019

Franks, Michael
151 El Camino Dr.
Beverly Hills, CA 90212

Frazier, Dallas
Route #5 (#133)
Gallatin, TN 37066

Free Flight
c/o Gurtman
162 W. 56th St.
New York, NY 10019

Freed, Bennett
8438 Sunset Blvd. (#103)
Los Angeles, CA 90069
Personal manager

Freed, Lance
c/o Almo Irving Music
1358 N. La Brea Ave.
Hollywood, CA 90028
Music publishing executive

Freedman, Arnold
South Park (#216)
U.S. Rt. 1
Walpole, MA 02081

Frehley, Ace
P.O. Box 968
Old Bridge, NJ 08857

Fresh!
P.O. Box 91878
Los Angeles, CA 90009
Fan magazine

Fresh, Doug E.
c/o General Talent
1700 Broadway
New York, NY 10019

Freston, Tom
c/o MTV
1775 Broadway
New York, NY 10019
Music television executive

Frets
20085 Stevens Creek
Cupertino, CA 95014
Musicians' magazine

Freud, James
c/o Geffen Records
9130 Sunset Blvd.
Los Angeles, CA 90069

Frey, Glenn
7250 Beverly Blvd. (#200)
Los Angeles, CA 90036-2560

Fricke, Janie
P.O. Box 798
Lancaster, TX 75146

Friday Night Videos
850 Seventh Ave. (#603)
New York, NY 10019
Music television series

Friedberg, Rick
c/o Suddleson, Irell & Manella
1800 Ave. of the Stars
Los Angeles, CA 90067
Music video director

Friedman, Emily
917 W. Wolfram
Chicago, IL 60651
Folk music magazine publisher

Friedman, Kim Paul
4425 Babcock Ave.
Studio City, CA 91604
Music video director

Friedman, Kinky (Richard)
511 Cozzens Ln.
North Brunswick, NJ 08902

Friendship
1901 Ave. of the Stars (#1240)
Los Angeles, CA 90067

Friesen, David
P.O. Box 29242
Oakland, CA 94604

Friesen, Gil
c/o A&M Records
1416 N. La Brea Ave.
Hollywood, CA 90028
Record company executive

Fripp, Robert
c/o EG Mgmt.
63A Kings Rd.
London SW3 4NT, England

Fritz, Ken
648 N. Robertson Blvd.
Los Angeles, CA 90069
Personal manager

Frizzell, David
1302 Division St. (#102)
Nashville, TN 37203

Front Row Films
87 Nottinghill Gate
London W11, England
Music video producers/directors

Frontier Booking
1776 Broadway
New York, NY 10019
Booking agent

Frontiere, Dominic
3815 W. Olive Ave. (#202)
Burbank, CA 91505
TV/film composer

Fuhrmann, Andre
c/o E/P/A Records
51 W. 52nd St.
New York, NY 10019
A&R executive

Full Force
217 Lafayette Ave.
Brooklyn, NY 11238

Fuller, Simon
c/o 19 Mgmt.
Unit 32, Ransomes Docks
35–37 Parkgate Rd.
London SW11 4NP, England
Personal manager

Fullerton, Sandi
c/o Dan Stevens
22420 Pacific Coast Highway
Malibu, CA 90265
Music television director

Funicello, Annette
c/o Rita Rose
10075 Dedham Dr.
Indianapolis, IN 46229
Fan club

• The Funkadelics
c/o Far Out
7417 Sunset Blvd.
Hollywood, CA 90046

Furlong, Michael
P.O. Box 878
Sonoma, CA 95476

Future Radio
P.O. Box 34005
Louisville, KY 40232-4005
Broadcasts original demos

Fuzzbox
P.O. Box 235
Balsall Heath
Birmingham B1Z 9RZ, England

G-Force
c/o Atlantic Records
6 W. 57th St.
New York, NY 10019

GTR
c/o Sun Artists
9 Hillgate St.
London W8 7SP, England

Gabriel, Howie
c/o Relativity/Combat Records
187-07 Henderson Ave.
Hollis, NY 11423
Record company executive

Gabriel, Peter
25 Ives St.
London SW3, England

Gaines, Rosie
807B Allston Way
Berkeley, CA 94710

Galante, Joe
c/o RCA Records
30 Music Square W.
Nashville, TN 37203
Record company executive

Galaxy
c/o Handle
1 Derby St., Mayfair
London W1Y 7HD, England

Gale, Eric
c/o Sanford Ross
1700 Broadway
New York, NY 10019

Gallico, Al
344 E. 49th St.
New York, NY 10017
Music publisher

Galway, James
c/o London Artists
73 Baker St.
London W1M 1AH, England

Gamble, Kenny
c/o Philadelphia Int.
309 S. Broad St.
Philadelphia, PA 19107
Songwriter/record company
executive

Game Theory
c/o Enigma Records
1750 E. Holly Ave.
El Segundo, CA 90245

Ganggajang
c/o Bottom Line
141 Brougham St.
Kings Cross, Sydney, NSW,
Australia

Ganis, Andrea
c/o Atlantic Records
75 Rockefeller Plaza
New York, NY 10019
Record company executive

Gannon, Oliver
P.O. Box 845
Concord, CA 94522

Gap Band
200 W. 51st St. (#1410)
New York, NY 10019

Garbarek, Jan
c/o Ted Kurland
173 Brighton Ave.
Boston, MA 02134

Garber, Jesus
c/o A&M Records
1416 N. La Brea Ave.
Hollywood, CA 90028
Record company executive

Garcia, Bob
c/o A&M Records
1416 N. La Brea Ave.
Hollywood, CA 90028
Record company executive

Garcia, Jerry
P.O. Box 1065
San Rafael, CA 94902

Garfunkel, Art
1619 Broadway
New York, NY 10019

Garland, Bob
c/o CBS Records
1801 Century Park W.
Los Angeles, CA 90067
Record company executive

Garr, Michael
1925 Oakden Dr.
Los Angeles, CA 90046
Music television producer/director

Garrett, Siedah
151 El Camino Dr.
Beverly Hills, CA 90212

Garrett, Snuff
4121½ Radford Ave.
Studio City, CA 91604
Record producer

Gaspar, Jerome
c/o A&M Records
1416 N. La Brea Ave.
Hollywood, CA 90028
A&R executive

The Gatlin Brothers
(Larry, Rudy, and Steve)
2 Maryland Farms (#322)
Brentwood, TN 37027

The Gavin Report
One Hallidie Plaza (#725)
San Francisco, CA 94102
Radio and record tip sheet

Gayle, Crystal (Brenda Webb)
51 Music Square E.
Nashville, TN 37203

Gaynor, Gloria
c/o Malcolm Feld
15 Atherton Pl., Southall
Middlesex UB1 3QT, England

Gazzari's
9039 Sunset Blvd.
Los Angeles, CA 90069
Nightclub

Geffen, David
c/o Geffen Records
9130 Sunset Blvd.
Los Angeles, CA 90069
Record company executive

J. Geils Band
8 Cadman Plaza W.
Brooklyn, NY 11201

Geldof, Sir Bob
Davington Priory
London, England

Gene Loves Jezebel
c/o Hempstead Assoc.
105 Hazlebury Rd.
London 2W6 2LY, England

General Talent International
1700 Broadway (10th Floor)
New York, NY 10019
Booking agent

Genesis
25 Ives St.
London SW3, England

Genteel, Linda
7060 Hollywood Blvd. (#1212)
Hollywood, CA 90028

George, Nelson
c/o Billboard
1515 Broadway
New York, NY 10036
Music critic

Georgia Satellites
1700 Hayes St. (#301)
Nashville, TN 37203

Georgio
c/o Motown Records
6255 Sunset Blvd.
Los Angeles, CA 90028

Germino, Mark
c/o Ten Ten
1010 16th Ave. S.
Nashville, TN 37212

Gerrity, George
c/o Warner Bros. Records
3300 Warner Blvd.
Burbank, CA 91510
Record company executive

Gerry and the Pacemakers
28-A Manor Row
Bradford BDL 3QU, England

Gersh, Gary
c/o Geffen Records
9130 Sunset Blvd.
Los Angeles, CA 90069
A&R executive

Gerston, Randy
c/o Arista Records
8370 Wilshire Blvd.
Los Angeles, CA 90211
A&R executive

Getz, Stan
Shadowbrook
Irvington, NY 10533

Geyer, Renne
476 Broome St. (#6A)
New York, NY 10013

Giant Steps
c/o A&M Records
1416 N. La Brea Ave.
Hollywood, CA 90028

Gibbs, Terry
c/o Willard Alexander
660 Madison Ave.
New York, NY 10021

Gibson
c/o Norlin Music
7373 N. Cicero Ave.
Lincolnwood, IL 60646
Guitar manufacturer

Gibson, Bob
P.O. Box 333
Evanston, IL 60204

Gibson, Debbie
P.O. Box 489
Merrick, NY 11566

Gibson, Don
38 Music Square E. (#300)
Nashville, TN 37203

Gig
17042 Devonshire St. (#209)
Northridge, CA 91325
Musicians' magazine

Gilberto, Astrud
c/o Abby Hoffer
223½ E. 48th St.
New York, NY 10017-1538

Gilder, Nick
c/o Carman Prods.
15456 Cabrito Rd.
Van Nuys, CA 91406

Gilkyson, Eliza
845 Via de la Paz (#365)
Pacific Palisades, CA 90272

Gill, Vince
7250 Beverly Blvd. (#200)
Los Angeles, CA 90036

Gillespie, Dizzy (John)
1995 Broadway (#501)
New York, NY 10023

Gillette, Steve
c/o Lloyd Segal
1116 N. Cory Ave.
Los Angeles, CA 90069

Gilley, Mickey
4500 Spencer Hwy.
Pasadena, TX 77504

Gilmour, David
200 W. 57th St. (#1403)
New York, NY 10019

Gimbel, Norman
P.O. Box 50013
Montecito, CA 93150
Songwriter

Gina Go-Go
c/o Capitol Records
1750 N. Vine St.
Hollywood, CA 90028

Gipsy Kings
c/o Elektra Records
9229 Sunset Blvd.
Los Angeles, CA 90069

Giraldi, Bob
c/o GASP!
581 Sixth Ave.
New York, NY 10011
Music video director

The Girls Next Door
207 Westport Rd. (#202)
Kansas City, MO 64111

Girlschool
c/o Barry Army
98 Puddleton Crescent
Canford Heath
Poole, Dorset, England

Gismonti, Egberto
c/o Ted Kurland
173 Brighton Ave.
Boston, MA 02134

Giuffria
c/o Winterland
890 Tennessee St.
San Francisco, CA 94107

Glaser, Jim
c/o Taylor
2401 12th Ave. S.
Nashville, TN 37204

Glass, Daniel
c/o Chrysalis Records
645 Madison Ave.
New York, NY 10022
Record company executive

Glass, Philip
853 Broadway (#2120)
New York, NY 10003
Avant-garde composer

✦ **Glass Tiger**
238 Davenport (#126)
Toronto, ON M6R 1J6, Canada

Glenn (Spove)
c/o Empire
Kocksgatan 28
Stockholm 11623, Sweden

Glenn, Garry
c/o Motown Records
6255 Sunset Blvd.
Los Angeles, CA 90028

Glew, Dave
c/o E/P/A Records
51 W. 52nd St.
New York, NY 10019
Record company executive

Gmeiner, Ray
c/o Elektra Records
9229 Sunset Blvd.
Los Angeles, CA 90069
Record company executive

The Go Betweens
c/o Capitol Records
1750 N. Vine St.
Hollywood, CA 90028

Go West
c/o Blueprint
81 Harley House, Marylebone Rd.
London NW1, England

The Godfathers
c/o Epic Records
51 W. 52nd St.
New York, NY 10019

Godley and Creme (Kevin and Lol)
c/o John Gaydon
Chelsea Wharf, 15 Lots Rd.
London SW10 0QH, England
Music video directors

Goffin, Louise
151 El Camino Dr.
Beverly Hills, CA 90212

Golde, Franne
c/o Chappell Music
810 Seventh Ave.
New York, NY 10019
Songwriter

Golden Earring
c/o Diversified
17650 W. Twelve Mile Rd.
Southfield, MI 48076

Goldenberg, Billy
3815 W. Olive Ave. (#202)
Burbank, CA 91505
Film/TV composer

Goldman, Albert
c/o William Morrow
105 Madison Ave.
New York, NY 10016
Controversial rock biographer

Goldman, Elliot
c/o RCA Records
1133 Ave. of the Americas
New York, NY 10036
Record company executive

Goldmark, Andy
11 W. 17th St.
New York, NY 10011
Songwriter

Goldmine
700 E. State St.
Iola, WI 54990
Record collectors' magazine

Goldsboro, Bobby
P.O. Box 5250
Ocala, FL 32678-5250

Goldsmith, Jerry
2049 Century Park E. (#3700)
Los Angeles, CA 90067
Film composer

Goldstein, Patrick
c/o Los Angeles Times
Times Mirror Square
Los Angeles, CA 90053
Music journalist

Goldstein, Wendy
c/o RCA Records
1133 Ave. of the Americas
New York, NY 10036
A&R executive

Goldstone, Mike
c/o PolyGram Records
3800 Alameda Ave. (#1500)
Burbank, CA 91505
Record company executive

Golson, Benny
c/o Helen Keane
49 E. 96th St.
New York, NY 10128

Gomm, Ian
c/o Charly
156–166 Ilderton Rd.
London SE15 1NT, England

' **Good Question**
c/o Craig Nowag
6037 Haddington Dr.
Memphis, TN 38119

Goodman, Jerry
14011 Ventura Blvd. (#200B)
Sherman Oaks, CA 91423

Goodman, Randy
c/o RCA Records
30 Music Square W.
Nashville, TN 37203
Record company executive

Gordon, Dexter
c/o MS Mgmt.
130 E. 31st St.
New York, NY 10016

Gordon, Robert
3 E. 54th St. (#1400)
New York, NY 10022

Gordon, Shep
c/o Alive Ent.
8271 Melrose Ave.
Los Angeles, CA 90046
Personal manager

Gordy, Berry, Jr.
c/o Motown Records
6255 Sunset Blvd.
Los Angeles, CA 90028
Record company executive

Gore, Mrs. Albert (Tipper)
Rt. #2
Carthage, TN 37030
Anti-obscenity spokesperson

Gore, Lesley
c/o Soundedge
332 Southdown Rd.
Lloyd Harbor, NY 11743

**The Gorfaine/Schwartz Agency
(Mike and Sam)**
3815 W. Olive Ave. (#202)
Burbank, CA 91505
Agents for film/TV music

Gorman, Tom
c/o Capitol Records
1750 N. Vine St.
Hollywood, CA 90028
Record company executive

Gorme, Eydie
P.O. Box 5140
Beverly Hills, CA 90210

Gormley, Mike
c/o L.A. Personal Direction
8335 Sunset Blvd.
Los Angeles, CA 90069
Personal manager

Gosdin, Vern
818 18th Ave. S. (#300)
Nashville, TN 37203

Gospel Music Association
38 Music Square W.
Nashville, TN 37203

Gould, Morton
c/o ASCAP
One Lincoln Plaza
New York, NY 10023
Pres., Performing rights
organization

Gouldman, Graham
Kennedy House
31 Stamford St., Altrincham
Cheshire WA14 1ES, England

Goulet, Robert
151 El Camino Dr.
Beverly Hills, CA 90212

Gowan
41 Britain St. (#200)
Toronto, ON M5A 1R7, Canada

Graceland Mansion
P.O. Box 16508
Memphis, TN 38186-0508
Elvis Presley's home/museum

Graffiti
151 John Street (#506)
Toronto, ON M5V 2T2, Canada
Fan magazine

Graham, Bill
201 11th St.
San Francisco, CA 94103
Concert promoter/personal
manager

Graham, Jaki
Harley House
Marylebone Rd.
London NW1 5HT, England

Gramm, Lou
1790 Broadway (PH)
New York, NY 10019

Grand Ole Opry House
2804 Opryland Dr.
Nashville, TN 37214

Grand Staff
P.O. Box 2144
Kankakee, IL 60901

Grandmaster Flash (Joseph Sadler)
200 W. 51st St. (#1410)
New York, NY 10019

Grant, Amy
Riverstone Farm
Moran Rd.
Franklin, TN 37064

Grant, Eddy
P.O. Box 212
London, England

The Grapes Of Wrath
1755 Robson St.
Vancouver, BC V6G 1C9, Canada

Grappelli, Stephane
c/o Abby Hoffer
223½ E. 48th St.
New York, NY 10017-1538

The Grass Roots
888 Seventh Ave. (#402)
New York, NY 10019

Grasso, Carl
c/o I.R.S. Records
100 Universal City Plaza
(Bldg. 422)
Universal City, CA 91608
Record company executive

Grateful Dead
P.O. Box 1073
San Rafael, CA 94901

Gray, Dobie
(Leonard Ainsworth, Jr.)
210 25th Ave. N. (#N-101)
Nashville, TN 37203

Gray, Gregory
1790 Broadway (PH)
New York, NY 10019

Gray, Mark
P.O. Box 22419
Nashville, TN 37202

Great White
P.O. Box 67487
Los Angeles, CA 90067

Greater Talent Network
150 Fifth Ave. (#1102)
New York, NY 10011
Speakers bureau

Greco, Buddy
9200 Sunset Blvd. (#621)
Los Angeles, CA 90069

Green, Al
9200 Sunset Blvd. (#823)
Los Angeles, CA 90069

Green on Red
P.O. Box 2896
Torrance, CA 90507

Greenberg, Jerry
c/o WTG Records
1801 Century Park W.
Los Angeles, CA 90067
Record company executive

Greene, Jack
P.O. Box 4966
Little Rock, AR 72214

Greene, Michael
c/o NARAS
4444 Riverside Dr. (#202)
Burbank, CA 91505
Pres., National music organization

Greenhill, Manny and Mitch
c/o Folklore
1671 Appian Way
Santa Monica, CA 90401
Agents/managers for folk artists

Greenwood, Lee
1204 17th Ave. S. (#300)
Nashville, TN 37212

Grein, Paul
c/o Billboard
9107 Wilshire Blvd.
Beverly Hills, CA 90210
Music journalist

Gretsch
908 W. Chestnut
Chanute, KS 66720
Instrument maker

Grey, Joel (Katz)
c/o Nina Fireman
2 W. 73rd St.
New York, NY 10023

Grierson, Don
c/o E/P/A Records
1801 Century Park W.
Los Angeles, CA 90067
Record company executive

Griff, Ray
P.O. Box 158925
Nashville, TN 37215

Griffey, Dick
c/o Solar Records
1635 N. Cahuenga Blvd.
Los Angeles, CA 90028
Record company executive

Griffin, Reggie
c/o Glo
98 Hamilton Park
Columbus, OH 43203

Griffith, Gerry
c/o EMI-Manhattan Records
1370 Ave. of the Americas
New York, NY 10019
A&R executive

Griffith, Nanci
P.O. Box 121684
Nashville, TN 37212

Griffiths, Richard
c/o Virgin Music
827 N. Hilldale Ave.
W. Hollywood, CA 90069
Music publishing executive

Grim Reaper
1133 Broadway (#735)
New York, NY 10010

Grisman, David
7957 Nita Ave.
Canoga Park, CA 91304

Gronenthal, Max
P.O. Box 4217
N. Hollywood, CA 91607

Gross, Henry
2600 Poplar (#324)
Memphis, TN 38111

Grossman, Stefan
c/o Folklore
1671 Appian Way
Santa Monica, CA 90401

Grusin, Dave
c/o GRP Records
555 W. 57th St. (#1228)
New York, NY 10019

Grusin, Don
c/o GRP Records
555 W. 57th St. (#1228)
New York, NY 10019

Guadalcanal Diary
P.O. Box 1584
Marietta, GA 30067

Guccione, Bob, Jr.
c/o Spin
6 W. 18th St.
New York, NY 10011-4608
Music magazine publisher

Guercio, James
P.O. Box 310
Nederland, CO 80466
Record producer

Guild
225 W. Grand St. (#203)
Elizabeth, NJ 07207
Guitar maker

Guitar
110 Midland Ave.
Port Chester, NY 10573-1490
Musicians' magazine

Guitar Center
7425 Sunset Blvd.
Los Angeles, CA 90046
Includes Rockwalk honoring
musicians

Guitar Player
20085 Stevens Creek Blvd.
Cupertino, CA 95014
Musicians' magazine

Gunn, Rhonda
P.O. Box 120897
Nashville, TN 37212

Guns N' Roses
9000 Sunset Blvd. (#405)
Los Angeles, CA 90069

Guthrie, Arlo
The Farm
Washington, MA 01223

Guthrie, Gwen
c/o Bob Caviano
254 W. 51st St.
New York, NY 10019

Gutter Boy
c/o Geffen Records
9130 Sunset Blvd.
Los Angeles, CA 90069

Guy
c/o MCA Records
70 Universal City Plaza
Universal City, CA 91608

Guy, Buddy
c/o American Famous
816 W. Evergreen
Chicago, IL 60622

The Gyrlz
c/o ICM
40 W. 57th St.
New York, NY 10019

Hackett, Steve
c/o Brian Gibbon
126 Great Portland St.
London W1, England

Haden, Charlie
c/o Abby Hoffer
223½ E. 48th St.
New York, NY 10022

Hagar, Sammy
9229 Sunset Blvd. (#625)
Los Angeles, CA 90069

The Hagers
P.O. Box 121153
Nashville, TN 37212

Haggard, Marty
c/o David Skepner
7 Music Square N.
Nashville, TN 37203

Haggard, Merle
P.O. Box 536
Palo Cedro, CA 96073

Hague, Stephen
1780 Broadway (#1200)
New York, NY 10019
Record producer

Bill Haley's Comets
2011 Ferry Ave. (#U19)
Camden, NJ 08104

Hall and Oates (Daryl and John)
130 W. 57th St. (#2A)
New York, NY 10019

Hall, Tom T.
P.O. Box 40209
Brentwood, TN 37027

Hall, Tony
c/o Manna Ent.
9 Carnaby St.
London W1V 1PG, England
Personal manager

♪ **Hallow's Eve**
18653 Ventura Blvd. (#311)
Tarzana, CA 91356

Halsey, Jim
24 Music Square W.
Nashville, TN 37203-3204
Booking agent/personal manager

Hamby, Larry
c/o CBS Records
34 Music Square E.
Nashville, TN 37203
A&R executive

Hamilton, Chico
c/o Arthur Shafman
723 Seventh Ave.
New York, NY 10019

Hamilton, George, IV
P.O. Box 727
Matthews, NC 28105

Hamilton, Vickie
c/o Geffen Records
9130 Sunset Blvd.
Los Angeles, CA 90069
A&R executive

Hamlisch, Marvin
c/o Songwriter's Guild
276 Fifth Ave.
New York, NY 10001
Songwriter

Hammer, Jan
3815 W. Olive Ave. (#202)
Burbank, CA 91505

Hammer, MC
2599 Stevenson Blvd.
Fremont, CA 94538

Hammond
4200 W. Diversey
Chicago, IL 66639
Organ manufacturer

Hammond, Jeremy
c/o EMI-Manhattan Records
1370 Ave. of the Americas
New York, NY 10019
Record company executive

Hammond, John
P.O. Box 210203
San Francisco, CA 94121

Hampton, Lionel
1995 Broadway
New York, NY 10023

Hancock, Herbie
1250 N. Doheny Dr.
Los Angeles, CA 90069

Hangman
c/o Capitol Records
1750 N. Vine St.
Hollywood, CA 90028

Hanna, Roland
c/o Abby Hoffer
223½ E. 48th St.
New York, NY 10017-1538

Hansen, Randy
c/o Adam's
827 Folsom St.
San Francisco, CA 94107

Hanson, Candice
9255 Sunset Blvd.
10th Floor
Los Angeles, CA 90069
Music attorney

Harbough, Lorie
c/o PolyGram Records
3800 Alameda Ave. (#1500)
Burbank, CA 91505
A&R executive

Hard, Bill
c/o The Hard Report
4 Trading Post Way
Medford Lakes, NJ 08055
Radio and records tip sheet

• **Hard Rock Cafe**
510 N. Robertson Blvd.
Los Angeles, CA 90048
Displays rock memorabilia

Hardcastle, Paul
c/o 19 Mgmt.
9 Disraeli Rd.
London SW, England

Hardin, Gus
c/o Jim Halsey Co.
24 Music Square W.
Nashville, TN 37203

Harlequin
41 Britain St. (#200)
Toronto, ON M5A 1R7, Canada

The Harmonica Rascals
P.O. Box 156
Roselle, NJ 07203

Harper, Roy
c/o Acorn
Winterfold House
46 Woodfield Rd., Kings Heath
Birmingham B13 9UJ, England

The Harptones
55 W. 119th St.
New York, NY 10026

Harris, Eddie
c/o DeLeon
4031 Panama Ct.
Piedmont, CA 94611

Harris, Emmylou
P.O. Box 1384
Brentwood, TN 37027

Harris, Jimmy "Jam"
c/o Flyte Tyme
4330 Nicollet Ave.
Minneapolis, MN 55409

Harris, Jordan
c/o Virgin Records
9247 Alden Dr.
Beverly Hills, CA 90210
Record company executive

Harris, Sam
9465 Wilshire Blvd. (#424)
Beverly Hills, CA 90212

Harrison, George
Friar Park Rd.
Henley-On-Thames, England

Harrison, Jerry
c/o Overland
1775 Broadway
New York, NY 10019

Harry, Deborah
c/o Overland
1775 Broadway
New York, NY 10019

Hart, Corey
1888 Century Park E. (#1400)
Los Angeles, CA 90067

Hart, Freddie
c/o Tessier-Marsh
505 Canton Pass
Madison, TN 37115

Hartford, John
P.O. Box 638
Indian Hills, CO 80454

Hartman, Bret
c/o MCA Records
70 Universal City Plaza
Universal City, CA 91608
Record company executive

Hartman, Dan
3 E. 54th St. (#1400)
New York, NY 10022

Hartman, Lisa
9145 Sunset Blvd. (#218)
Los Angeles, CA 90069

Harvey, Alex
c/o Renthal-Kaufman
1900 Ave. of the Stars
Los Angeles, CA 90067

Harvey, Hilary
P.O. Box 421268
San Francisco, CA 94142

Havana
6253 Hollywood Blvd. (#810)
Hollywood, CA 90028

Havens, Richie
10 E. 44th St. (#700)
New York, NY 10017

Hawkins, Edwin
c/o Glitter Mgmt.
1833 N. Orange Grove Ave.
Los Angeles, CA 90046

Hawkins, Ronnie
3015 Kennedy Rd. (#1)
Scarborough, ON M1V 1E7,
Canada

Hawkins, Screamin' Jay (Jalacy)
1833 N. Orange Grove Ave.
Los Angeles, CA 90046

Hawkins, Tramaine
339 S. Robertson Blvd. (#102)
Beverly Hills, CA 90211

Hawkins, Walter
10100 Santa Monica Blvd. (#1600)
Los Angeles, CA 90067

Hay, Colin James
575 Madison Ave. (#600)
New York, NY 10022

Hayes, Bonnie
c/o Chrysalis Records
645 Madison Ave.
New York, NY 10022

Hayes, Isaac
c/o Hush Prods.
231 W. 58th St.
New York, NY 10010

Haywoode
c/o Mr. I. Mouse
920 Dickson St.
Marina del Rey, CA 90292

Haza, Ofra
c/o Sire Records
3300 Warner Blvd.
Burbank, CA 91510

Head, Murray
273A King's Rd.
London SW3, England

Head, Roy
c/o Hugh Dancy
3095 Hwy. 301 N.
Lake Cornorant, MS 38641

Healey, Jeff
c/o Forte Records
326½ Howland Ave.
Toronto, ON M5R 3B9, Canada

• **Heart**
219 First Avenue N. (#333)
Seattle, WA 98109
Fan club

The Heaters
c/o KP Prods.
132 N. Doheny Dr.
Los Angeles, CA 90048

Heathen
c/o Combat Records
187-07 Henderson Ave.
Hollis, NY 11423

Heaven
c/o ATI
888 Seventh Ave.
New York, NY 10106

Heaven 17
3 Notting Hill Gate
London W11 3HX, England

Heavy D and the Boyz
c/o ICM
40 W. 57th St.
New York, NY 10019

Hedges, Michael
P.O. Box 9532
Madison, WI 53715

Hee Haw
2806 Opryland Dr.
Nashville, TN 37214
Television country music program

Hein, Wesley and William
c/o Enigma Records
1750 E. Holly Ave.
El Segundo, CA 90245
Record company executives

Helix
P.O. Box 577
Waterloo, ON N2J 4B8, Canada
Fan club

Heller, Liz
c/o MCA Records
70 Universal City Plaza
Universal City, CA 91608
Music video executive

Hellion
18653 Ventura Blvd. (#307)
Ventura, CA 91532

Helloween
c/o IRD
149-03 Guy R. Brewer Blvd.
Jamaica, NY 11434

Helm, Levon
c/o Magna
595 Madison Ave.
New York, NY 10022

Hemmert, Terri
c/o WXRT
4949 W. Belmont Ave.
Chicago, IL 60641
Disc jockey

Henderson, Florence
9000 Sunset Blvd. (#1200)
Los Angeles, CA 90069

Henderson, Michael
c/o EMI-Manhattan Records
1370 Ave. of the Americas
New York, NY 10019

**Jimi Hendrix Information
Management Institute**
P.O. Box 374
Des Plaines, IL 60016
Fan newsletter

Hendryx, Nona
130 W. 57th St. (#8B)
New York, NY 10019

Henke, James
c/o Rolling Stone
745 Fifth Ave.
New York, NY 10151
Music critic

Henley, Don
10880 Wilshire Blvd. (#2110)
Los Angeles, CA 90024

Henry, Clarence "Frogman"
c/o Bob Aster
23 Holly Dr.
La Place, LA 70068

Hensley, Tari
c/o McFadden
818 18th Ave. S.
Nashville, TN 37203

Herbert, Herbie
2051 Third St.
San Francisco, CA 94107
Personal manager

Herman, Jerry
c/o ASCAP
One Lincoln Plaza
New York, NY 10023
Songwriter

Woody Herman Orchestra
417 Marawood Dr.
Woodstock, IL 60098

Herman's Hermits
P.O. Box 81, Brighton, Oldham
Manchester OLD 5DG, England

Heroes
c/o Sounz
1 Brunswick Park Rd.
Wednesbury
West Midlands WS10 9HL,
England

Herschel
c/o WDVE
200 Fleet St. (#3999)
Pittsburgh, PA 15220
Program director/disc jockey

Herzog, Doug
c/o MTV
1775 Broadway
New York, NY 10019
Music television executive

Hewett, Howard
c/o Elektra Records
9229 Sunset Blvd.
Los Angeles, CA 90069

Heyward, Nick
c/o Reprise Records
3300 Warner Blvd.
Burbank, CA 91510

Heyward, Sharon
c/o Virgin Records
9247 Alden Dr.
Beverly Hills, CA 90210
Record company executive

Hiatt, John
1700 Hayes St. (#301)
Nashville, TN 37203

Hicks, Dan (and His Hot Licks)
c/o Savoy Music
1111 Kearney St.
San Francisco, CA 94133

Higgins, Bertie
16 E. Broad St. (PH)
Columbus, OH 43215

Highway 101
P.O. Box 120897
Nashville, TN 37212

Hilburn, Robert
c/o Los Angeles Times
Times Mirror Square
Los Angeles, CA 90053
Music critic

Hill, Dan
c/o Propas Mgmt.
6A Wellesley St. W.
Toronto, ON M4Y 1E7, Canada

Himmelman, Peter
South Park (#216)
U.S. Rt. 1
Walpole, MA 02081

Hindsight
c/o Virgin Records
9247 Alden Dr.
Beverly Hills, CA 90210

Hine, Rupert
23241 Ventura Blvd. (#100)
Woodland Hills, CA 91364

Hinton, Bruce
c/o MCA Records
1701 West End Ave.
Nashville, TN 37203
Record company executive

Hipsway
30 E. End Ave. (#2P)
New York, NY 10028

Hirax
18653 Ventura Blvd. (#311)
Tarzana, CA 91356

Hiroshima
6404 Wilshire Blvd. (#800)
Los Angeles, CA 90048

Hirt, Al
809 St. Louis St.
New Orleans, LA 70112

Hit and Run Music
25 Ives St.
London SW3, England
Personal manager

Hit Factory
237 W. 54th St.
New York, NY 10019
Recording studio

Hit Parader
Charlton Bldg.
Derby, CT 06418
Fan magazine

Hit Video USA
1000 Louisiana Ave.
Houston, TX 77002
Music video programming

●**Hitchcock, Robyn**
(and the Egyptians)
c/o A&M Records
1416 N. La Brea Ave.
Hollywood, CA 90028

Hitmakers
20847 Sherman Way (#205)
Canoga Park, CA 91306
Radio and records tip sheet

Hits
15477 Ventura Blvd. (#300)
Sherman Oaks, CA 91403
Industry magazine

Ho, Don
2005 Kalia Rd.
Honolulu, HI 96815

Hobbs, Becky
c/o Kathy Woods
220 A. Craighead
Nashville, TN 37205

Hochberg, Victoria
9000 Sunset Blvd. (#1200)
Los Angeles, CA 90069
Music video director

Hodgson, Roger
P.O. Box 1656
Nevada City, CA 95959

Hoenig, Michael
P.O. Box 775
Bryn Mawr, PA 19010

Hoffer, Abby
223½ E. 48th St.
New York, NY 10017-1538
Jazz booking agent

Hoffman, Janie
c/o MCA Records
70 Universal City Plaza
Universal City, CA 91608
Record company executive

Hofmann, Peter
Schloss Schoenreuth
Schoenreuth 8581, West Germany

Hohner
P.O. Box 15035
Richmond, VA 23227
Instrument manufacturer

Holden, Stephen
c/o New York Times
229 W. 43rd St.
New York, NY 10036
Music critic

Holdsworth, Allan
17609 Ventura Blvd. (#212)
Encino, CA 91316

Holland, Jools
c/o Prestige
Bugle House
21A Noel St.
London W1V 3PD, England

Holliday, Jennifer
9000 Sunset Blvd. (#1200)
Los Angeles, CA 90069

Hollier, Jill
P.O. Box 69180
Los Angeles, CA 90069

Hollywood Beyond
c/o Warner Bros. Records
3300 Warner Blvd.
Burbank, CA 91510

Hollywood Reporter
6715 Sunset Blvd.
Hollywood, CA 90028
Trade magazine

Hollywood Walk of Fame
c/o Hollywood Chamber of
Commerce
6290 Sunset Blvd.
Hollywood, CA 90028

Holmes, Clint
151 El Camino Dr.
Beverly Hills, CA 90212

Holmes, Rupert
c/o Spotlite
221 W. 57th St.
New York, NY 10019

Holstein, Fred and Ed
1040 W. Granville (#222)
Chicago, IL 60660

Holt, David
c/o Folklore
1671 Appian Way
Santa Monica, CA 90401

Holy Soldier
P.O. Box 7000-123
Rancho Palos Verdes, CA 90274

Holzman, Allan
10351 Santa Monica Blvd. (#211)
Los Angeles, CA 90025
Music video director

Home and Studio Recording
c/o Music Maker
22024 Lassen St. (#118)
Chatsworth, CA 91311
Magazine for engineers and
producers

Honeymoon Suite
41 Britain St. (#103)
Toronto, ON M5A 1R7, Canada

Hoodoo Gurus
c/o Harbour
63 William St.
Sydney, NSW 2000, Australia

Hooker, John Lee
P.O. Box 210103
San Francisco, CA 94121

Hooper, Stix
151 El Camino Dr.
Beverly Hills, CA 90212

The Hooters
P.O. Box 205
Ardmore, PA 19003

Hopkins, Linda
151 El Camino Dr.
Beverly Hills, CA 90212

Hopkins, Nicky
45A Moreton Terrace, Westminster
London SW1 V2NS, England

Horn, Jim
P.O. Box 120897
Nashville, TN 37212

Horn, Paul
P.O. Box 6193, Station C
Victoria, BC V8P 5L5, Canada

Horne, Lena
1200 S. Arlington Ave.
Los Angeles, CA 90024

Horner, James
3815 W. Olive Ave. (#202)
Burbank, CA 91505
Film composer

Hornsby, Bruce (and The Range)
10513 Cushdon Ave.
Los Angeles, CA 90069

Horowitz, Vladimir
1995 Broadway
New York, NY 10023

Horowitz, Zach
c/o MCA Records
70 Universal City Plaza
Universal City, CA 91608
Record company executive

Horton, Steve
c/o Capitol Records
1111 16th Ave. S.
Nashville, TN 37212

Hot House
c/o Kollectiv
132 Liverpool Rd.
London N1 1LA, England

Hot Locks
8951 Sunset Blvd.
Los Angeles, CA 90069
Rock 'n' roll hairstylists

•**Hot Tuna**
611 Broadway (#822)
New York, NY 10012

Hothouse Flowers
3 E. 54th St. (#1400)
New York, NY 10022

House, James
c/o MCA Records
1701 West End Ave.
Nashville, TN 37203

◾ **House of Lords**
c/o RCA Records
1133 Ave. of the Americas
New York, NY 10036

House of Schock
6201 Sunset Blvd. (#206)
Los Angeles, CA 90028

Houston, Cissy
P.O. Box 82
Great Neck, NY 11021

Houston, David
c/o TFE
324 Johnson Building
Shreveport, LA 71101

Houston, Thelma
c/o Abby Hoffer
223½ E. 48th St.
New York, NY 10017-1538

Houston, Whitney
410 E. 50th St.
New York, NY 10022-8071

Howard, George
c/o MCA Records
70 Universal City Plaza
Universal City, CA 91608

Howard, Jan
c/o Tessier-Marsh
505 Canton Pass
Madison, TN 37115

Howard, Miki
c/o Tammi
1800 S. Robertson Blvd.
Los Angeles, CA 90035

Howe, Bones
c/o The FK Mgmt. Co.
D6, Metropolitan Wharf
Wapping Wall
London E1, England

Howe, Steve
c/o Arista Records
6 W. 57th St.
New York, NY 10019

Hubbard, Freddie
17609 Ventura Blvd. (#212)
Encino, CA 91316

Hudson, Al
c/o Capitol Records
1750 N. Vine St.
Hollywood, CA 90028

Hudson, Susan
c/o Mercury Records
10 Music Square S.
Nashville, TN 37203

Hudson Brothers
10100 Santa Monica Blvd. (#1600)
Los Angeles, CA 90067

Hues Corporation
P.O. Box 5295
Santa Monica, CA 90405

Huff, Leon
c/o Philadelphia Int.
309 S. Broad St.
Philadelphia, PA 19107
Songwriter/record company
executive

Huffam, Teddy
P.O. Box 22707
Nashville, TN 37202

Huggins, Charles
c/o Hush Prods.
231 W. 58th St.
New York, NY 10019
Personal manager

Hugh, Grayson
c/o RCA Records
1133 Ave. of the Americas
New York, NY 10036

Hughes, John
c/o Hughes Music
100 Universal City Plaza
(Bldg. 507)
Universal City, CA 91608
Record company executive

Hugo Largo
c/o Warner Bros. Records
3300 Warner Blvd.
Burbank, CA 91510

Hulett, Tom
c/o WEG/Concerts West
11111 Santa Monica Blvd.
Los Angeles, CA 90025
Concert promoter

Human League
P.O. Box 153
Sheffield SL 1DR, England

Humble Pie (also **Steve Marriott**)
1800 N. Highland Ave. (#411)
Los Angeles, CA 90028

**Humperdinck, Englebert
(Arnold Dorsey)**
c/o Michelle Marx
9044 Melrose Ave.
Los Angeles, CA 90069

Hunley, Con
P.O. Box 121321
Nashville, TN 37203

Hunt, Brad
c/o Elektra Records
75 Rockefeller Plaza
New York, NY 10019
Record company executive

Hunter
476 Broome St. (#6A)
New York, NY 10013

Hunter, John
c/o Arnold Stiefel
9200 Sunset Blvd.
Los Angeles, CA 90069

Hunter, Tom
c/o MTV
1775 Broadway
New York, NY 10019
Music video executive

Hunters and Collectors
P.O. Box 216
Albert Park, VIC 3206, Australia

Huntington Station
663 S. Mallard Dr.
Palatine, IL 60067

Huntsberry, Howard
c/o MCA Records
70 Universal City Plaza
Universal City, CA 91608

Hurley, Libby
c/o Trey Turner
818 19th Ave. S.
Nashville, TN 37203

Hurrah!
c/o Kitchenware
Saint Thomas St. Table
Saint Thomas St.
Newcastle-Upon-Tyne NE1 4LE,
England

Hurricane
14755 Ventura Blvd. (#1-962)
Sherman Oaks, CA 91403

• **Husker Du**
P.O. Box 1304
Burbank, CA 91507

Husky, Ferlin
P.O. Box 48833
Chicago, IL 60648

Hutcherson, Bobby
c/o Fantasy Records
Tenth & Parker Sts.
Berkeley, CA 94710

Hutchinson, Earl
c/o Elektra Records
75 Rockefeller Plaza
New York, NY 10019
Record company executive

Hyman, Kate
c/o Chrysalis Records
645 Madison Ave.
New York, NY 10022
A&R executive

Hyman, Phyllis
1608 Walnut St. (#1302)
Philadelphia, PA 19103

INXS
8 Hayes St. (#1)
Neutral Bay, NSW 20891, Australia

I Napoleon
c/o Geffen Records
9130 Sunset Blvd.
Los Angeles, CA 90069

Iam Siam
c/o David Sonnenberg
83 Riverside Dr.
New York, NY 10024

Ian, Janis
9200 Sunset Blvd. (#1102)
Los Angeles, CA 90069

Ibrahim, Abdullah
(Dollar Brand)
c/o DeLeon
4031 Panama Ct.
Piedmont, CA 94611

Icehouse
Village Centre, Kings Cross 27A
Sydney, Australia

Ice-T
c/o Sire Records
75 Rockefeller Plaza
New York, NY 10019

The Icicle Works
c/o Side One
1775 Broadway
New York, NY 10019

Idle Tears
P.O. Box 69180
Los Angeles, CA 90069

Idol, Billy (Broad)
c/o Eastend
8209 Melrose Ave.
Los Angeles, CA 90046

Ienner, Don
c/o CBS Records
51 W. 52nd Street
New York, NY 10019
Record company executive

Iglauer, Bruce
c/o Alligator Records
P.O. Box 60234
Chicago, IL 60660
Record company executive

Iglesias, Julio
(Julio Jose Iglesias de la Cueva)
4500 Biscayne Blvd.
Miami, FL 33137

Illinois Entertainer
2200 E. Devon (#192)
Des Plaines, IL 60018
Fan and musicians' magazine

Illinois Jacquet
c/o Atlantic Records
75 Rockefeller Plaza
New York, NY 10019

Immaculate Fools
c/o Playhouse
1 Eversham St.
London W11 4AJ, England

The Impalas
168 Orchid Dr.
Pearl River, NY 10965

The Imperials
P.O. Box 17272
Memphis, TN 38187

Imperiet
P.O. Box 1018
Lidingo, Sweden

The Impressions
50 Music Square W. (#804)
Nashville, TN 37203

In Pursuit
c/o Side One
1775 Broadway
New York, NY 10019

In Vitro
10513 Cushdon Ave.
Los Angeles, CA 90064

Information Society
c/o Reprise Records
3300 Warner Blvd.
Burbank, CA 91510

Ingram, James
9200 Sunset Blvd. (#823)
Los Angeles, CA 90069

Ingram, Luther
c/o Don Dortch
904 Raynor St.
Memphis, TN 38114

‣ **Ink Spots**
P.O. Box 70218
Fort Lauderdale, FL 33307

Inner City
c/o Virgin Records
9247 Alden Dr.
Beverly Hills, CA 90210

Insiders
P.O. Box 437
Excelsior, MN 55331

**International Bluegrass
Music Association**
326 St. Elizabeth St.
Owensboro, KY 42301

**International Creative
Management (ICM)**
40 W. 57th St.
New York, NY 10019

**International Fan Club
Organization**
P.O. Box 177
Wild Horse, CO 80862

Iovine, Jimmy
c/o A&M Records
1416 N. La Brea Ave.
Los Angeles, CA 90028
Record producer

Iris, Donnie
c/o ATI
888 Seventh Ave.
New York, NY 10106

Irish Rovers
P.O. Box 4486
Vancouver, BC, Canada

Iron Butterfly
223 Colonial Homes Dr.
Atlanta, GA 30309

Iron Maiden
P.O. Box 1AP
London W1 L1P, England
Fan club

Isaak, Chris
c/o Warner Bros. Records
3300 Warner Blvd.
Burbank, CA 91510

Isaak, Wayne
c/o A&M Records
595 Madison Ave.
New York, NY 10022
Publicity executive

Isham, Mark
234 Cabot St (#6)
Beverly, MA 01915

Isham, Wayne
c/o The Company
1041 N. Highland Ave.
Hollywood, CA 90038
Music video director

The Isley Brothers
(Rudolph, Ronald and O'Kelly)
446 Liberty Rd.
Inglewood, NJ 07631

Isquith, Jack
c/o E/P/A Records
51 W. 52nd St.
New York, NY 10019
Record company executive

Israelson, Peter
900 Broadway (#604)
New York, NY 10003
Music video director

It Bites
P.O. Box 2
Egremont, Cumbria CA22 2BL,
England

❭ **Ives, Burl (Icle Ivanhoe)**
427 N. Canon Dr. (#205)
Beverly Hills, CA 90210

Iyall, Debora
c/o David Rubinson
1734 Fell St.
San Francisco, CA 94117

JJ Fadd
c/o General Talent
1700 Broadway
New York, NY 10019

Jack Mack and the Heart Attack
c/o Rightrack
7952 W. Norton Ave.
Los Angeles, CA 90046

Jackson, Freddie
c/o Hush Prods.
231 W. 58th St.
New York, NY 10019

Jackson, Janet
c/o A&M Records
1416 N. La Brea Ave.
Hollywood, CA 90028

Jackson, Jermaine
c/o Arista Records
6 W. 57th St.
New York, NY 10019

Jackson, Joe
c/o Basement Music
6 Pembridge Rd
Trinity House
London W11, England

Jackson, LaToya
c/o ICM
40 W. 57th St.
New York, NY 10019

Jackson, Marlon
15445 Ventura Blvd. (#10-246)
Sherman Oaks, CA 91403

Jackson, Michael
5455 Wilshire Blvd.
Suite 2200
Los Angeles, CA 90036

The World of Michael Jackson
P.O. Box 1804
Encino, CA 91426
Fan club

The Jacksons
P.O. Box 1804
Encino, CA 91426

Jackson, Millie
c/o Keishvalent
1650 Broadway
New York, NY 10019

Jackson, Milt
211 Thompson St (#1D)
New York, NY 10012

Jackson, Nisha
c/o Capitol Records
1111 16th Ave. S.
Nashville, TN 37212

Jackson, Paul, Jr.
10100 Santa Monica Blvd. (#1600)
Los Angeles, CA 90067

Jackson, Randy
c/o John McClain
1416 N. La Brea Ave.
Hollywood, CA 90028

Jackson, Rebbie
200 W. 51st St. (#1410)
New York, NY 10019

Jackson, Wanda
P.O. Box 7007
Oklahoma City, OK 73153

Jacobs, Fred
31800 Northwestern Hwy. (#385)
Farmington Hills, MI 48018
Radio programming consultant

Jacoves, Aaron
c/o A&M Records
1416 N. La Brea Ave.
Hollywood, CA 90028
A&R executive

Jagger, Mick
c/o Jim Wiatt
8899 Beverly Blvd.
Suite 721
Los Angeles, CA 90048

Jagiello, Li'l Wally
P.O. Box 4155, Normandy Branch
Miami Beach, FL 33141

Jailhouse
8600 Wilbur Ave.
Northridge, CA 91324

Jam Productions
207 W. Goethe
Chicago, IL 60610
Concert promoter

Jamal, Ahmad
c/o Abby Hoffer
223½ E. 48th St.
New York, NY 10017-1538

James, Bob
c/o IMG Artists
22 E. 71st St.
New York, NY 10021

Dick James Organization
1040 N. Las Palmas Ave.
Los Angeles, CA 90038
Music publisher

James, Etta
(Etta James Hawkins)
c/o DeLeon
4031 Panama Ct.
Piedmont, CA 94611

The Harry James Orchestra
c/o Willard Alexander
660 Madison Ave.
New York, NY 10021

James, Melvin
16530 Ventura Blvd. (#201)
Encino, CA 91436

James, Rick (James Johnson)
c/o Mary Jane
104 Chapin Pkwy.
Buffalo, NY 14209

James, Sonny (Jimmy Loden)
c/o McFadden
818 18th Ave. S.
Nashville, TN 37203

James, Tommy (Thomas Jackson)
c/o Stephen Frank
458 W. 55th St.
New York, NY 10019

Jamieson, Bob
c/o PolyGram Records
810 Seventh Ave.
New York, NY 10019
Record company executive

Jamm
10100 Santa Monica Blvd. (#1600)
Los Angeles, CA 90067

Jan and Dean (Berry and Torrance)
8912 Burton Way
Beverly Hills, CA 90211

Jane's Addiction
c/o Overland
1775 Broadway
New York, NY 10019

Jankel, Chaz
c/o Andrew Heath
5 Poland St.
London W1, England

Janz, Paul
c/o Michael Godin
218 W. 19th St.
Vancouver, BC V5Y 2B7, Canada

Jarreau, Al
c/o Patrick Rains
8752 Holloway Dr.
Los Angeles, CA 90069

Jarrett, Keith
c/o Vincent Ryan
135 W. 16th St.
New York, NY 10011

Jason and the Scorchers
P.O. Box 120-235
Nashville, TN 37212

Jasper, Chris
c/o E/P/A Records
51 W. 52nd St.
New York, NY 10019

Jay and the Americans
c/o William Rezey
1775 Broadway
New York, NY 10019

Jaye, Miles
c/o Sedonia Walker
107 Stratton Lane
Mt. Laurel, NJ 08054

Jazz Butcher
c/o Big Time Records
6777 Hollywood Blvd.
Los Angeles, CA 90028

Jazz Times
8055 13th St. (#301)
Silver Spring, MD 20910
Fan magazine

Jazziz
3620 NW 43rd St. (#D)
Gainesville, FL 32606
Jazz magazine

Jeffreys, Garland
c/o ICM
40 W. 57th St.
New York, NY 10019

Jeffries, Nancy
c/o Virgin Records
30 W. 21st St.
New York, NY 10010
A&R executive

Jellybean (Benitez)
1888 Century Park E. (#1400)
Los Angeles, CA 90067

Jennings, Waylon
c/o Mark Rothbaum
225 Main St.
Danbury, CT 06811

The Jesus and Mary Chain
c/o Frontier
1776 Broadway
New York, NY 10019

Jeter, Genobia
1995 Broadway (#501)
New York, NY 10023

Jethro Tull
12 Stratford Pl.
London W1N 9AF, England

The Jets
P.O. Box 290097, Brooklyn Center
Minneapolis, MN 55429

Jett, Joan
P.O. Box 600
Long Beach, NY 11561

Jim and Jesse (McReynolds)
P.O. Box 304
Gallatin, TN 37066

Jimmy the Hoover
c/o Handle
1 Derby St.
Mayfair, London W1Y 7HD,
England

Jimmy Z (Zavala)
100 Universal City Plaza
(Bldg. 422)
Universal City, CA 91608

The Jitters
41 Britain St. (#200)
Toronto, ON M5A 1R7, Canada

Jo Jo and the Real People
P.O. Box 79
Liverpool L69 1SL, England

Jobete Music
6255 Sunset Blvd.
Los Angeles, CA 90028
Music publisher

Joboxers
21 Wigmore St.
London W1, England

Joel, Billy
375 N. Broadway
Jericho, NY 11753

John, Elton (Reginald Dwight)
c/o Constant Communications
51 Holland St.
London W8 7JB, England

Johnny Hates Jazz
c/o Virgin Records
Kensall House
533/579 Harrow Rd.
London W10 4RH, England

The Johnnys
c/o 135 Music
11/79 Old South Head Rd.
Bondi Junction, Sydney,
NSW 2022, Australia

Johnson, Cynthia
c/o Arista Records
8370 Wilshire Blvd.
Los Angeles, CA 90211
Record company executive

Johnson, Don
3575 Cahuenga Blvd. W. (#470)
Los Angeles, CA 90068

Johnson, Eric
P.O. Box 162197
Austin, TX 78716

Johnson, Holly
c/o MCA Records
70 Universal City Plaza
Universal City, CA 91608

Johnson, Jay
c/o WTLC
2126 Meridian St.
Indianapolis, IN 46206
Program director/disc jockey

Johnson, Jesse
c/o American Artists
312 Washington Ave. N.
Minneapolis, MN 55401

Johnson, Marc
c/o Mogul
9570 Wilshire Blvd.
Beverly Hills, CA 90212

Johnson, Michael
P.O. Box 40661
Nashville, TN 37204

Johnson, Slack
c/o EMI-Manhattan Records
1370 Ave. of the Americas
New York, NY 10019
Record company executive

Johnson, Step
c/o Capitol Records
1750 N. Vine St.
Hollywood, CA 90028
Record company executive

Johnson, Varnell
c/o EMI-Manhattan Records
1370 Ave. of the Americas
New York, NY 10019
Record company executive

The Johnson Brothers
9200 Sunset Blvd. (#823)
Los Angeles, CA 90069

Johnson Mountain Boys
P.O. Box 160
Hendersonville, TN 37077

Johnstone, Davey
9595 Wilshire Blvd. (#505)
Beverly Hills, CA 90212

Joint Communications
1311 Johnson Ferry Rd. (#252)
Marietta, GA 30068
Radio programming consultants

Jones, David Lynn
c/o PolyGram Records
10 Music Square S.
Nashville, TN 37203

Jones, Davy
P.O. Box 400
Beavertown, PA 17813

Jones, Elvin
c/o Keiko Jones Mgmt.
415 Central Park W.
New York, NY 10025

Jones, George
38 Music Square, E. (#300)
Nashville, TN 37203

Jones, Glenn
c/o West Mgmt.
1775 Broadway
New York, NY 10019

Jones, Grace
P.O. Box 82
Great Neck, NY 11022

Jones, Grandpa
P.O. Box 57
Mountain View, AR 72560

Jones, Howard
P.O. Box 185
High Wycom
Buckinghamshire HP11 2E2,
England

Jones, Jack
508 N. Kings Rd. (#2)
Los Angeles, CA 90048

Jones, Jonah
c/o Counterpoint
10 Munson Ct.
Melville, NY 11747

Jones, Marti
5 W. Hargett St. (#1004)
Raleigh, NC 27601

Jones, Oran "Juice"
298 Elizabeth St.
New York, NY 10012

Jones, Quincy
7250 Beverly Blvd. (#207)
Los Angeles, CA 90036

Jones, Rickie Lee
10100 Santa Monica Blvd. (#1600)
Los Angeles, CA 90067

Jones, Ronnie
c/o Motown Records
6255 Sunset Blvd.
Los Angeles, CA 90028
Record company executive

Jones, Shirley
132 Lasky Dr.
Beverly Hills, CA 90212

Jones, Shirley Y.
c/o EMI-Manhattan Records
1370 Ave. of the Americas
New York, NY 10019

Jones, Spike, Jr.
631 N. La Cienega Blvd.
Los Angeles, CA 90069

Jones, Tom (Woodward)
10100 Santa Monica Blvd. (#205)
Los Angeles, CA 90067

Jones, Waymon
c/o PolyGram Records
810 Seventh Ave.
New York, NY 10019
Record company executive

The Jones Girls
P.O. Box 6010, Dept. 761
Sherman Oaks, CA 91413-6010

Jopson, John
c/o Dana Cioffi
8428 Melrose Ave.
Los Angeles, CA 90069
Music video director

Jordan, Marc
c/o RCA Records
1133 Ave. of the Americas
New York, NY 10036

Jordan, Stanley
c/o Don Dickson Mgmt.
55 Grand St.
New York, NY 10013

Jordan, Traci
c/o Motown Records
6255 Sunset Blvd.
Los Angeles, CA 90028
Music video executive

Jordanaires
c/o World Class
1522 Demonbreun St.
Nashville, TN 37203

Journey
P.O. Box 5952
San Francisco, CA 94101

Joy Division
c/o Qwest Records
3300 Warner Blvd.
Burbank, CA 91510

Joyner, Tom
c/o WGCI
6 N. Michigan Ave.
Chicago, IL 60602
Disc jockey

Judas Priest
3 E. 54th St. (#1400)
New York, NY 10022

The Judds (Wynonna and Naomi)
Old Charlotte Rd.
Franklin, TN 37064

Juicy
c/o Arista Records
6 W. 57th St.
New York, NY 10019

Jukeboxes Unlimited
12655 McLennan Ave.
Granada Hills, CA 91344
Jukebox expert

Julian and the Gents
9017 Reseda Blvd. (#210)
Northridge, CA 91324

Jungklas, Rob
P.O. Box 1994
San Francisco, CA 94101

Junkyard
c/o Geffen Records
9130 Sunset Blvd.
Los Angeles, CA 90069

K-9 Posse
c/o Arista Records
6 W. 57th St.
New York, NY 10019

KBC
P.O. Box 15-584
San Francisco, CA 94115

K.C. and the Sunshine Band
(Harry Wayne Casey)
774 NW 71st St.
Miami, FL 33166

Kane, Big Daddy
c/o Warner Bros. Records
75 Rockefeller Plaza
New York, NY 10019

Kane, Kieran
P.O. Box 121089
Nashville, TN 37212

The Kane Gang
c/o Kitchenware
St. Thomas Street Stables
St. Thomas Street
Newcastle-Upon-Tyne NE1 4LE,
England

Kansas
c/o E/P/A Records
1801 Century Park W.
Los Angeles, CA 90067

Kantner, Paul
P.O. Box 15-584
San Francisco, CA 94115

Kappus, Mike
P.O. Box 210103
San Francisco, CA 94121
Personal manager/booking agent

Kasem, Casey
America's Top 10
c/o KTLA
5800 Sunset Blvd.
Los Angeles, CA 90028
Radio personality

Kashif
c/o Raymond Katz
9255 Sunset Blvd.
Los Angeles, CA 90069

Katrina and the Waves
28 Addison Close
Feltwell RR, Thetford
Norfolk 1P2 64DJ, England

Kaufman, Bennett
c/o RCA Records
6363 Sunset Blvd.
Los Angeles, CA 90028
A&R executive

Kaufman, Matthew "King"
2054 University Ave. (#400)
Berkeley, CA 94704
Record producer/personal
manager

Kaukonen, Jorma
c/o Bowman
2300 Fulton St.
San Francisco, CA 94118

Kawai
2-8-8 Shinbashi
Minato-ku, Tokyo 105, Japan
Piano and organ maker

Kay, Arnie
c/o Mars Talent
168 Orchid Dr.
Pearl River, NY 10965
Booking agent/personal manager

Kay, John (and Steppenwolf)
(Joachim Krauledat)
9454 Wilshire Blvd. (#206)
Beverly Hills, CA 90212

Kaye, Chuck
c/o Windswept Pacific
4450 Lakeside Dr. (#200)
Burbank, CA 91505
Music publisher

Kaye, Sylvia Fine
8955 Beverly Blvd.
Los Angeles, CA 90048
Musical theatre historian

Kaye, Tony
P.O. Box 775
Bryn Mawr, PA 19010

Kazan, Lainie (Levine)
9903 Santa Monica Blvd. (#283)
Beverly Hills, CA 90212

Kean, Sherry
6A Wellesley St. W.
Toronto, ON M4Y 1E7, Canada

Keel
14755 Ventura Blvd. (#1-710)
Sherman Oaks, CA 91403
Fan club

Keene, Tommy
P.O. Box 1304
Burbank, CA 91507

Keep it Dark
60B Cornwall Gardens
London SW7 4BG, England

Kelley, Irene
c/o MCA Records
1701 West End Ave.
Nashville, TN 37203

Kellow, Khris
c/o Ellipsis
252 Robby Lane
New Hyde Park, NY 11040

Kelly, Gene
8899 Beverly Blvd.
Los Angeles, CA 90048

Kelly, Karen
c/o I.R.S. Records
100 Universal City Plaza
(Bldg. 422)
Universal City, CA 91608
Record company executive

Kelly, Paul (and the Messengers)
P.O. Box 192, Kings Cross
Sydney, NSW 2011, Australia

Kemp, Johnny
c/o Jim Tyrrell
828 E. 222nd St.
New York, NY 10467

Kemp, Wayne
P.O. Box 390
Pontotoc, MS 38863

Kendall, Charlie
c/o WSHE
3000 SW 60th Ave.
Ft. Lauderdale, FL 33314
Disc jockey

The Kendalls (Royce and Jeannie)
1522 Demonbreun St.
Nashville, TN 37203

Kendrick, Eddie
1510 W. 50th St.
Los Angeles, CA 90062

Kennedy, Jerry
54 Music Square E.
Nashville, TN 37203
Record producer

Kenny G (Gorelick)
648 N. Robertson Blvd.
Los Angeles, CA 90048

Kenyon, Kathy
c/o Island Records
14 E. 4th St.
New York, NY 10012
Record company executive

Kerrang!
40 Long Acre
London WC2, England
Heavy metal magazine

Kershaw, Doug
8899 Beverly Blvd.
Los Angeles, CA 90048

Kershaw, Nik
c/o Arctic King
Avon House
360 Oxford St.
London W1N 9HA, England

Kessel, Barney
c/o Bennett Morgan
119 W. 57th St.
New York, NY 10019

Keyboard Magazine
20085 Stevens Creek Blvd.
Cupertino, CA 95014
Musicians' magazine

Khan, Chaka (Yvette Stevens)
P.O. Box 3125
Beverly Hills, CA 90212

Kiara
c/o Arista Records
6 W. 57th St.
New York, NY 10019

Kick Axe
P.O. Box 127
Winnipeg, MB R3C 2G1, Canada

Kid Creole and the Coconuts
130 W. 57th St. (#2A)
New York, NY 10019

Kid Flash
9229 Sunset Blvd. (#311)
Los Angeles, CA 90069

Kidd, Eddie
c/o Warner Bros. Records
3300 Warner Blvd.
Burbank, CA 91510

Kihn, Greg
P.O. Box 387
Fremont, CA 94537

Kiley, Richard
Ryerson Rd.
Warwick, NY 10990

Killen, Buddy
c/o Tree International
8 Music Square W.
Nashville, TN 37203
Music publisher

Killer Dwarfs
238 Davenport Rd. (#319)
Toronto, ON M5R 1J6, Canada

Killing Joke
c/o EG Mgmt.
63A Kings Rd.
London SW3 4NT, England

Kilzer, John
644 N. Doheny Dr.
Los Angeles, CA 90069

Kimmel, Tom
c/o John Baruck
1046 Carol Dr.
W. Hollywood, CA 90069

King
c/o Perry Haines
2 Alma Place
London SE19, England

King, Albert
c/o Associated Booking
1995 Broadway
New York, NY 10023

King, B.B.
(Riley "Blues Boy" King)
P.O. Box 16707
Memphis, TN 38131

King, Ben E. (Benjamin Nelson)
c/o Knight
185 Clinton
Staten Island, NY 10301

King, Carole (Klein)
P.O. Box 7308
Carmel, CA 93921

King, Evelyn "Champagne"
119 W. 57th St. (#901)
New York, NY 10019

King, Jackie
c/o Brad Simon
445 E. 80th St.
New York, NY 10021

King, Jay
414 12th St.
Sacramento, CA 95814
Record producer

King, Morgana
c/o Muse Records
160 W. 71st St.
New York, NY 10023

King, Paul
c/o Outlaw Mgmt.
36–38 West St.
London WC2, England

King Crimson
c/o EG Mgmt.
161 W. 54th St.
New York, NY 10019

King Diamond
P.G. Rams Alle 66
2000 Copenhagen, Denmark
Fan club

King Kobra
P.O. Box 69780
Los Angeles, CA 90069

King Tee
c/o Capitol Records
1750 N. Vine St.
Hollywood, CA 90028

Kingdom Come
12652 Killion St.
N. Hollywood, CA 91607

The Kings
41 Britain St. (#400)
Toronto, ON M5A 1R7, Canada

Kings X
P.O. Box 968
Old Bridge, NJ 08857

The Kingsmen
c/o Sterling
1139 SW Lakewood Ct.
Tigard, OR 97223

The Kingston Trio
107 Degas Rd.
Portola Valley, CA 94025

Kinison, Sam
c/o Warner Bros. Records
3300 Warner Blvd.
Burbank, CA 91510

The Kinks
c/o Larry Page
29 Ruston Mews
London W11 1RB, England

Kinley, Kathryn
c/o VH-1
1775 Broadway
New York, NY 10019
Veejay

Kirkup, Martin
c/o Direct Mgmt.
945A La Cienega Blvd.
Los Angeles, CA 90069
Personal manager

KISS
P.O. Box 77505
San Francisco, CA 94107

Kitaro (Masanori Takahashi)
c/o Geffen Records
9130 Sunset Blvd.
Los Angeles, CA 90069

Kitt, Eartha
c/o ICM
40 W. 57th St.
New York, NY 10019

Kix
P.O. Box 2679
Hagerstown, MD 21741
Fan club

Klein, Marty
c/o Agency for the
Performing Arts
9000 Sunset Blvd. (#1200)
Los Angeles, CA 90069
Booking agent

Klein, Roger
c/o E/P/A Records
1801 Century Park W.
Los Angeles, CA 90067
A&R executive

Kleinbaum, Janet
c/o Island Records
14 E. 4th St.
New York, NY 10012
Publicity/music video executive

Klemmer, John
c/o Alive Ent.
1775 Broadway
New York, NY 10019

Kline, Dickie
c/o Epic Records
51 W. 52nd St.
New York, NY 10019
Record company executive

Klugh, Earl
c/o Warner Bros. Records
3300 Warner Blvd.
Burbank, CA 91510

Klymaxx
3580 Wilshire Blvd. (#1840)
Los Angeles, CA 90010

Knight, Gladys (and the Pips)
P.O. Box 42942
Las Vegas, NV 89104

Knight, Holly
c/o Chrysalis Records
645 Madison Ave.
New York, NY 10022

Knopfler, Mark
10 Southwick Mews
London SW2, England

Kobrin, Barry
c/o Relativity/Combat Records
187-07 Henderson Ave.
Hollis, NY 11423
Record company executive

Koloc, Bonnie
1040 W. Granville (#222)
Chicago, IL 60660

Kolotkin, Glen
4 Pegs Lane
Huntington, NY 11743
Record producer

Kon Kan
c/o Atlantic Records
75 Rockefeller Plaza
New York, NY 10019

Konjoyan, Jon
c/o A&M Records
1416 N. La Brea Ave.
Hollywood, CA 90028
Record company executive

Koo De Tah
c/o PolyGram Records
810 Seventh Ave.
New York, NY 10019

Kool and the Gang
641 Lexington Ave. (#1450)
New York, NY 10022

Kool Moe Dee
c/o General Talent
1700 Broadway
New York, NY 10019

Koppelman, Charles
810 Seventh Ave.
New York, NY 10019
Industry executive

Kostich, Craig
c/o Warner Bros. Records
3300 Warner Blvd.
Burbank, CA 91510
Record company executive

Kottke, Leo
P.O. Box 7308
Carmel, CA 93923

Kovac, Allen
c/o Left Bank
2519 Carmen Crest Dr.
Los Angeles, CA 90068
Personal manager

Kraftwerk
c/o Marvin Katz
75 Rockefeller Plaza
New York, NY 10019

Kragen, Ken
1112 N. Sherbourne Dr.
Los Angeles, CA 90069
Personal manager

Kranes, Bob
c/o PolyGram Records
810 Seventh Ave.
New York, NY 10019
Record company executive

Krasnow, Bob
c/o Elektra Records
75 Rockefeller Plaza
New York, NY 10019
Record company executive

Krebs, David
155 E. 55th St. (#6H)
New York, NY 10022
Personal manager

Kristofferson, Kris
8899 Beverly Blvd.
Los Angeles, CA 90048

Krokus
c/o Arista Records
6 W. 57th St.
New York, NY 10019

Kubernik, Harvey
c/o Freeway Records
P.O. Box 67930
Los Angeles, CA 90067
Record producer

Kujala, Steve
845 Via de la Paz (#365)
Pacific Palisades, CA 90272

Kurfirst, Gary
c/o Overland Prods.
1775 Broadway
New York, NY 10019
Personal manager

Kurland, Ted
173 Brighton Ave.
Boston, MA 02134
Agent/manager for jazz artists

Kushnick, Ken
327 N. Orlando Ave.
Los Angeles, CA 90048
Personal manager

L.A. Dream Team
3610 W. 6th St. (#536)
Los Angeles, CA 90020

L.A. Guns
10966 Le Conte Rd. (#A)
Los Angeles, CA 90024

LL Cool J
298 Elizabeth St.
New York, NY 10012

La La
c/o Jim Tyrrell
828 E. 222nd St.
New York, NY 10467

LaBelle, Patti
c/o MCA Records
70 Universal Plaza
Universal City, CA 91608

LaBeque, Katia and Marielle
c/o ICM
40 W. 57th St.
New York, NY 10019

Laboe, Art
c/o Original Sound
7120 Sunset Blvd.
Hollywood, CA 90046
Nostalgia record company
executive

LaBounty, Bill
9454 Wilshire Blvd. (#309)
Beverly Hills, CA 90212
Songwriter

Lace (Bobbi)
c/o Wide Country
402 NE 1st St.
Pompano Beach, FL 33060

Ladanyi, Greg
1592 Crossroads of the World
Hollywood, CA 90022
Record producer

Ladysmith Black Mambazo
1619 Broadway (#510)
New York, NY 10019

Lagrene, Bireli
c/o Abby Hoffer
223½ E. 48th St.
New York, NY 10017-1538

Laguna, Kenny
P.O. Box 1158
New York, NY 10101
Personal manager

Laine, Cleo (Clementina)
(and John Dankworth)
The Old Rectory, Wavedon
Milton Keynes MK17 8LT,
England

Laine, Frankie (LoVecchio)
c/o Thomas Cassidy
417 Marawood Dr.
Woodstock, IL 60098

Lake, Greg
c/o ATI
888 Seventh Ave.
New York, NY 10106

Lakeside
c/o The Griff Co.
1630 N. Cahuenga Blvd.
Los Angeles, CA 90028

LaMarche, Jim
58 Phoebe St.
Toronto, ON M5T 1A9, Canada

Lambert, Craig
c/o Atco Records
75 Rockefeller Plaza
New York, NY 10019
Record company executive

Lambert, Mary
c/o Sharon Oreck
5636 Melrose Ave.
Los Angeles, CA 90038
Music video director

Lambert, Rick
c/o KLOL
510 Lovett
Houston, TX 77006
Program director/disc jockey

Landau, Jon
136 E. 57th St.
New York, NY 10022
Personal manager/record producer

Landers, Audrey and Judy
3151 Cahuenga Blvd. W. (#235)
Los Angeles, CA 90068

Landreth, Sonny
c/o CBS Records
34 Music Square E.
Nashville, TN 37203

Lane, Brian
c/o Sun Artists
9 Hillgate St.
London W8 7SP, England
Personal manager

lang, k.d. (and the Reclines)
41 Britain St. (#200)
Toronto, ON M5A 1R7, Canada

Larrabee Sound
8811 Santa Monica Blvd.
Los Angeles, CA 90069
Recording studio

Larsen, Neil
9034 Sunset Blvd. (#250)
Los Angeles, CA 90069

Larson, Nicolette
P.O. Box 150973
Nashville, TN 37215

Laser Media
2046 Armacost Ave.
Los Angeles, CA 90025
Concert laser light effects

Last Tango
119 W. 57th St. (#901)
New York, NY 10019

Lathower, Mauri
c/o CBS Records
1801 Century Park W.
Los Angeles, CA 90067
A&R executive

Latin Quarter
c/o Arista Records
6 W. 57th St.
New York, NY 10019

Lattisaw, Stacy
c/o William Morris
1350 Ave. of the Americas
New York, NY 10019

Lauderdale, Jim
c/o Epic Records
1801 Century Park W.
Los Angeles, CA 90067

Lauper, Cyndi
65 W. 55th St. (#4G)
New York, NY 10019

Laurence, Paul
c/o Hush Prods.
231 W. 58th St.
New York, NY 10019

Laurence, Sherisse
c/o RCA Records
1133 Ave. of the Americas
New York, NY 10036

Laventhol and Horwath
1776 Broadway
New York, NY 10019
Business managers

Laverty, Marilyn
c/o CBS Records
51 W. 52nd St.
New York, NY 10019
Publicity executive

Lawrence, Carol (Laraia)
P.O. Box 1895
Studio City, CA 91604

Lawrence, Steve
c/o Arnold Lipsman & Assoc.
8961 Sunset Blvd.
Los Angeles, CA 90069

Laws, Hubert
c/o John Mason
9200 Sunset Blvd.
Los Angeles, CA 90069

Laws, Ronnie
c/o Mr. I. Mouse
920 Dickson St.
Marina del Rey, CA 90292

Leach, David
c/o PolyGram Records
810 Seventh Ave.
New York, NY 10019
Record company executive

The Leahy Family
P.O. Box 1282
Peterborough, ON K9J 7H5,
Canada

Lear, Amanda
Postfach 800149
D-8000 Munich 80, West Germany

Leatherwolf
P.O. Box 7542
Huntington Beach, CA 92615-7542

Leber, Steve
155 E. 55th St. (#6H)
New York, NY 10022
Personal manager

Lee, Albert
6399 Wilshire Blvd. (PH)
Los Angeles, CA 90048

Lee, Alvin
9454 Wilshire Blvd. (#206)
Beverly Hills, CA 90212

Lee, Barbara
P.O. Box 110033
Nashville, TN 37222

Lee, Brenda
(Brenda Mae Tarpley)
P.O. Box 24727
Nashville, TN 37202

Lee, Buddy
38 Music Square E. (#300)
Nashville, TN 37203
Country music booking agent

Lee, Jake E.
P.O. Box 792
Wilkes Barre, PA 18702
Fan club

Lee, Johnny
818 18th Ave. S.
Nashville, TN 37203

Lee, Peggy
(Norma Jean Egstrom)
744 Collier Dr.
San Leandro, CA 94577
Fan club

Leeds, Harvey
c/o E/P/A Records
51 W. 52nd St.
New York, NY 10019
Record company executive

Lefevre, Mylon
P.O. Box 723591
Atlanta, GA 30339

Leffler, Edward S.
c/o E.L. Mgmt.
9229 Sunset Blvd. (#625)
Los Angeles, CA 90067
Personal manager

Legacy
c/o Manna
9 Carnaby St.
London W1V 1PG, England

Legal Reins
c/o Arista Records
6 W. 57th St.
New York, NY 10019

Legal Weapon
23241 Ventura Blvd. (#100)
Woodland Hills, CA 91364

LeGrand, Michel
c/o Jim DiGiovanni
157 W. 57th St.
New York, NY 10019

Leikin, Molly-Ann
P.O. Box 93759
Hollywood, CA 90093
Songwriter's consultant

Lemaire, Sonny
P.O. Box 1273
Nashville, TN 37202
Songwriter

Lembo, Jerry
c/o CBS Records
51 W. 52nd St.
New York, NY 10019
Record company executive

Lembo, Mike
c/o Mike's Artist Mgmt.
225 W. 57th St. (#301)
New York, NY 10019

Lennon, Julian
P.O. Box 1060
Lenox Hill Station
New York, NY 10021

Lennon Sisters
944 Harding Ave.
Venice, CA 90291

Leo, Kid
c/o CBS Records
51 W. 52nd St.
New York, NY 10019
Record company executive

Leonard, Pat
c/o Fitzgerald-Hartley
7250 Beverly Blvd.
Los Angeles, CA 90036
Record producer

Leroi Brothers
6908 Cherry Meadow
Austin, TX 78745

LeRoux
P.O. Box U
Tarzana, CA 91356

Lessner, Michael
c/o Motown Records
6255 Sunset Blvd.
Los Angeles, CA 90028
Record company executive

Let's Active
37 Lee St.
Waterbury, CT 06708

The Lettermen
15910 Ventura Blvd. (#712)
Encino, CA 91436-2834

Level 42
c/o Outlaw Mgmt.
145 Oxford St.
London W1, England

Levert (Gerald)
c/o Associated Booking
1995 Broadway
New York, NY 10023

Levin, Neal
9595 Wilshire Blvd. (#505)
Beverly Hills, CA 90212
Business manager

Levine, Arnold
231 E. 55th St.
New York, NY 10022
Music television director

Levine, Michael
8730 Sunset Blvd.
Los Angeles, CA 90069
Author of *The Music Address Book*

Leviticus
c/o Lennart Soderlund
Gamlakungsvagen 53B
54132 Skovde, Sweden

Levy, Paige
c/o Warner Bros. Records
P.O. Box 120897
Nashville, TN 37212
A&R executive

Lewis, Gary (and the Playboys)
P.O. Box 53664
Indianapolis, IN 46253

Lewis, Huey (and the News)
P.O. Box 819
Mill Valley, CA 94942

Lewis, Jerry Lee
P.O. Box 3864
Memphis, TN 38173

Lewis, Jim
c/o PolyGram Records
810 Seventh Ave.
New York, NY 10019
A&R executive

Lewis, Marcus
c/o Epic Records
51 W. 52nd St.
New York, NY 10019

Lewis, Mel
c/o Abby Hoffer
223½ E. 48th St.
New York, NY 10022

Lewis, Ramsey
c/o R. Chiaro
2 W. 86th St.
New York, NY 10024

Lewis, Terry
c/o Flyte Tyme
4330 Nicollet Ave.
Minneapolis, MN 55409
Record producer

Lewisohn, Mark
c/o Harmony Books
225 Park Ave. S.
New York, NY 10003
Beatles expert/author

Lia
c/o Virgin Records
30 W. 23rd St.
New York, NY 10010

Libman-Moore Prods.
6311 Romaine St. (#7311)
Los Angeles, CA 90038
Music video producers/directors

Libow, Judy
c/o Atlantic Records
75 Rockefeller Plaza
New York, NY 10019
Record company executive

Licata, Sal
c/o EMI-Manhattan Records
1370 Ave. of the Americas
New York, NY 10019
Record company executive

Liege Lord
18653 Ventura Blvd. (#311)
Tarzana, CA 91356

Life By Night
c/o Mogul
9570 Wilshire Blvd.
Beverly Hills, CA 90212

Light, Rob
c/o Creative Artists Agency
1888 Century Park E. (#1400)
Los Angeles, CA 90067
Booking agent

Lightfoot, Gordon
1364 Yonge St. (#207)
Toronto, ON M4T 2P7, Canada

Lillywhite, Steve
250 W. 57th St. (#2028)
New York, NY 10107
Record producer

Limahl
c/o Gaff Mgmt.
2 New Kings Rd.
London SW6 4SA, England

Limelight
1724 Whitley Ave.
Los Angeles, CA 90028
Music video producers/directors

The Limeliters
17350 Ventura Blvd. (#108)
Encino, CA 91316

Limited Warranty
P.O. Box 437
Excelsior, MN 55331

Lind, Jon
c/o Virgin Music
827 Hilldale Ave.
W. Hollywood, CA 90069
Songwriter

Linde, Dennis
Route #1, Lakeview Rd.
Hermitage, TN 37076

Lindley, David (and El Rayo-X)
c/o Elektra Records
9229 Sunset Blvd.
Los Angeles, CA 90069

Linehan, Michael
c/o Reprise Records
3300 Warner Blvd.
Burbank, CA 91510
Record company executive

Lion
P.O. Box 15812
N. Hollywood, CA 91615

Lion Share
8255 Beverly Blvd.
Los Angeles, CA 91356
Recording studio

Lions and Ghosts
10100 Santa Monica Blvd. (#1600)
Los Angeles, CA 90067

Lippman, Peter
6879 Camrose Dr.
Hollywood, CA 90068
Music video director

Lipsius, Marilyn
c/o RCA Records
1133 Ave. of the Americas
New York, NY 10036
Publicity executive

LiPuma, Tommy
c/o Warner Bros. Records
75 Rockefeller Plaza
New York, NY 10019
Record company executive

Lisa Lisa (and Cult Jam)
P.O. Box 284
Brooklyn, NY 11203

Little America
16161 Ventura Blvd. (#481)
Encino, CA 91436

Little Anthony (Gourdine)
8033 Sunset Blvd. (#222)
Los Angeles, CA 90046

Little Caesar
c/o Geffen Records
9130 Sunset Blvd.
Los Angeles, CA 90069

Little Feat
8899 Beverly Blvd.
Los Angeles, CA 90048

Little Kings
P.O. Box 1309
Studio City, CA 91604

Little Mountain Sound Studios
201 W. Seventh Ave.
Vancouver, BC V5Y 1L9, Canada

Little Richard (Penniman)
9200 Sunset Blvd. (#415)
Los Angeles, CA 90069

Little River Band
98-91 Palmerston Crescent
Albert Park
Melbourne, VIC 3206, Australia

Little Steven
9200 Sunset Blvd. (#915)
Los Angeles, CA 90069

Living Blues
2615 N. Wilton Ave.
Chicago, IL 60614
Blues magazine

Living Colour
c/o Epic Records
51 W. 52nd St.
New York, NY 10019

The Living Daylights
P.O. Box 2276
Garden Grove, CA 92642

Living In A Box
c/o Chrysalis Records
9225 Sunset Blvd.
Los Angeles, CA 90069

Lizzy Borden
18653 Ventura Blvd. (#309)
Tarzana, CA 91356

Lloyd, Michael
10960 Wilshire Blvd. (#826)
Los Angeles, CA 90024
Record producer

Lloyd, Richard
c/o Dare Mgmt.
227 Waverly Place
New York, NY 10014

Lock Up
c/o Geffen Records
9130 Sunset Blvd.
Los Angeles, CA 90069

LoCurto, Sal
c/o VH-1
1775 Broadway
New York, NY 10019
Music video executive

Loder, Kurt
c/o Rolling Stone
745 Fifth Ave.
New York, NY 10151
Music journalist

Lodgic
1918 Pacific (#3)
Venice, CA 90291

Loeb and Loeb
10100 Santa Monica Blvd. (#2200)
Los Angeles, CA 90067
Attorneys/personal managers

Loebl, Jocelyn
c/o Relativity/Combat Records
187-07 Henderson Ave.
Hollis, NY 11423
Publicity executive

Lofgren, Nils
1801 Century Park E. (#1132)
Los Angeles, CA 90067

Logan, Bud
821 19th Ave. S.
Nashville, TN 37203
Record producer

Logan, Johnny
Unit 32, Ransomes Docks
35–37 Parkgate Rd.
London SW11 4NP, England

Loggins, Kenny
P.O. Box 10905
Beverly Hills, CA 90213

Lolita Pop
P.O. Box 19003
Stockholm, Sweden

Lomax, John, III
2128 Acklen Ave.
Nashville, TN 37212
Personal manager/music critic

London
22458 Ventura Blvd. (#E)
Woodland Hills, CA 91364

Lone Justice
c/o Geffen Records
9130 Sunset Blvd.
Los Angeles, CA 90069

Lone Star Cafe
61 Fifth Ave.
New York, NY 10003
Nightclub

Long Hair Rocks
2513 E. Colorado Blvd.
Pasadena, CA
Hairstylists

Long Live Rock
P.O. Box 131662 (Dept. MS)
Staten Island, NY 10313-006
Posters, t-shirts, etc.

The Long Ryders
7523 Hollywood Blvd. (#313)
Hollywood, CA 90046

Look Up
P.O. Box 723591
Atlanta, GA 30339

Loose Ends
c/o Manna
9 Carnaby St.
London W1, England

The Looters
c/o Morrison & James
5024 3rd St.
San Francisco, CA 94124

Lopez, Denise
c/o A&M Records
1416 N. La Brea Ave.
Hollywood, CA 90028

Lopez, Trini
7060 Hollywood Blvd. (#610)
Los Angeles, CA 90028

Lorber, Jeff
2519 Carmen Crest Dr.
Los Angeles, CA 90068

Lords of the New Church
c/o Frontier
1775 Broadway
New York, NY 10019

Lorelei
218 S. 16th St. (#300)
Philadelphia, PA 19107

Loren, Bryan
c/o John McClain
1416 N. La Brea Ave.
Hollywood, CA 90028

Loring, Gloria
8730 Sunset Blvd. (PH W)
Los Angeles, CA 90069

Los Angeles Songwriters Showcase
P.O. Box 93759
Hollywood, CA 90093
Songwriter organization

Los Lobos
P.O. Box 1304
Burbank, CA 91507

Lott, Roy
c/o Arista Records
6 W. 57th St.
New York, NY 10019
Record company executive

Loudness
8899 Beverly Blvd.
Los Angeles, CA 90048

Love and Money
321 Fulham Rd.
London SW10 9QL, England

Love and Rockets
c/o Big Time Records
6777 Hollywood Blvd.
Los Angeles, CA 90028

Loveless, Patty
c/o MCA Records
1514 South St.
Nashville, TN 37212

The Lover Speaks
c/o Reg Freeman
18 Longfield, Upton-upon-Severn
Worcestershire, England

Loverboy
406-68 Water St., Gastown
Vancouver, BC VGB 1AY, Canada

Lovesin, Johnny
c/o Amber
735 Queen St. W.
Toronto, ON M6J 1G1, Canada

Lovett, Lyle
6865 S. Dayton (#1300)
Englewood, CO 80111

Lovich, Lene
c/o ATI
888 Seventh Ave.
New York, NY 10106

Low, Simon
c/o RCA Records
1133 Ave. of the Americas
New York, NY 10036
A&R executive

Lowe, Nick
c/o ICM
40 W. 57th St.
New York, NY 10019

The Lowery Group
3051 Clairmont Rd. NE
Atlanta, GA 30329
Music publisher

L'Trimm
c/o General Talent
1700 Broadway
New York, NY 10019

Luba
154 Grande Cote
Rosemere, PQ J7A 1H3, Canada

Lubin, Peter
c/o PolyGram Records
810 Seventh Ave.
New York, NY 10019
A&R executive

Lucas, Carrie
200 W. 51st St. (#1410)
New York, NY 10019

The Lucy Show
16530 Ventura Blvd. (#202)
Encino, CA 91436

Ludwig
1728 Damen Ave.
Chicago, IL 60647
Drum manufacturer

Lukather, Steve
10100 Santa Monica Blvd. (#1600)
Los Angeles, CA 90067

Lundvall, Bruce
c/o EMI-Manhattan Records
1370 Ave. of the Americas
New York, NY 10019
Record company executive

Lupone, Patti
8899 Beverly Blvd.
Los Angeles, CA 90048

Lyman, Shelby
c/o CBS Records
34 Music Square E.
Nashville, TN 37203

Lynn, Cheryl
200 W. 51st St. (#1410)
New York, NY 10019

Lynn, Loretta
P.O. Box 120369
Nashville, TN 37212

Lynne, Jeff
c/o Sam Sylvester
Clintons, Wellington House
6–9 Upper St. Martins
London W, England

Lynyrd Skynyrd
3 E. 54th St. (#1400)
New York, NY 10022

Lyons, Barry
c/o I.R.S. Records
100 Universal City Plaza
(Bldg. 422)
Universal City, CA 91608
Record company executive

M&M
41 Britain St. (#200)
Toronto, ON M5A 1R7, Canada

M/A/R/R/S
c/o Island Records
14 E. 4th St.
New York, NY 10012

MC5
P.O. Box 82
Great Neck, NY 11021

MCA Music
70 Universal City Plaza
Universal City, CA 91608
Music publisher

MGMM
191 Wardour St.
London W1V 3FA, England
Music video producers/directors

MPL Communications
39 W. 54th St.
New York, NY 10019
Music publisher

MTB
1830 S. Robertson Blvd. (#201)
Los Angeles, CA 90035

MTV (Music Television)
1775 Broadway
New York, NY 10019
Music video network

Ma, Yo-Yo
c/o ICM
40 W. 57th St.
New York, NY 10019

The Mac Band
10100 Santa Monica Blvd. (#1600)
Los Angeles, CA 90067

Mack, Lonnie (McIntosh)
P.O. Box 20043
Columbus Circle Station
New York, NY 10023

Macon, Steve
c/o A&M Records
1416 N. La Brea Ave.
Hollywood, CA 90028
Music video executive

MacPherson, Fraser
P.O. Box 845
Concord, CA 94522

Madame Wong's West
2900 Wilshire Blvd.
Santa Monica, CA 94403
Nightclub

Madness
c/o Sterling Artists Mgmt.
167 Caledonian Rd.
London N1 OSL, England

Madonna (Ciccone)
9200 Sunset Blvd. (#915)
Los Angeles, CA 90069

Maglia, Lou
c/o Island Records
14 E. 4th St.
New York, NY 10012
Record company executive

Magnoli, Albert
8899 Beverly Blvd.
Los Angeles, CA 90048
Film director/personal manager

Mahal, Taj
(Henry St. Claire Fredericks)
c/o Folklore
1671 Appian Way
Santa Monica, CA 90401

Mahogany Rush
5 W. 55th St. (#306)
New York, NY 10019

The Main Attraction
2600 Nonconnah Blvd. (#390)
Memphis, TN 38132

Maitland, Mark
c/o Reprise Records
3300 Warner Blvd.
Burbank, CA 91510
Record company executive

Makaface
c/o Mismanagement
55 Fulham High St.
London SW6 3JJ, England

Makeba, Miriam
14011 Ventura Blvd. (#200-B)
Sherman Oaks, CA 91423

Malchak, Tim
1522 Demonbreun St.
Nashville, TN 37203

Maldonado, David
1674 Broadway (#703)
New York, NY 10019
Personal manager

Maldonado, Shirley
c/o WPOW
18350 NW 2nd Ave.
Miami, FL 33169
Radio station music director

Malice
c/o Atlantic Records
75 Rockefeller Plaza
New York, NY 10019

Mallet, David
191 Wardour St.
London W1V 3FA, England
Music video director

Malloy, David
1033 16th Ave. S.
Nashville, TN 37212
Record producer

Malmsteen, Yngwie
c/o ICM
40 W. 57th St.
New York, NY 10019

Malone, Michelle
c/o Arista Records
6 W. 57th St.
New York, NY 10019

Mama's Boys
c/o Jive Records
1348 Lexington Ave.
New York, NY 10128

The Mamas and the Papas
805 Third Ave. (#2900)
New York, NY 10022

Mamis, "Famous" Toby
c/o Alive Ent.
1775 Broadway
New York, NY 10019
Personal manager

Mammoth
c/o ARC
8 Cleveland Rd., Chiswick
London W4 5HP, England

Man Friday
c/o Bob Caviano
254 W. 51st St.
New York, NY 10019

Manatt, Phelps, Rothenberg, and Phillips
11355 W. Olympic Blvd.
Los Angeles, CA 90064
Music attorneys

Manchester, Melissa
10100 Santa Monica Blvd.
16th Floor
Los Angeles, CA 90067

Mancini, Henry
9200 Sunset Blvd. (#823)
Los Angeles, CA 90069

Mandel, Johnny
3815 W. Olive Ave. (#202)
Burbank, CA 91505
Film music composer

Mandrell, Barbara
P.O. Box 332
Hendersonville, TN 37075

Mandrell, Erline
P.O. Box 23110
Nashville, TN 37202

Mandrell, Louise
Old Hickory Lane
Hendersonville, TN 37202

Mangione, Chuck
c/o Gates Music
1845 Clinton Ave. N.
Rochester, NY 14621

Manhattan Transfer
3805 W. Magnolia Blvd.
Burbank, CA 91505

The Manhattans
c/o Worldwide Ent.
641 Lexington Ave.
New York, NY 10022

Manilow, Barry
P.O. Box 4095
Beverly Hills, CA 90213

Mann, Barry
3815 W. Olive Ave. (#202)
Burbank, CA 91505
Songwriter

Mann, Herbie
c/o Atlantic Records
75 Rockefeller Plaza
New York, NY 10019

Mann, Johnny
17530 Ventura Blvd. (#105)
Encino, CA 91316

Mann, Lou
c/o MCA Records
70 Universal City Plaza
Universal City, CA 91608
Record company executive

Mann, Manfred
c/o Lloyd Segal
1116 N. Cory Ave.
Los Angeles, CA 90069

Mannheim Steamroller (Chip Davis)
c/o American Gramaphone
Records
9130 Mormon Bridge Rd.
Omaha, NE 68152

Manor, Katie
c/o XTRA
4891 Pacific Highway
San Diego, CA 92110
Disc jockey

The Manor
Manor House, Shipton-on-Cherwell
Oxford, England
Recording studio

Mantronix
175 Fifth Ave. (#2229)
New York, NY 10010

Manzanera, Phil
c/o EG Records
242 E. 62nd St.
New York, NY 10021

March, Peggy
c/o Arnie Harris
26011 Redbluff Dr.
Calabasas, CA 91302

Marcovicci, Andrea
c/o Stone
1052 Carol Dr.
Los Angeles, CA 90069

Marcucci, Bob
10600 Holman Ave.
Los Angeles, CA 90024
Personal manager

Marcus, Greil
c/o Rolling Stone
745 Fifth Ave.
New York, NY 10151
Music critic

The Marcy Brothers
P.O. Box 120897
Nashville, TN 37212

Mardones, Benny
c/o Panacea
2705 Glendower Ave.
Los Angeles, CA 90027

Maria, Tania
c/o EMI-Manhattan Records
1370 Ave. of the Americas
New York, NY 10019

Marie, Teena
c/o General Talent
1700 Broadway
New York, NY 10019

Marillion
c/o The Station Agency
132 Liverpool Rd.
London N1 1LA, England

Marin, Cheech (Richard Marin)
8899 Beverly Blvd.
Los Angeles, CA 90048

Marks, Johnny
1619 Broadway
New York, NY 10019
Songwriter

Marley, Ziggy (and the Melody Makers)
151 El Camino Dr.
Beverly Hills, CA 90212

Marley Marl
c/o Warner Bros. Records
3300 Warner Blvd.
Burbank, CA 91510

Mars Talent Agency
168 Orchid Dr.
Pearl River, NY 10965
Nostalgia acts

Marsalis, Branford
P.O. Box 55398
Washington, DC 20040

Marsalis, Wynton
9000 Sunset Blvd. (#1200)
Los Angeles, CA 90069

Marsh, Dave
P.O. Box 2060
Teaneck, NJ 07666
Critic/"Rock & Roll Confidential"

Marshall
c/o Korg USA
89 Frost St.
Westbury, NY 11590
Equipment manufacturer

Marshall, Terry
c/o Daily Insider
2050 Elinora Dr.
Pleasant Hill, CA 94523
Industry insider newsletter

Marshall Tucker Band
c/o Sugar Pine
300 E. Henry St.
Spartanburg, SC 69302

Martika
c/o CBS Records
1801 Century Park W.
Los Angeles, CA 90067

Martin, Dean (Dino Crocetti)
9000 Sunset Blvd. (#1200)
Los Angeles, CA 90069

Martin, Eric
P.O. Box 5952
San Francisco, CA 94101

Martin, J.D.
c/o Hallmark
15 Music Square W.
Nashville, TN 37203

Martin, Marilyn
1841 Broadway (#411)
New York, NY 10023

Martin, Mary
c/o RCA Records
30 Music Square W.
Nashville, TN 37203
A&R executive

Martinez, Nancy
c/o Atlantic Records
75 Rockefeller Plaza
New York, NY 10019

Martone, James
c/o Enigma Records
1750 E. Holly Ave.
El Segundo, CA 90245
Record company executive

The Marvelettes
141 Dunbar Ave.
Fords, NJ 08863

Marx, Richard
2519 Carmen Crest Dr.
Los Angeles, CA 90068

The Mary Jane Girls
c/o Seidman & Seidman
135 Delaware Ave.
Buffalo, NY 14202

Mascolo, Eddie
c/o RCA Records
1133 Ave. of the Americas
New York, NY 10036
Record company executive

Masekela, Hugh
14011 Ventura Blvd. (#200-B)
Sherman Oaks, CA 91423

Mason, Dave
16121 Sunset Blvd. (#3)
Pacific Palisades, CA 90272

Mason Dixon
P.O. Box 57291
Dallas, TX 75207

Masser, Michael
8033 Sunset Blvd. (#1113)
Los Angeles, CA 90046
Songwriter/record producer

Massey, Wayne
c/o PolyGram Records
810 7th Avenue
New York, NY 10019

Material
c/o Georgiakarakos
45 W. 81st St.
New York, NY 10024

Mathieu, Mireille
122 Ave. de Wagram
Paris 75017, France

Mathis, Johnny
3500 W. Olive Ave. (#750)
Burbank, CA 91505

Matsui, Keiko
c/o MCA Records
70 Universal City Plaza
Universal City, CA 91608

Mattea, Kathy
P.O. Box 24475
Nashville, TN 37202

Matthews, Ian
(Ian Matthew MacDonald)
845 Via de la Paz (#365)
Pacific Palisades, CA 90272

Matthews, Rachel
c/o Capitol Records
1750 N. Vine St.
Hollywood, CA 90028
A&R executive

Mattiussi, Jeanne
c/o RCA Records
1133 Ave. of the Americas
New York, NY 10036
Music video executive

Maxi Priest
c/o Virgin Records
9247 Alden Dr.
Beverly Hills, CA 90210

May, Brian
P.O. Box 562
Beverly Hills, CA 90213
Film composer

Mayall, John
P.O. Box 210103
San Francisco, CA 94188

Mayfield, Curtis
P.O. Box 724677
Atlanta, GA 30339

Mays, Lyle
c/o Ted Kurland
173 Brighton Ave.
Boston, MA 02134

Mazarati
c/o Paisley Park/Warner Bros.
3300 Warner Blvd.
Burbank, CA 91510

Maze featuring Frankie Beverly
c/o V. Jones
805 Moraga Dr.
Lafayette, CA 94549

Mazer, Larry
c/o Cinema Records
P.O. Box 775
Bryn Mawr, PA 19010
Record company executive

McAnally, Mac
P.O. Box 2831
Muscle Shoals, AL 35660

McAuley-Schenker Group
8899 Beverly Blvd.
Los Angeles, CA 90048

McCabe's Guitar Shop
3101 Pico Blvd.
Santa Monica, CA 90404
Center for folk music

McCall, C.W. (Bill Fries)
c/o Bill Fries
Office of the Mayor
Ouray, CO 81427

McCandless, Paul
845 Via de la Paz (#365)
Pacific Palisades, CA 90272

McCann, Les
c/o DeLeon
4031 Panama Ct.
Piedmont, CA 94611

McCardle, Andrea
c/o William Morris
1350 Ave. of the Americas
New York, NY 10019

McCarrell, Ron
c/o Capitol Records
1750 N. Vine St.
Hollywood, CA 90028
Record company executive

The McCarters
P.O. Box 120897
Nashville, TN 37212

McCartney, Paul
(James Paul McCartney)
Waterfall Estate
Peamarsh, St. Leonard-on-Sea
Sussex, England

McCasland, Sue
P.O. Box 6581
San Jose, CA 95150
Elvis expert

McCaslin, Mary (and **Jim Ringer**)
c/o Folklore
1671 Appian Way
Santa Monica, CA 90401

McClain, Charly
P.O. Box 2757
Nashville, TN 37219

McClain, John
c/o A&M Records
1416 N. La Brea Ave.
Hollywood, CA 90028
A&R executive

McClinton, Delbert
P.O. Box 9482
Fort Worth, TX 76102

McCoo, Marilyn
10100 Santa Monica Blvd. (#1600)
Los Angeles, CA 90067

McDaniel, Mel
c/o Top Billing
1114 17th Ave. S
Nashville, TN 37212

McDonald, Brian
c/o American Artists
312 Washington Ave. N.
Minneapolis, MN 55401

McDonald, "Country" Joe
17337 Ventura Blvd. (#300)
Encino, CA 91316

McDonald, Michael
80 Universal City Plaza
Universal City, CA 91608

McDowell, Carrie
c/o Motown Records
6255 Sunset Blvd.
Los Angeles, CA 90028

McDowell, Ronnie
P.O. Box 53
Portland, TN 37148

McElroy, Donna
P.O. Box 120897
Nashville, TN 37212

McEntire, Pake
1114 17th Ave. S. (#101)
Nashville, TN 37212

McEntire, Reba
Star Route
Stringtown, OK 74569

McEuen, John
9000 Sunset Blvd. (#1200)
Los Angeles, CA 90069

McFadden, Jack
818 18th Ave. S.
Nashville, TN 37203
Personal manager

McFadden and Whitehead
(Gene and John)
200 W. 51st St. (#1410)
New York, NY 10019

McFerrin, Bobby
9000 Sunset Blvd. (#1200)
Los Angeles, CA 90069

McGarrigle, Kate and Anna
2067 Broadway (#B)
New York, NY 10023

McGhee, Doc
9145 Sunset Blvd. (#100)
Los Angeles, CA 90069
Personal manager

McGhee, Walter "Brownie"
c/o APA
120 W. 57th St.
New York, NY 10019

McGovern, Maureen
c/o Warner Bros. Records
3300 Warner Blvd.
Burbank, CA 91510

McGuinn, Roger
P.O. Box 1265
Morro Bay, CA 93442

McGuire, Barry
P.O. Box 320
Lindale, TX 75771

McGuire Sisters
(Phyllis, Dorothy, and Christine)
100 Rancho Circle
Las Vegas, NV 89119

McKay, Kris
c/o Arista Records
6 W. 57th St.
New York, NY 10019

McKee, Maria
c/o Geffen Records
9130 Sunset Blvd.
Los Angeles, CA 90069

McKeon, Jim
c/o RCA Records
1133 Ave. of the Americas
New York, NY 10036
Record company executive

McKuen, Rod
P.O. Box G
Beverly Hills, CA 90213

McKusick, Hal
c/o Counterpoint
10 Munson Ct.
Melville, NY 11747

McLagan, Ian
P.O. Box 2276
Garden Grove, CA 92642

McLaughlin, John
c/o CBS Records
51 W. 52nd St.
New York, NY 10019

McLaughlin, Pat
10513 Cushdon Ave.
Los Angeles, CA 90064

McLaughlin, Sarah
c/o Arista Records
6 W. 57th St.
New York, NY 10019

McLean, Don
Old Manitou Rd.
Garrison, NY 10524

McLeese, Don
c/o Chicago Sun-Times
401 N. Wabash Ave.
Chicago, IL 60611
Music critic

McMahon, Ed
c/o NBC-TV
3000 W. Alameda Ave.
Burbank, CA 91505
Host of Star Search

McNeill, Dugan
c/o Good Music
200 Third Ave. N.
Minneapolis, MN 55401

McRae, Carmen
c/o Abby Hoffer
223½ E. 48th St.
New York, NY 10017-1538

McTell, Ralph
c/o Bruce May
11 Oxford Circus Ave.
London W1R 1AD, England

McVicker, Dana
c/o Capitol Records
1111 16th Ave. S.
Nashville, TN 37212

McVie, Christine
8306 Wilshire Blvd. (#1008)
Beverly Hills, CA 90211

McVie, John
P.O. Box 69180
Los Angeles, CA 90069

Meade, Donna
10 Music Square S.
Nashville, TN 37203

The Meat Puppets
P.O. Box 110
Tempe, AZ 85281

Meatloaf (Marvin Lee Aday)
P.O. Box 68, Stockport
Cheshire SK3 OJY, England

Medeiros, Glenn
c/o Carefree Mgmt.
1762 Main St.
Buffalo, NY 14208

Medley, Bill
1112 N. Sherbourne Dr.
Los Angeles, CA 90069

The Meeting
c/o Cameron
822 Hillgrove Ave.
Western Springs, IL 60558

Megadeth
9145 Sunset Blvd. (#100)
Los Angeles, CA 90069

Mehta, Zubin
c/o New York Philharmonic
Avery Fisher Hall
1941 Broadway
New York, NY 10023

Melanie (Safka)
c/o Dennis Vaughan
Heathcoat House
18–20 Savile Rd.
London W1, England

Melle-Mel (Melvin Glover)
200 W. 51st St. (#1410)
New York, NY 10019

Mellencamp, John Cougar
Rt. 1 (#361)
Nashville, IN 47448

Melodia (USA)
4265 Marina City Dr. (#415)
Marina del Rey, CA 90292
USSR-USA record company

Melody Maker
Berkshire House
168–173 High Holborn
London WC1, England
Fan magazine

**Melvin, Harold (and the
Bluenotes)**
P.O. Box 82
Great Neck, NY 11021

Men At Work
P.O. Box 289
Abbotsford, VIC 2067, Australia

Men Without Hats
c/o Outlaw Mgmt.
145 Oxford St.
London W1R 1TD, England

Mendes, Sergio
P.O. Box 118
Los Angeles, CA 90028

Mensch, Peter
80 Warwick Gardens
London W14 8PR, England
Personal manager

o **Mental As Anything**
79 Old South Head Rd. (#17)
Bondi Junction, NSW 2022,
Australia

Menudo
Padosa Hato Rey
157 Ponce de Leon
San Juan, Puerto Rico

Merlis, Bob
c/o Warner Bros. Records
3300 Warner Blvd.
Burbank, CA 91510
Publicity executive

Merrill, Helen
c/o Abby Hoffer
223½ E. 48th St.
New York, NY 10022

Merrill, Robert
c/o William Morris
1350 Ave. of the Americas
New York, NY 10019

Mertens, Wim
c/o Crepuscule
Greepstraat 4
Brussels 1000, Belgium

Messiah Prophet
48 A St.
Northumberland, PA 17857

Metal
185 Franklin St.
New York, NY 10013
Fan magazine

Metal Church
P.O. Box 6632
Kent, WA 98031

Metal Edge
355 Lexington Ave.
New York, NY 10017
Fan magazine

Metal Muscle
63 Grand Ave. (#230)
River Edge, NJ 07661
Fan magazine

Metal Network
P.O. Box 1241M
Bayshore, NY 11706
Fan magazine

Metalhead Earpiercers
c/o PCA, Inc.
427 Plain St.
Marshfield, MA 02050
At-home earpiercing kits

Metallica
P.O. Box 1347
Roslyn Heights, NY 11577
Fan club

Metalshop
355 Lexington Ave.
New York, NY 10017
Fan magazine

Metheny, Mike
c/o Ted Kurland
173 Brighton Ave.
Boston, MA 02134

Metheny, Pat
c/o Ted Kurland
173 Brighton Ave.
Boston, MA 02134

The Metros
8752 Monticello Lane
Maple Grove, MN 55369

Meyer, Steve
c/o MCA Records
70 Universal City Plaza
Universal City, CA 91608
Record company executive

Michael, George
8800 Sunset Blvd. (#401)
Los Angeles, CA 90069

Michaels, Lorne
1619 Broadway
New York, NY 10019
Producer of Saturday Night Live

Michaels, Marilyn
162 W. 56th St. (#506)
New York, NY 10019
Impressionist

Midler, Bette
P.O. Box 46703
Los Angeles, CA 90046

Midnight Oil
P.O. Box 186, Glebe
Sydney, NSW 2037, Australia

Midnight Star
P.O. Box 9481
Columbus, OH 43209

The Mighty Clouds of Joy
c/o Glickman/Marks
655 Madison Ave.
New York, NY 10021

The Mighty Lemon Drops
c/o Sire Records
75 Rockefeller Plaza
New York, NY 10019

Mike and the Mechanics
P.O. Box 107
London N65 ARU, England

Miles, Buddy
1800 N. Highland Ave. (#411)
Los Angeles, CA 90028

Miles, John
c/o Allied
76 Tottenham Court Rd.
London W1P 9PA, England

Milgrim, Hale
c/o Elektra Records
75 Rockefeller Plaza
New York, NY 10019
Record company executive

Miller, Alonzo
c/o MCA Records
70 Universal City Plaza
Universal City, CA 91608
A&R executive

Miller, Bernie
c/o E/P/A Records
51 W. 52nd St.
New York, NY 10019
A&R executive

Glenn Miller Society
18 Crendon St., High Wycombe
Buckinghamshire, England
Fan club

Miller, Roger
P.O. Box 2689
Danbury, CT 06813

Miller, Steve
P.O. Box 4127
Bellevue, WA 98040

Milli Vanilli
c/o Arista Records
6 W. 57th St.
New York, NY 10019

Millions Like Us
c/o Virgin Records
9247 Alden Dr.
Beverly Hills, CA 90210

Mills, Darby
c/o S.L. Feldman
1534 W. 2nd Ave.
Vancouver, BC V6J 1H2, Canada

Mills, Frank
4881 Yonge St. (#412)
Toronto, ON M4S 2B9, Canada

Mills, Stephanie
P.O. Box K (#350)
Tarzana, CA 91356

The Mills Brothers
8899 Beverly Blvd.
Los Angeles, CA 90048

Milnes, Sherrill
1776 Broadway (#504)
New York, NY 10019

Milsap, Ronnie
P.O. Box 23109
Nashville, TN 37202

Mink DeVille
c/o Stevens Enterprises
240 Central Park S.
New York, NY 10019

Minnelli, Liza
c/o ICM
40 W. 57th St.
New York, NY 10022

Minogue, Kylie
9 Dundas Lane
Albert Park, VIC 3206, Australia

Minor, Charlie
c/o A&M Records
1416 N. La Brea Ave.
Hollywood, CA 90028
Record company executive

•Mr. Mister
P.O. Box 69343
Los Angeles, CA 90069

Mitchell, George
c/o Robert Luff
294 Earls Court Rd.
London SW5 9BB, England

Mitchell, Joni
(Roberta Joan Anderson)
644 N. Doheny Dr.
Los Angeles, CA 90069

Mitchell, Kim
41 Britain St. (#305)
Toronto, ON M5A 1R7, Canada

Mix
6400 Hollis St. (#12)
Emeryville, CA 94608
Recording engineer magazine

Moby Grape
c/o Matthew Katz
555 Post St.
San Francisco, CA 94102

The Models
8 Hayes St. (#1)
Neutral Bay, NSW 20891, Australia

Modern Drummer
P.O. Box 480
Mount Morris, IL 61054-0480
Musicians' magazine

Modern English
c/o Side One
1775 Broadway
New York, NY 10019

Modern Jazz Quartet
c/o Ted Kurland
173 Brighton Ave.
Boston, MA 02134

The Modernaires
17752 Skypark Blvd. (#265)
Irvine, CA 92714

Moffett, Charnett
9000 Sunset Blvd. (#1200)
Los Angeles, CA 90069

Molly Hatchet
P.O. Box 6600
Macon, GA 51215

Moman, Chips
646 W. Iris Dr.
Nashville, TN 37203
Record producer

Mondo Rock
c/o Management House
3 Seymour Ave.
Armadale, VIC 3143, Australia

Money, Eddie (Mahoney)
P.O. Box 1994
San Francisco, CA 94101

Monkees
1775 Broadway (#700)
New York, NY 10019

Monroe, Bill
c/o MCA Records
70 Universal City Plaza
Universal City, CA 91608

Monterey Peninsula Artists
P.O. Box 7308
Carmel, CA 93921
Booking agent

Montgomery, Melba
1300 Division St. (#103)
Nashville, TN 37203

Montoya, Carlos
1501 Broadway (#201)
New York, NY 10036

Montreaux International Festival
P.O. Box 97
CH-1820, Montreaux, Switzerland

Montrose, Ronnie
10966 Le Conte Ave. (#A)
Los Angeles, CA 90024

The Moody Blues
c/o WEG/Concerts West
11111 Santa Monica Blvd.
Los Angeles, CA 90025

Moog
2500 Walden Ave.
Buffalo, NY 14225
Synthesizer maker

Moore, Melba
c/o Hush Productions
231 W. 58th St.
New York, NY 10019

Moore, Rene
c/o PolyGram Records
810 Seventh Ave.
New York, NY 10019

Moore, Sam
141 Dunbar Ave.
Fords, NJ 08863

Morahan, Andy
155–157 Oxford St.
London W1R 1TB, England
Music video director

Moraz, Patrick
P.O. Box 775
Bryn Mawr, PA 19010

Moreno, Rita (Rosita Alverio)
151 El Camino Dr.
Beverly Hills, CA 90212

Morgan, Bennett
119 W. 57th St.
New York, NY 10019
Booking agent

Morgan, Lorrie
c/o RCA Records
30 Music Square W.
Nashville, TN 37203

Morgan, Meli'sa
c/o Hush Productions
231 W. 58th St.
New York, NY 10019

Morgenstern, Jay
c/o Warner-Chappell Music
9000 Sunset Blvd.
Los Angeles, CA 90069
Music publishing executive

Moroder, Giorgio
4162 Lankershim Blvd.
Universal City, CA 91602
Record producer/composer

Morris, Chris
c/o Billboard
9107 Wilshire Blvd.
Beverly Hills, CA 90210
Music journalist

Morris, Doug
c/o Atlantic Records
75 Rockefeller Plaza
New York, NY 10019
Record company executive

Morris, Gary
6027 Church Dr.
Sugar Land, TX 77478

Morris, John
3815 W. Olive Ave. (#202)
Burbank, CA 91505
Film music composer

Morris, Nick
191 Wardour St.
London W1V 3FA, England
Music video director

Morrison, Van
12304 Santa Monica Blvd. (#300)
Los Angeles, CA 90025

Morrissey (Steven)
c/o Frontier
1776 Broadway
New York, NY 10019

Morrow, Cousin Brucie
c/o WCBS-FM
51 W. 52nd St.
New York, NY 10019
Disc jockey

Morse, Steve
c/o Entertainment Services
212 Race St.
Philadelphia, PA 19106

Moss, Jerry
c/o A&M Records
1416 N. La Brea Ave.
Hollywood, CA 90028
Record company executive

Mother's Finest
c/o Capitol Records
1750 N. Vine St.
Hollywood, CA 90028

Motley Crue
9145 Sunset Blvd. (#100)
Los Angeles, CA 90069

Motorhead
98 Puddletown Crescent
Poole, Dorset BH17 8AN, England

Motown Museum
2648 W. Grand Blvd.
Detroit, MI 48208
Birthplace of Motown Records

Mottola, Tommy
c/o CBS Records
51 W. 52nd St.
New York, NY 10019
Record company executive

Mouse, Stanley
c/o ArtRock
225 E. Liberty Plaza
Ann Arbor, MI 48104
Rock poster artist

Mouzon, Alphonse
17337 Ventura Blvd. (#300C)
Encino, CA 91316

Mox Nix
c/o Shatter Records
119 W. 57th St.
New York, NY 10019

Moyet, Alison
c/o TBA
144 New King's Rd.
London SW6, England

Muchoney, Kelly
c/o Chrysalis Records
9255 Sunset Blvd.
Los Angeles, CA 90069
A&R executive

Muench, Teri
P.O. Box 10003
Van Nuys, CA 91410-0003
Songwriter's consultant

Mulcahy, Russell
191 Wardour St.
London W1V 3FA, England
Music video director

Muldaur, Maria
P.O. Box 5535
Mill Valley, CA 94942-5525

Mull, Martin
9000 Sunset Blvd. (#1200)
Los Angeles, CA 90069

Mulligan, Gerry
1501 Broadway (#201)
New York, NY 10036

Muni, Scott
c/o WNEW
655 Third Ave.
New York, NY 10017
Disc jockey

Murdock, Shirley
c/o Larry Troutman
2010 Salem Ave.
Dayton, OH 45406

Murphy, Eddie
P.O. Box 1028
Englewood Cliffs, NJ 07632

Murphy, Matt "Guitar"
c/o Concerted Efforts
110 Madison Ave.
Newtonville, MA 02160

Murphy, Michael Martin
P.O. Box FFF
Taos, NM 87571

Murray, Anne
4881 Yonge St. (#412)
Toronto, ON M4S 2B9, Canada

Muscle Shoals Recording Studio
1000 Alabama Ave.
Sheffield, AL 35660

Music City News
50 Music Square W. (#601)
Nashville, TN 37202
Country music fan magazine

Music, Computers and Software
190 E. Main St.
Huntington, NY 11743
Musicians' magazine

Music Connection
6640 Sunset Blvd.
Hollywood, CA 90028
Musicians' magazine

Music Technology
22024 Lassen St. (#118)
Chatsworth, CA 91311
Musicians' magazine

Music Video Association
900 Third Ave.
New York, NY 10022

Musical Youth
c/o Old Gold
126 Great Portland St.
London W1, England

Musician Magazine
P.O. Box 701
Gloucester, MA 01930

Musicland (also **Sam Goody**)
7500 Excelsior Blvd.
St. Louis Park, MN 55426
Retail music chain

Myrick, Gary
P.O. Box 7308
Carmel, CA 93921

Nabors, Jim
c/o CBS Records
51 W. 52nd St.
New York, NY 10019

Naftaly, Keith
c/o KMEL
55 Francisco St. (#400)
San Francisco, CA 94133
Radio station program director

Najee
c/o EMI-Manhattan Records
1370 Ave. of the Americas
New York, NY 10019

Nantucket
c/o CMC
3924 Browning Pl.
Raleigh, NC 27609

Napoliello, Peter
c/o Geffen Records
9130 Sunset Blvd.
Los Angeles, CA 90069
Record company executive

Narell, Andy
c/o Bradshaw
859 O'Farrell St.
San Francisco, CA 94109

Nascimento, Milton
Rua Dos Timbiras, 301
30.000 Belo Horizonte
Minas Geraes, Brazil

Nash, Graham
P.O. Box 838
Hanaleo, HI 96714

Nash, Richard
c/o Atlantic Records
75 Rockefeller Plaza
New York, NY 10019
Record company executive

The Nashville Network
2806 Opryland Dr.
Nashville, TN 37214
Country music television network

Nasty Savage
18653 Ventura Blvd. (#311)
Tarzana, CA 91356

Nathan, Marc
c/o Atlantic Records
75 Rockefeller Plaza
New York, NY 10019
Record company executive

**National Academy of Recording
Arts and Sciences (NARAS)**
303 N. Glenoaks Blvd. (#140M)
Burbank, CA 91502
Awards Grammys

National Association of Fan Clubs
2730 Baltimore Ave.
Pueblo, CO 81003
Publishes directory

**National Association
of Music Merchants**
500 N. Michigan Ave. (#2010)
Chicago, IL 60611

National Association of
Recording Merchandisers
3 Eves Dr. (#307)
Marlton, NJ 08053

National Music Publishers
Association
205 E. 42nd St.
New York, NY 10017

National Velvet
41 Britain St. (#200)
Toronto, ON M5A 1R7, Canada

Native
c/o Charlie Brusco
1593 Monroe Dr.
Atlanta, GA 30324

Naumann, Jeffrey
c/o Virgin Records
9247 Alden Dr.
Beverly Hills, CA 90210
Record company executive

Nazareth
3101 Eisenhower Hwy. (#3)
Ann Arbor, MI 48104

N'Dour, Youssou
c/o Soundscape
500 W. 52nd St.
New York, NY 10019

Near, Holly
c/o Redwood Records
476 MacArthur Blvd.
Oakland, CA 94609

Neece, Tim
10513 Cushdon Ave.
Los Angeles, CA 90064
Personal manager

Nelson, B.J.
c/o EMI-Manhattan Records
1370 Ave. of the Americas
New York, NY 10019

Nelson, Kathy
c/o MCA Records
70 Universal City Plaza
Universal City, CA 91608
A&R executive

Nelson, Phyllis
1515 Market St. (#700)
Philadelphia, PA 19102

Nelson, Tracy
P.O. Box 1343
Marietta, GA 30061

Nelson, Tyka
c/o Chrysalis Records
645 Madison Ave.
New York, NY 10022

Nelson, Willie
P.O. Box 2689
Danbury, CT 06813

Nena (Gabriele Kerner)
c/o Jim Rakete
Leibnitzstrasse 47
1 Berlin 12, West Germany

Neptune, John "Kaizau"
150 Fifth Ave. (#1103)
New York, NY 10011

Nesmith, Mike
50 N. La Cienega Blvd.
Beverly Hills, CA 90211

Nevermore
c/o Def American Records
9157 Sunset Blvd.
Los Angeles, CA 90069

Nevil, Robbie
9200 Sunset Blvd. (PH 15)
Los Angeles, CA 90069

Neville, Ivan
P.O. Box 1994
San Francisco, CA 94101

The Neville Brothers
P.O. Box 24752
New Orleans, LA 70184

Nevison, Ron
8800 Sunset Blvd. (#401)
Los Angeles, CA 90069
Record producer

The New Christy Minstrels
8467 Beverly Blvd. (#100)
Los Angeles, CA 90048

New Edition
P.O. Box 604
San Francisco, CA 94101

New Grass Revival
P.O. Box 4003
Beverly Hills, CA 90213

New Kids on the Block
P.O. Box 7001
Quincy, MA 02269

New Model Army
c/o Frog
Front Unit, 2nd Floor
87 Great Eastern St.
London EC2A 3HY, England

New Music Seminar
1747 First Ave.
New York, NY 10128
Organization for new music

New Musical Express
5–7 Carnaby St.
London W1V 1PG, England
Fan magazine

New Order
c/o Warner Bros. Records
3300 Warner Blvd.
Burbank, CA 91510

New Riders of the Purple Sage
150 Fifth Ave. (#1103)
New York, NY 10011

The New York Samba Band
c/o Abby Hoffer
223½ E. 48th St.
New York, NY 10022

Newbury, Mickey
2510 Franklin Rd.
Nashville, TN 37204

Newley, Anthony
4419 Van Nuys Blvd.
Sherman Oaks, CA 91403

Newman, David "Fathead"
c/o Bennett Morgan
119 W. 57th St.
New York, NY 10019

Newman, Pam
c/o Enigma Records
1750 E. Holly Ave.
El Segundo, CA 90245
Record company executive

Newman, Randy
644 N. Doheny Dr.
Los Angeles, CA 90069

Newton, Juice
P.O. Box 7308
Carmel, CA 93921

Newton, Tony
8306 Wilshire Blvd. (#6042)
Beverly Hills, CA 90211

Newton, Wayne
3180 S. Highland Dr. (#1)
Las Vegas, NV 89109-1042

Newton-John, Olivia
P.O. Box 2710
Malibu, CA 90265

Nice n' Wild
c/o Atlantic Records
75 Rockefeller Plaza
New York, NY 10019

Nicks, Stevie
c/o Warner Bros. Records
3300 Warner Blvd.
Burbank, CA 91510

Night Ranger
P.O. Box 1000
Glen Ellen, CA 95442

Night Tracks
6311 Romaine St. (#7225)
Hollywood, CA 90038
Music video programming

The Nighthawks
P.O. Box 210103
San Francisco, CA 94121

Nightnoise
8144A Big Bend
St. Louis, MO 63119

Nikki
c/o Geffen Records
9130 Sunset Blvd.
Los Angeles, CA 90069

Nilsson, Harry
(Harry Nelson III)
11330 Ventura Blvd.
Studio City, CA 91604

The Nits
Bontekoekade dg
Denhaag, The Netherlands

Nitty Gritty Dirt Band
c/o Feyline
2175 S. Cherry St.
Denver, CO 80222

Nitzsche, Jack (Bernard)
3815 W. Olive Ave. (#202)
Burbank, CA 91505
Record producer/composer

Niven, Alan
1830 S. Robertson Blvd. (#201)
Los Angeles, CA 90035
Record producer/personal
manager

Nixon, Mojo (and Skid Roper)
611 Broadway (#526)
New York, NY 10012

Nixon, Nick
13704 Clayton Rd.
St. Louis, MO 63011

Noble, Mike
c/o Running Dog Mgmt.
27 Queensdale Pl.
London W11 4SQ, England
Personal manager

Noel
c/o Island Records
14 E. 4th St.
New York, NY 10012

Noiseworks
c/o CBS Records
51 W. 52nd St.
New York, NY 10019

Nolan, Kenny
c/o Bennett
211 S. Beverly Dr.
Beverly Hills, CA 90219

Noone, Peter
9200 Sunset Blvd. (#1210)
Los Angeles, CA 90069

Norman, Jim Ed
P.O. Box 120897
Nashville, TN 37212

The Northern Pikes
41 Britain St. (#200)
Toronto, ON M5A 1R7, Canada

Norum, John
c/o Epic Records
51 W. 52nd St.
New York, NY 10019

Nu Shooz
c/o Sosumi
3233 SW Newby Terrace
Portland, OR 97201

Nuclear Assault
P.O. Box 4164
Osbornville, NJ 08723

Nugent, Ted
9229 Sunset Blvd.
Suite 710
Los Angeles, CA 90069

Numan, Gary (Webb)
c/o Beggar's
8 Hogarth Rd.
London SW5, England

Nuri, Erik
c/o Arista Records
6 W. 57th St.
New York, NY 10019
A&R executive

The Nylons
366 Adelaide St. E. (#436)
Toronto, ON M5A 3X9, Canada

Nyro, Laura
P.O. Box 186
Shoreham, NY 11786

OFB
1700 Hayes St. (#301)
Nashville, TN 37203

OMD
(Orchestral Maneuvers in the Dark)
c/o Direct Mgmt.
945A N. La Cienega Blvd.
Los Angeles, CA 90069

Oak Ridge Boys
329 Rockland Rd.
Hendersonville, TN 37075

Ober, Ken
c/o MTV
1775 Broadway
New York, NY 10019
Host of "Remote Control"

Oberheim
2015 Davie Ave.
City of Commerce, CA 90040-1704
Synthesizer manufacturer

Oberman, Ron
c/o CBS Records
1801 Century Park W.
Los Angeles, CA 90067
A&R executive

O'Bryan
P.O. Box 48306
Los Angeles, CA 90048

Obsession
P.O. Box 9591
New Haven, CT 06535-0591

Ocasek, Ric
8800 Sunset Blvd. (#401)
Los Angeles, CA 90069

Ocean, Billy
32 Willesden Lane
London NW6, England

O'Connell, Helen
7060 Hollywood Blvd. (#1212)
Hollywood, CA 90028

O'Connor, Mark
7957 Nita Ave.
Canoga Park, CA 91304

O'Connor, Sinead
10 Halsey House
13 Red Lion Sq.
London WC1, England

O'Day, Anita
P.O. Box 123
North Haven, CT 06473

O'Dell, Kenny
(Kenneth Gist, Jr.)
c/o Gelfand/Breslauer
7 Music Circle N.
Nashville, TN 37203

Odetta
c/o Producers, Inc.
5109 Oak Haven Lane
Tampa, FL 33617

Oedipus
c/o WBCN
1265 Boylston St.
Boston, MA 02215
Radio station program director

O'Hearn, Patrick
14011 Ventura Blvd. (#200-B)
Sherman Oaks, CA 91423

The Ohio Players
888 Eighth Ave. (#1-F)
New York, NY 10019

Ohlson, Curtis
P.O. Box 29242
Oakland, CA 94604

Oingo Boingo
8335 Sunset Blvd. (3rd Floor)
Los Angeles, CA 90069

O'Jays
113 N. Robertson Blvd.
Los Angeles, CA 90048

The O'Kanes
c/o Steve Greil
59 Music Square W.
Nashville, TN 37203

O'Keefe, Vikki
30 Tara St., Sylvania
Sydney, NSW 2224, Australia

Oken, Alan
c/o A&M Records
1416 N. La Brea Ave.
Hollywood, CA 90028
Record company executive

Oldfield, Mike
Little Halings
Tilehouse Lane, Denham
Buckinghamshire, England

Ole
c/o Arista Records
6 W. 57th St.
New York, NY 10019

Olivor, Jane
10100 Santa Monica Blvd. (#1600)
Los Angeles, CA 90067

The Olympics
c/o Monach Prods.
9227 Bellflower St.
Bellflower, CA 90706

Omar and the Howlers
c/o ICM
40 W. 57th St.
New York, NY 10019

Omarr, Dwayne
c/o Capitol Records
1750 N. Vine St.
Hollywood, CA 90028

Omartian, Michael
4400 Coldwater Canyon (#225)
Studio City, CA 91604
Record producer

Omen
18653 Ventura Blvd. (#311)
Tarzana, CA 91356

One Way
c/o Perk's Music
1866 Penobscot Blvd.
Detroit, MI 48226

O'Neal, Alexander
200 W. 51st St. (#1410)
New York, NY 10019

O'Neal, Jim and Amy
c/o Rooster Blues Records
102 S. Lemar Blvd.
Oxford, MS 38655
Blues record company executives

Ono, Yoko
c/o William Morris
1350 Ave. of the Americas
New York, NY 10019

Opus
340 W. 28th St. (#13G)
New York, NY 10001

Roy Orbison Memorial Fund
c/o Sarah McMullen
8425 W. 3rd St. (#307)
Los Angeles, CA 90048

Orbit, William
100 Universal City Plaza
(Bldg. 422)
Universal City, CA 91608

Oregon
c/o Ted Kurland
173 Brighton Ave.
Boston, MA 02134

Oreman, Alan
c/o CBS Records
1801 Century Park W.
Los Angeles, CA 90067
Record company executive

Orienza, Rick
c/o Enigma Records
1750 E. Holly Ave.
El Segundo, CA 90245
Record company executive

Orlando, Tony
(Michael Anthony Orlando
Cassavitis)
151 El Camino Dr.
Beverly Hills, CA 90212

Orr, Benjamin
c/o Lookout
506 Santa Monica Blvd.
Santa Monica, CA 90401

Osamu
845 Via de la Paz (#365)
Pacific Palisades, CA 90272

Osborne, Jeffrey
c/o Jack Nelson
5800 Valley Oak Dr.
Los Angeles, CA 90068

Osbourne, Ozzy
34 Windmill St.
London W1, England

Oslin, K.T.
c/o Moress-Nanas
2128 Pico Blvd.
Santa Monica, CA 90405

Osmond, Donny
3 Corporate Plaza (#220)
Newport Beach, CA 92664

Osmond, Marie
1799 N. State St.
Orem, UT 84057

The Osmonds
1420 E. 800 North
Orem, UT 84059

Ostin, Michael
c/o Warner Bros. Records
3300 Warner Blvd.
Burbank, CA 91510
A&R executive

Ostin, Mo
c/o Warner Bros. Records
3300 Warner Blvd.
Burbank, CA 91510
Record company executive

Ostin, Randy
c/o RCA Records
1133 Ave. of the Americas
New York, NY 10036
Record company executive

O'Sullivan, Gilbert
(Raymond O'Sullivan)
Saint George's Hill
Weybridge, England

Other Ones
c/o AGM
6412 Hollywood Blvd.
Hollywood, CA 90028

Otis, Johnny
P.O. Box 6024
Chicago, IL 60660

Out of the Blue
c/o Blue Note Records
1370 Ave. of the Americas
New York, NY 10019

The Outfield
c/o Kip Krones
Essex House
19–20 Poland St.
London W1V 3DD, England

Outlaw Management
36–38 West St.
London WC2, England
Personal manager

The Outlaws
c/o Jerry Womack
217 Smoke Rise Circle
Marietta, GA 30067

Ovation
Blue Hills Ave.
Bloomfield, CT 06002
Guitar maker

Overkill
P.O. Box 968
Old Bridge, NJ 98857

Overland Prods.
1775 Broadway
New York, NY 10019
Personal manager

Overstreet, Paul
P.O. Box 120555
Nashville, TN 37212
Songwriter

Overstreet, Tommy
P.O. Box 82
Greenbrier, TN 37073

Overton, Toi
9200 Sunset Blvd. (#1220)
Los Angeles, CA 90069

Owens, Buck (Alvis Edgar, Jr.)
1225 N. Chester Ave.
Bakersfield, CA 93308

Owens, Gary
P.O. Box 76860
Los Angeles, CA 90076
Disc jockey

Ozark Mountain Daredevils
54 Music Square E. (#305)
Nashville, TN 37203

Ozone, Makoto
c/o Ted Kurland
173 Brighton Ave.
Boston, MA 02134

PM
c/o Warner Bros. Records
3300 Warner Blvd.
Burbank, CA 91510

Pablo Cruise
P.O. Box 779
Mill Valley, CA 94941

Pacificoncerts
9229 Sunset Blvd. (#310)
Los Angeles, CA 90069
Concert promoters

Page, Jimmy
c/o Geffen Records
9130 Sunset Blvd.
Los Angeles, CA 90069

Page, Patti (Clara Ann Fowler)
P.O. Box 1105
Rancho Santa Fe, CA 92067

Paich, David
P.O. Box 6008
Sherman Oaks, CA 91413

Paisley, Bob
P.O. Box 156
Roselle, NJ 07203

Pallas, Laura
86 Clarence Ave., Clapham Park
Clapham, London SW4 8JR,
England

Palmer, Robert
10100 Santa Monica Blvd. (#1600)
Los Angeles, CA 90067

Palmese, Richard
c/o MCA Records
70 Universal City Plaza
Universal City, CA 91608
Record company executive

Palmieri, Eddie
c/o Third World
200 Varick St.
New York, NY 10014

The Palomino
6907 Lankershim Blvd.
N. Hollywood, CA 91605
Country music nightclub

Pandemonium
18653 Ventura Blvd. (#311)
Tarzana, CA 91356

Pandoras
P.O. Box 49217
Los Angeles, CA 90049

Pantera
2210 Raper Blvd.
Arlington, TX 76013
Fan club

Paper Cuts
24307 Magic Mountain Pkwy.
(#309)
Valencia, CA 91355
Creates comic books from songs

Pappalardi, Felix
3 E. 54th St. (#1400)
New York, NY 10022

Parachute Club
41 Britain St. (#200)
Toronto, ON M5A 1R7, Canada

Pareles, Jon
c/o New York Times
229 W. 43rd St.
New York, NY 10036
Music critic

Parents' Music Resource Center (PMRC)
1500 Arlington Blvd. (#300)
Arlington, VA 22209
Anti-obscenity organization

Paris, Jeff
2519 Carmen Crest Dr.
Los Angeles, CA 90068

Parkening, Christopher
c/o CAMI
165 W. 57th St.
New York, NY 10019

Parker, Graham
c/o Ernest Chapman
11 Old Lincoln's Inn
London WC2, England

Parker, Ray, Jr.
11340 W. Olympic Blvd. (#357)
Los Angeles, CA 90064

Parker, Shann Lee
P.O. Box 421268
San Francisco, CA 94142

Parks, Bert
Skyridge Rd.
Greenwich, CT 06830

Parks, John Andrew, III
c/o Capitol Records
1111 16th Ave. S.
Nashville, TN 37212

Parks, Van Dyke
P.O. Box 1207
Studio City, CA 91604

Parliament
100 W. 51st St. (#1410)
New York, NY 10019

Parr, John
c/o Atlantic Records
75 Rockefeller Plaza
New York, NY 10019

Parris, Fred (and the Satins)
168 Orchid Dr.
Pearl River, NY 10965

Parsons, Alan
c/o Woolsongs Co.
30 The Ave. Muswell Hill
London N10, England

Partland Brothers
c/o EMI-Manhattan Records
1370 Ave. of the Americas
New York, NY 10019

Parton, Dolly
c/o Amy Grossman
1888 Century Park E.
14th Floor
Los Angeles, CA 90067

Parton, Stella
P.O. Box 120295
Nashville, TN 37212

Pasetta, Marty
8322 Beverly Blvd. (#205)
Los Angeles, CA 90048
Music television director

Pass, Joe
c/o Salle
451 N. Canon Dr.
Beverly Hills, CA 90210

Passick, David
30 East End Ave. (#2P)
New York, NY 10028
Personal manager

Passport
Konzertbuero Claus Schreiner
Postfach 2230, Market 22
Marburg/Lahn, West Germany

Patrick, Kevin
c/o Elektra Records
75 Rockefeller Plaza
New York, NY 10019
A&R executive

Patti, Sandi
c/o Helvering
530 Grand Ave.
Anderson, IN 46012

Pattiz, Norm
c/o Westwood One
9540 Washington Blvd.
Culver City, CA 90232
Radio executive

Pavarotti, Luciano
c/o Herbert Breslin
119 W. 57th St.
New York, NY 10019

Paxton, Tom
5109 Oak Haven Ln.
Tampa, FL 33617

Paycheck, Johnny
38 Music Square E. (#300)
Nashville, TN 37203

Payne, Bill
644 N. Doheny Dr.
Los Angeles, CA 90069

Payne, Freda
1995 Broadway (#501)
New York, NY 10023

Peaches and Herb
(Linda Greene and Herb Fame)
18034 Ventura Blvd. (#190)
Encino, CA 91316

Peacock, Michelle
c/o Capitol Records
1750 N. Vine St.
Hollywood, CA 90028
Music video executive

Pearlman, Sandy
888 Seventh Ave.
New York, NY 10019
Personal manager

Peaston, David
c/o Geffen Records
9130 Sunset Blvd.
Los Angeles, CA 90069

Pebbles
364 14th St. (5th Floor)
Oakland, CA 94612

Peck, Greg
c/o Island Records
14 E. 4th St.
New York, NY 10012
Record company executive

Peebles, Ann
c/o MCA Records
70 Universal City Plaza
Universal City, CA 91608

Peel, John
c/o Shurwood Mgmt.
Sarabee Ridgeway, Pyford
Woking, Surrey GU22 8PW,
England
Disc jockey

Peer, Ralph
1740 Broadway
New York, NY 10019
Music publisher

Pendergrass, Teddy
P.O. Box 243
Gladwyne, PA 19035

The Penguins
708 W. 137th St.
Gardena, CA 90247

Pennington, J.P.
c/o Tree International
8 Music Square W.
Nashville, TN 37203
Songwriter

Pepsi and Shirlie
c/o ICM
40 W. 57th St.
New York, NY 10019

Percussion
310 Cedar Lane
Teaneck, NJ 07666
Musicians' magazine

Pere Ubu
611 Broadway (#822)
New York, NY 10022

Perez, Tony
P.O. Box 120897
Nashville, TN 37212

Performance
1203 Lake St. (#200)
Fort Worth, TX 76102
Industry magazine

Perkins, Carl
P.O. Box 17087
Nashville, TN 37217

Perlman, Itzak
c/o ICM
40 W. 57th St.
New York, NY 10019

Perry, Joe
P.O. Box 703
Allston, MA 02134

Perry, Richard
5505 Melrose Ave.
Los Angeles, CA 90038
Record producer

Perry, Steve
P.O. Box 5952
San Francisco, CA 94101

Perry, Steven Paul
7715 Sunset Blvd. (#210)
Los Angeles, CA 90046

The Persuasions
101 W. 57th St. (#2A)
New York, NY 10019

6 Pet Shop Boys
478 Welbeck St.
London W1, England

Peter, Paul, and Mary
(Yarrow, Stookey, and Travers)
648 S. Robertson Blvd.
Los Angeles, CA 90069

Peters, Bernadette (Lazzara)
8500 Wilshire Blvd. (#520)
Beverly Hills, CA 90211

Peters, Roberta
c/o ICM
40 W. 57th St.
New York, NY 10019

Peterson, Al
3397 Wrightwood Dr.
Studio City, CA 91604
Radio programming consultant

Peterson, Oscar
c/o Salle
451 N. Canon Dr.
Beverly Hills, CA 90210

Petrucciani, Michel
c/o DeLeon
4031 Panama Ct.
Piedmont, CA 94611

Petty, Kyle
P.O. Box 120308
Nashville, TN 37212

Petty, Tom
c/o MCA Records
70 Universal City Plaza
Universal City, CA 91608

Pfeifer, Robert
c/o E/P/A Records
1801 Century Park W.
Los Angeles, CA 90067
A&R executive

Phantom, Rocker & Slick
c/o Panacea
2705 Glendower Ave.
Los Angeles, CA 90027

Philbin, Peter
c/o Elektra Records
9229 Sunset Blvd.
Los Angeles, CA 90069
A&R executive

Phillips, Lee
11355 W. Olympic Blvd.
Los Angeles, CA 90064
Attorney

Phillips, Maurice
1680 N. Vine St. (#501)
Los Angeles, CA 90028
Music video director

Phillips, Sam
639 Madison Ave.
Memphis, TN 38103
Record producer

Phillips, Shawn
c/o TWM
641 Lexington Ave.
New York, NY 10022

Phranc
c/o Twist Mgmt.
652 Angelus Place
Venice, CA 90291

Pickett, Wilson
P.O. Box 322
Ingomar, PA 15127

Picture Music International
1750 N. Vine St.
Hollywood, CA 90028
Music video producers

Pieces Of A Dream
1127 E. Hortter St.
Philadelphia, PA 19138

Pierce, Webb
c/o Joyce
2028 Chestnut St.
Philadelphia, PA 19103

Pine, Courtney
c/o Island Records
14 E. 4th St.
New York, NY 10012

Pink Floyd
43 Portland Rd.
London W11, England

Pinkard and Bowen
P.O. Box 120897
Nashville, TN 37212

Pitchford, Dean
1880 Century Park E. (#900)
Los Angeles, CA 90067
Songwriter

Pitney, Gene
P.O. Box 537
Somers, CT 06071

Pittman, Bob
c/o QMI Music
75 Rockefeller Plaza
New York, NY 10019
MTV founder/industry executive

Place, Mary Kay
9744 Wilshire Blvd. (#206)
Beverly Hills, CA 90212

Plant, Robert
c/o Atlantic Records
75 Rockefeller Plaza
New York, NY 10019

Platinum Blonde
P.O. Box 1223, Station F
Toronto, ON M4Y 2T8, Canada

The Platters
P.O. Box 39
Las Vegas, NV 89101

Plen, Michael
c/o Virgin Records
9247 Alden Dr.
Beverly Hills, CA 90210
Record company executive

Poco
P.O. Box 24475
Nashville, TN 37202

Podell, Doug
c/o WLLZ
31555 14 Mile Rd.
Farmington Hills, MI 48018
Program director/disc jockey

The Pogues
P.O. Box 2428
El Segundo, CA 90245

Poindexter, Buster
(David Johansen)
c/o Steve Paul
106 E. 19th St.
New York, NY 10003

Pointer, Bonnie
200 W. 51st St. (#1410)
New York, NY 10019

Pointer, Noel
11 Bailey Ave.
Ridgefield, CT 06877

Pointer Sisters
(Anita, June, and Ruth)
10100 Santa Monica Blvd.
16th Floor
Los Angeles, CA 90067

Poison
P.O. Box 6668
San Francisco, CA 94101
Fan club

• The Police
41-B Blenheim Crescent
London W11, England

Pollack, Jeff
984 Monument St. (#105)
Pacific Palisades, CA 90272
Radio programming consultant

Pollack, Matt
c/o Relativity/Combat Records
187-07 Henderson Ave.
Hollis, NY 11423
Record company executive

PolyGram Music
810 Seventh Ave.
New York, NY 10019
Music publisher

Pond, Steve
c/o Rolling Stone
745 Fifth Ave.
New York, NY 10022
Music journalist

Ponty, Jean-Luc
3805 W. Magnolia Blvd.
Burbank, CA 91505

Pop, Iggy
(James Jewell Osterberg)
449 S. Beverly Dr. (#102)
Beverly Hills, CA 90212

The Pop
6430 Sunset Blvd. (#1516)
Los Angeles, CA 90028

Pope, Tim
c/o GLO Prods.
1–5 Midford Place
London W1, England
Music video director

Posner, Mel
c/o Geffen Records
9130 Sunset Blvd.
Los Angeles, CA 90069
Record company executive

Post, Mike
3815 W. Olive Ave. (#202)
Burbank, CA 91505
TV/film composer

Potts, Simon
c/o Capitol Records
1750 N. Vine St.
Hollywood, CA 90028
A&R executive

Pousette-Dart Band
3 E. 54th St. (#1400)
New York, NY 10022

Power Station
441 W. 53rd St.
New York, NY 10019
Recording studio

Powerline
P.O. Box 4426
Stamford, CT 06907-0426
Fan magazine

Prager, Bud
c/o E.S.P. Mgmt.
1790 Broadway (PH)
New York, NY 10019
Personal manager

Praxis International
1700 Hayes St. (#301)
Nashville, TN 37203
Personal manager

Prefab Sprout
c/o Kitchenware
Saint Thomas St. Stable
Saint Thomas St.
Newcastle-upon-Tyne NE1 4LE,
England

Premier Talent Agency
3 E. 54th St.
New York, NY 10022
Booking agent

Prendatt, Tony
c/o PolyGram Records
810 Seventh Ave.
New York, NY 10019
A&R executive

Preservation Hall Jazz Band
726 St. Peter St.
New Orleans, LA 70116

Preston, Billy
1680 N. Vine St. (#214)
Hollywood, CA 90028

Preston, Frances
c/o BMI
320 W. 57th St.
New York, NY 10019
Pres., Performing rights
organization

Preston, Johnny
P.O. Box 1830
Gretna, LA 70053

The Pretenders
3 E. 54th St. (#1400)
New York, NY 10022

Pretty Maids
c/o Epic Records
51 W. 52nd St.
New York, NY 10019

Pretty Poison
c/o City Lights
2037 Pine St.
Philadelphia, PA 19103

• **Previn, Andre**
c/o The Music Center
135 N. Grand Ave.
Los Angeles, CA 90012
Classical conductor/composer

Price, Alan
c/o Cromwell Mgmt.
The Coach House, 9A The
Broadway
Huntingdon, Cambs PE17 4BX,
England

Price, Leontyre
c/o CAMI
165 W. 57th St.
New York, NY 10019

Price, Ray
P.O. Box 1986
Mt. Pleasant, TX 75455

Pride, Charley
3198 Royal Lane (#204)
Dallas, TX 75229

The Primitives
c/o Wasted Talent
321 Fulham Rd.
London SW10 9QL, England

Prince (Prince Rogers Nelson)
P.O. Box 10118
Minneapolis, MN 55401

Prince, Michael
c/o WTG Records
1801 Century Park W.
Los Angeles, CA 90067
A&R executive

Princess
c/o Mr. I. Mouse
920 Dickson St.
Marina del Rey, CA 90292

Princess Pang
18653 Ventura Blvd. (#311)
Tarzana, CA 91356

Prine, John
4121 Wilshire Blvd. (#215)
Los Angeles, CA 90010

Process and Doo-Rags
P.O. Box 158
Buffalo, NY 14209

The Proclaimers
c/o Chrysalis Records
645 Madison Ave.
New York, NY 10022

Proffer, Spencer
c/o Pasha Music
5615 Melrose Ave.
Hollywood, CA 90038
Record producer

Propaganda Films
413 S. La Brea Ave.
Los Angeles, CA 90036
Music video producers/directors

Prophet
P.O. Box 968
Old Bridge, NJ 08857

Prophet, Ronnie
c/o RCA Records
30 Music Square W.
Nashville, TN 37203

Pruett, Jeanne
1300 Division St. (#103)
Nashville, TN 37203

Prysock, Arthur
c/o D. Palmer
211 W. 53rd St.
New York, NY 10019

Pseudo Echo
c/o Wheatley
49 Bank St.
South Melbourne, VIC 3205,
Australia

The Psychedelic Furs
c/o Amanita
1 Cathedral St.
London SE1, England

Public Enemy
298 Elizabeth St.
New York, NY 10012

● **Public Image Ltd.**
c/o ICM
40 W. 57th St.
New York, NY 10019

Pucci, Mark
450 14th St. NW (#201)
Atlanta, GA 30318
Public relations

Puckett, Gary
151 El Camino Dr.
Beverly Hills, CA 90212

Puente, Tito
c/o Ralph Mercado Mgmt.
1650 Broadway
New York, NY 10019

Pugh, Eddie
c/o CBS Records
1801 Century Park W.
Los Angeles, CA 90067
Record company executive

Pullen, Don
c/o Bridge
106 Fort Greene Pl.
Brooklyn, NY 11217

Pure Prairie League
c/o Mike Reilly
1113 Park Dr.
Park Hills, CA 91011

Purim, Flora (and Airto)
c/o MPM Mgmt.
518 N. La Cienega Blvd.
Los Angeles, CA 90048

Purple Haze Experience
15236 Victory Blvd. (#267)
Van Nuys, CA 91406
Jimi Hendrix tribute act

The Pursuit of Happiness
c/o Chrysalis Records
645 Madison Ave.
New York, NY 10022

Puvogel, Kenny
c/o Warner Bros. Records
3300 Warner Blvd.
Burbank, CA 91510
Record company executive

Quartararo, Phil
c/o Virgin Records
9247 Alden Dr.
Beverly Hills, CA 90210
Record company executive

Quarterflash
P.O. Box 8231
Portland, OR 97207

Quatro, Suzi
c/o ATI
888 Seventh Ave.
New York, NY 10106

Que Pasa
1086 Teaneck Rd.
Teaneck, NJ 07666
Hispanic music fan magazine

Queen
46 Pemberidge Rd.
London W11 3HN, England

Queensryche
P.O. Box 70503
Bellevue, WA 98007

The Quick
c/o Worlds End
134 Lots Rd.
London SW10, England

Quiet Riot
3208 Cahuenga Blvd. W.
(#107)
Los Angeles, CA 90068

R.E.M.
P.O. Box 8032
Athens, GA 30603

REO Speedwagon
c/o E/P/A Records
1801 Century Park W.
Los Angeles, CA 90067

R.J.'s Latest Arrival
c/o ICM
40 W. 57th St.
New York, NY 10019

Ra, Sun (Le Sony'R Ra)
P.O. Box 7124
Chicago, IL 60607

Rabbitt, Eddie
(Edward Thomas)
9229 Sunset Blvd. (9th Floor)
Los Angeles, CA 90069

Radiance
c/o Glo
98 Hamilton Park
Columbus, OH 43203

Radiators
c/o E/P/A Records
51 W. 52nd St.
New York, NY 10019

Radio and Records
1930 Century Park W.
Los Angeles, CA 90067
Industry trade magazine

Radio City Music Hall
1260 Ave. of the Americas
New York, NY 10020

Radio Vision International
7060 Hollywood Blvd. (#525)
Hollywood, CA 90028
Music program distributor

Rafferty, Gerry
c/o Michael Gray
51 Paddington St.
London W1, England

Raffi
c/o Heidi Robinson
120 S. Victory Blvd. (#201)
Burbank, CA 91502
Singer of children's songs

Rain Parade
c/o Malibu Mgmt.
22003 Pacific Coast Hwy.
Malibu, CA 90265

The Rainmakers
P.O. Box 437
Excelsior, MN 55331

Rains, Patrick
8752 Holloway Dr.
Los Angeles, CA 90069
Personal manager

Raitt, Bonnie
P.O. Box 626
Los Angeles, CA 90078

Ralbovsky, Steve
c/o A&M Records
1416 N. La Brea Ave.
Hollywood, CA 90028
A&R executive

Rambeau, Leonard
c/o Balmur Ltd.
4881 Yonge St. (#412)
Toronto, ON M2N 5X3, Canada
Personal manager

Rambo, Reba
9200 Sunset Blvd. (#823)
Los Angeles, CA 90069

Ramone, Phil
322 W. 48th St.
New York, NY 10019
Record producer

The Ramones
c/o Overland
1775 Broadway
New York, NY 10019

Rampal, Jean-Pierre
111 W. 57th St.
New York, NY 10019

Randi, Don
c/o The Baked Potato
3787 Cahuenga Blvd. W.
Studio City, CA 91604

Randolph, Boots
c/o Purcell
964 Second Ave.
New York, NY 10022

Rankin, Kenny
8033 Sunset Blvd. (#1037)
Los Angeles, CA 90046

Ranking Roger
c/o Frontier
1776 Broadway
New York, NY 10019

Rap Masters
63 Grand Ave. (#230)
River Edge, NJ 07661
Fan magazine

Raphael
c/o William Morris
1350 Ave. of the Americas
New York, NY 10019

Rappaport, Paul
c/o CBS Records
51 W. 52nd St.
New York, NY 10019
Record company executive

Rappin' Duke
P.O. Box 252
Hollywood, CA 90078

Rare Earth
c/o Northern Int.
5224 S. Logan St.
Lansing, MI 48910

Raspberry, Larry
P.O. Box O
Minneapolis, MN 55331

Rated X
71 Dogwood Way
Hollywood, FL 33026

Ratner, Marc
c/o Reprise Records
3300 Warner Blvd.
Burbank, CA 91510
Record company executive

Ratt
P.O. Box 93519
Los Angeles, CA 90093
Fan club

Rattlesnake Annie
P.O. Box 2977
Hendersonville, TN 37077

Raven
c/o Headquarters
9 Eccleston St., Belgravia
London SW1 9LX, England

Raven, Eddy
P.O. Box 1402
Hendersonville, TN 37075

The Rave-Ups
P.O. Box 1818
Beverly Hills, CA 90213

Rawls, Lou
9200 Sunset Blvd. (#823)
Los Angeles, CA 90069

**Ray, Goodman, and Brown
(Harry, Al, and Billy)**
c/o Hush Prods.
231 W. 58th St.
New York, NY 10019

Ray, Johnny
P.O. Box C
River Edge, NJ 07661

Raze
c/o CBS Records
51 W. 52nd St.
New York, NY 10019

Razorback Band
P.O. Box 22419
Nashville, TN 37202

Rea, Chris
c/o Real Life
11 Cross Keys Close
London W1H 5FY, England

Ready for the World
c/o AMI
1776 Broadway
New York, NY 10019

The Real Thing
c/o Manna
9 Carnaby St.
London W1V 1PG, England

Record Plant (LA)
8456 W. 3rd St.
Los Angeles, CA 90048
Recording studio

Record Plant (NY)
321 W. 44th St.
New York, NY 10036
Recording studio

Record Review
P.O. Box 91878
Los Angeles, CA 90069
Magazine

Record World
6255 Sunset Blvd.
Los Angeles, CA 90028
Trade magazine

**Recording Artists Against
Drunk Driving**
120 S. Victory Blvd. (#201)
Burbank, CA 91502

Recording Engineer/Producer
c/o Intertec
9221 Quivira Rd.
Overland Park, KS 66215
Magazine

**Recording Industry Association
of America (RIAA)**
888 Seventh Ave.
New York, NY 10106

Red 7
P.O. Box 2210
Novato, CA 94948

Red Flag
c/o Enigma Records
1750 E. Holly Ave.
El Segundo, CA 90245

Red Hot Chili Peppers
11116 Aqua Vista St. (#39)
Studio City, CA 91602

Redbeard
c/o KTXQ
4131 N. Central Expy.
Dallas, TX 75204
Disc jockey

Redbone, Leon
c/o Beryl Handler
179 Aquetong Rd.
New Hope, PA 18938

Redd, Toby
P.O. Box 114
Fraser, MI 48026

The Reddings
1995 Broadway (#501)
New York, NY 10023

Reddy, Helen
10100 Santa Monica Blvd. (#1600)
Los Angeles, CA 90067

Redgum
c/o Sweet Conspiracy
500 Oxford St., Bondi Junction
Sydney, NSW 2022, Australia

Dan Reed Network
P.O. Box 1994
San Francisco, CA 94101

Reed, Jerry (Hubbard)
P.O. Box 38
Thompsons Station, TN 37179

Reed, Lou
38 E. 68th St.
New York, NY 10021

Reeves, Dianne
c/o William Morris
1350 Ave. of the Americas
New York, NY 10019

Reeves, Martha
168 Orchid Dr.
Pearl River, NY 10965

Refugee
c/o Falcon
3080 Lenworth Dr.
Mississauga, ON L4X 2G1, Canada

Regina
c/o Broadbeard
29 Greene St.
New York, NY 10013

Reid, Antonio "L.A."
9229 Sunset Blvd. (#311)
Los Angeles, CA 90069
Record producer

Reid, John
c/o Renegade Mgmt.
145 Oxford St.
London W1, England
Personal manager

The Reivers
P.O. Box 3094
Austin, TX 78764

Relix
P.O. Box 94
Brooklyn, NY 11229
Fan magazine

Remler, Emily
P.O. Box 845
Concord, CA 94522

Renbourn, John
c/o Folklore
1671 Appian Way
Santa Monica, CA 90401

The Replacements
c/o Sire Records
75 Rockefeller Plaza
New York, NY 10019

The Residents
109 Minna St. (#391)
San Francisco, CA 94105

Resnik, Steve
c/o A&M Records
1416 N. La Brea Ave.
Hollywood, CA 90028
Record collector

Restless Heart
7250 Beverly Blvd. (#200)
Los Angeles, CA 90036

Paul Revere and the Raiders
9000 Sunset Blvd. (#315)
Los Angeles, CA 90069

Rex
c/o La La La Prods.
Krukmakargatan 29
Stockholm S-11851, Sweden

Reyne, James
3575 Cahuenga Blvd. W. (#580)
Los Angeles, CA 90068

Reynolds, Debbie
(Mary Francis Reynolds)
151 El Camino Dr.
Beverly Hills, CA 90212

Rez Band
c/o Tone Zone
4707 N. Malden
Chicago, IL 60640

Rhythm
c/o Music Maker
22024 Lassen St. (#118)
Chatsworth, CA 91311
Magazine for percussionists

Rhythm and Business
11631 Victory Blvd. (#206)
N. Hollywood, CA 91609
Music industry magazine

The Rhythm Corps
P.O. Box 37044
Detroit, MI 48237

Rice, Tim
c/o Land
118 Wardour St.
Chichester, Sussex, England
Songwriter

Rich, Charlie
8229 Rockcreek Pkwy.
Cordova, TN 38018

Richard, Cliff (Harry Webb)
P.O. Box 46-C
Esher, Surrey KT10 9AF, England

Richards, Keith
"Redlands" West Whittering
Chichester, Sussex, England

Richey, George
6 Music Circle N.
Nashville, TN 37203

Richie, Lionel
P.O. Box 1862
Encino, CA 91426-1862

Richman, Jonathan
644 N. Doheny Dr.
Los Angeles, CA 90069

Rickenbacker
3895 S. Main
Santa Ana, CA 92707
Guitar maker

The Nelson Riddle Orchestra
c/o Willard Alexander
660 Madison Ave.
New York, NY 10021

Ride The River
c/o Our Gang
1012 16th Ave. S.
Nashville, TN 37212

Riders In The Sky
c/o David Skepner
7 Music Circle N.
Nashville, TN 37203

Ridgeley, Andrew
8800 Sunset Blvd. (#401)
Los Angeles, CA 90069

Ridgway, Stan
c/o Geffen Records
9130 Sunset Blvd.
Los Angeles, CA 90069

Riggio, Jaye
c/o EMI-Manhattan Records
1370 Ave. of the Americas
New York, NY 10019
Record company executive

The Right Profile
c/o Arista Records
6 W. 57th St.
New York, NY 10019

The Righteous Brothers
c/o Select Artists
7300 Camelback Rd.
Scottsdale, AZ 85251

Rigor Mortis
c/o Epic Records
51 W. 52nd St.
New York, NY 10019

Riley, Jeannie C.
P.O. Box 454
Brentwood, TN 37027

Ring-Ginsberg, Sherry
c/o Elektra Records
75 Rockefeller Plaza
New York, NY 10019
Publicity executive

Rip
9171 Wilshire Blvd. (#300)
Beverly Hills, CA 90210
Fan magazine

The Rippingtons
9157 Sunset Blvd. (#200)
Los Angeles, CA 90069

Rissmiller, Jim
c/o Rissky Business
10966 Le Conte Ave. (#A)
Los Angeles, CA 90024
Booking agent

The Ritchie Family
4100 W. Flagler (#B-2)
Miami, FL 33134

Ritenour, Lee
P.O. Box 3122
Burbank, CA 91504

The Ritz
254 W. 54th St.
New York, NY 10022
Nightclub

Rivers, Johnny (Ramistella)
9255 Sunset Blvd. (#411)
Los Angeles, CA 90069

Riviera, Jake
Setstar Estate
Transport Ave., Brentford
Middlesex TW8 0QP, England
Personal manager

Roach, Max
c/o Brad Simon
122 E. 57th St.
New York, NY 10022

Roach, Raoul
c/o Elektra Records
75 Rockefeller Plaza
New York, NY 10019
A&R executive

Rob Base and E-Z Rock
c/o General Talent
1700 Broadway
New York, NY 10019

Robbins, Dennis
c/o Robert Porter
1100 17th Ave. S.
Nashville, TN 37212

Roberts, Bruce
3815 W. Olive Ave. (#202)
Burbank, CA 91505
Songwriter

Roberts, Judy
c/o Brad Simon
122 E. 57th St.
New York, NY 10022

Robertson, Robbie
c/o Geffen Records
9130 Sunset Blvd.
Los Angeles, CA 90069

Robinson, Anne
c/o Windham Hill Records
247 High St.
Palo Alto, CA 94305
Record company executive

Robinson, Bert
c/o Capitol Records
1750 N. Vine St.
Hollywood, CA 90028

Robinson, Fenton
c/o Rooster Blues Records
2615 N. Wilton Ave.
Chicago, IL 60614

Robinson, Heidi Ellen
c/o Jensen Communications
120 S. Victory Blvd. (#201)
Burbank, CA 91502
Public relations

Robinson, Lisa
c/o N.Y. Times Syndicate
130 Fifth Ave.
New York, NY 10011
Music journalist

Robinson, Primus
c/o Elektra Records
75 Rockefeller Plaza
New York, NY 10019
Record company executive

Robinson, Smokey (William)
c/o Michael Roshkind
6255 Sunset Blvd.
Los Angeles, CA 90028

Robinson, Sonya
P.O. Box 4836
Atlanta, GA 30302

Robinson, Tom
250 W. 57th St. (#603)
New York, NY 10107

Robinson, Vicki Sue
1650 Broadway (#611)
New York, NY 10019

Rochelle and Fresh Heir
141 Dunbar Ave.
Fords, NJ 08863

• The Roches
P.O. Box 1333
Montclair, NJ 07042

Rock
1112 N. La Cienega Blvd.
Los Angeles, CA 90069
Fan magazine

Rock, Bob
c/o Little Mountain Studios
201 Seventh Ave.
Vancouver, BC V5Y 1L9, Canada
Record producer/musician

Rock, Monti, III
c/o Mosman
395 NE 21st St.
Miami, FL 33137

Rock Against Drugs
3575 Cahuenga Blvd. W. (#204)
Los Angeles, CA 90068

Rock and Roll Hall of Fame
c/o Ahmet Ertegun
75 Rockefeller Plaza
New York, NY 10019

Rock 'n' Roll Fantasy Camp
P.O. Box 460159
San Francisco, CA 94146-0159
Summer camp for rock 'n' roll
wannabes

Rock Beat
9171 Wilshire Blvd. (#525)
Beverly Hills, CA 90210
Fan magazine

Rock City Angels
2 Drury Ct.
Holtsville, NY 11742

Rock Legends
40-19 164th St. (Dept. E)
Flushing, NY 11358
Posters, t-shirts, etc.

Rock Scene
475 Park Ave. (#2201)
New York, NY 10016
Fan magazine

Rock Tops
Dept. ME4, Box D, Main St.
Bloomington, NY 12411
Posters, t-shirts, etc.

Rockabilia
P.O. Box 24591 (Dept. 52)
Edina, MN 55424
Posters, t-shirts, etc.

Rockfield Studios
Amberley Court
Rockfield Rd.
Monmouth, Gwent, South Wales,
UK
Recording studio

Rock-O-Graphs (Joe Long)
520 Miller St.
Hellertown, PA 18055
Buys and sells rock autographs

Rockstar
P.O. Box 16912
N. Hollywood, CA 91615
Fan magazine

Rockwell (Kenneth Gordy)
c/o Motown Records
6255 Sunset Blvd.
Los Angeles, CA 90028

Rodgers, Jimmie
17530 Ventura Blvd. (#108)
Encino, CA 91316

Rodgers, Michael
c/o WTG Records
1801 Century Park W.
Los Angeles, CA 90067

Rodgers, Nile
48 Signal Rd.
Stamford, CT 06902
Record producer

Rodman, Judy
c/o Sandy Neese
21 Music Square E.
Nashville, TN 37203

Rodney, Red
c/o Muse Records
160 W. 71st St.
New York, NY 10023

Rodriguez, Johnny
c/o World Class
1522 Demonbreun St.
Nashville, TN 37203

Rodriguez, Ruben
c/o CBS Records
51 W. 52nd St.
New York, NY 10019
Record company executive

Roe, Tommy
P.O. Box 26037
Minneapolis, MN 55426

Roger (Troutman)
2010 Salem Ave.
Dayton, OH 45406

Rogers, Al
4805 Wellington Ct.
Temple, TX 76502

Rogers, Dann
c/o Carman Prods.
15456 Cabrito Rd.
Van Nuys, CA 91406

Rogers, Evan
c/o Capitol Records
1750 N. Vine St.
Hollywood, CA 90028

Rogers, Gamble
P.O. Box 1556
Gainesville, FL 32602

Rogers, Kenny
1112 N. Sherbourne Dr.
Los Angeles, CA 90069

Rogers, Melani
c/o Arista Records
6 W. 57th St.
New York, NY 10019
Publicity executive

Rogers, Roy (and Dale Evans)
(Leonard Slye and Francis Smith)
15650 Seneca Rd.
Victorville, CA 92392

Rogue Male
c/o New Thunder
8 Carnaby St.
London W1V 1PG, England

Rolling Stone
745 Fifth Ave.
New York, NY 10022
Fan magazine

The Rolling Stones
1776 Broadway (#507)
New York, NY 10019

Rollins, Henry
P.O. Box 2461
Redondo Beach, CA 90278

Rollins, Sonny
Route #9-G
Germantown, NY 12526

The Romantics
P.O. Box 133-LV
Lathrop Village, MI 48076

Romeo Void
c/o ICM
40 W. 57th St.
New York, NY 10019

The Ronettes
5218 Almont St.
Los Angeles, CA 90032

Ronstadt, Linda
644 N. Doheny Dr.
Los Angeles, CA 90069

⨍ **Roomful of Blues**
c/o Chickles
15 Mansfield St.
Boston, MA 02134

Rose, Richard and Gary
c/o Capitol Records
1111 16th Ave. S.
Nashville, TN 37212

Rose Royce
7751 Alabama Ave. (#13)
Canoga Park, CA 91304

Rose Tattoo
P.O. Box 442
Kings Cross, NSW 2011, Australia

The Rosebud Agency
P.O. Box 210103
San Francisco, CA 94121
Booking agent/personal manager

Rosen, Larry
c/o GRP Records
555 W. 57th St. (#1228)
New York, NY 10019
Record company executive

Rosenblatt, Ed
c/o Geffen Records
9130 Sunset Blvd.
Los Angeles, CA 90069
Record company executive

Rosenblatt, Michael
c/o Geffen Records
75 Rockefeller Plaza
New York, NY 10019
A&R executive

Rosenman, Leonard
3815 W. Olive Ave. (#202)
Burbank, CA 91505
Film/TV music composer

Rosenthal, Laurence
3815 W. Olive Ave. (#202)
Burbank, CA 91505
Film/TV music composer

Ross, Diana
P.O. Box 1683
New York, NY 10185

Ross, Tom
c/o Creative Artists
1888 Century Park E.
Los Angeles, CA 90067
Booking agent

Rossington
c/o Charlie Brusco
1593 Monroe Dr.
Atlanta, GA 30324

Roth, David Lee
3960 Laurel Canyon Blvd. (#430)
Studio City, CA 91604

Rothbaum, Mark
P.O. Box 2689
Danbury, CT 06813
Booking agent/personal manager

Rough Cutt
18653 Ventura Blvd. (#307)
Tarzana, CA 91356

Rough House
c/o CBS Records
51 W. 52nd St.
New York, NY 10019

Roussos, Demis
c/o Denis Vaughan
Bond St. House
14 Clifford St.
London W1X 2JD, England

Rowan, Brent
P.O. Box 120665
Nashville, TN 37212

Rowan, Peter
c/o Keith Case
1016 16th Ave. S.
Nashville, TN 37212

Roxx Gang
c/o Virgin Records
9247 Alden Dr.
Beverly Hills, CA 90210

Roxy
9009 Sunset Blvd.
Los Angeles, CA 90069
Nightclub

Royal, Billy Joe
c/o Entertainment Artists
819 18th Ave. S.
Nashville, TN 37203

Royal Court of China
P.O. Box 7308
Carmel, CA 93921

Rubin, Rick
c/o Def American Records
9157 Sunset Blvd.
Los Angeles, CA 90069
Producer/record company
executive

Ruffin, David
200 W. 57th St. (#907)
New York, NY 10019

Ruffner, Mason
c/o CBS Records
51 W. 52nd St.
New York, NY 10019

Rufus
7250 Beverly Blvd. (#200)
Los Angeles, CA 90036

Run-D.M.C.
298 Elizabeth St.
New York, NY 10012

Rundgren, Todd
c/o Panacea
2705 Glendower Rd.
Los Angeles, CA 90027

Runner
c/o Prologue Records
1674 Broadway
New York, NY 10019

Rush
41 Britain St. (#200)
Toronto, ON M5A 1R7, Canada

Rush, Jennifer
c/o Moress-Nanas
2128 Pico Blvd.
Santa Monica, CA 90405

Rush, Marilee
2701 NW Vaughn (#766)
Portland, OR 97210

Rush, Tom
P.O. Box 16
Hillsboro, NH 03244

Rush Artist Mgmt.
298 Elizabeth St.
New York, NY 10012
Personal manager

Rushen, Patrice
c/o Class Act
1090 S. La Brea Ave.
Los Angeles, CA 90010

Russell, Brenda
(Brenda Gordon)
P.O. Box 3875
Hollywood, CA 90028

Russell, Leon (Hank Wilson)
P.O. Box 638
Indian Hills, CO 80454

Ruth, Peter "Madcat"
P.O. Box 8125
Ann Arbor, MI 48107

Rydell, Bobby (Ridarelli)
230 W. 55th St. (#17D)
New York, NY 10019

Ryder, Mitch
(William Levise, Jr.)
c/o Diversified
17650 W. Twelve Mile Rd.
Southfield, MI 48076

Ryles, John Wesley
P.O. Box 1470
Hendersonville, TN 37075

Ryser, Jimmy
c/o Arista Records
6 W. 57th St.
New York, NY 10019

16
157 W. 57th St.
New York, NY 10019
Teen fan magazine

The 7A3
c/o Regina Jones
1230 S. Van Ness Ave.
Los Angeles, CA 90019

SBK Entertainment
810 Seventh Ave.
New York, NY 10019
Music publisher

S.O.S. Band
119 W. 57th St. (#901)
New York, NY 10019

Saatchi, Philip
c/o Metric Music
194 Kensington Park Rd.
London W11, England

Sade
c/o I.B.C.
1–3 Mortimer St.
London W1, England

Sa-Fire
1674 Broadway (#703)
New York, NY 10019

Saga
11 Harley St.
London W1, England

Sager, Carole Bayer
c/o Chapell Music
810 Seventh Ave.
New York, NY 10019

Saint
P.O. Box 12974
Salem, OR 97309

Sainte-Marie, Buffy
RR #1 (#368)
Kapaa, Kauai, HI 96746

Saisse, Philippe
34 Hemlock Shore Dr.
Atkinson, NH 03811

Sakamoto, Ryuichi
c/o Virgin Records
Kensall House
533/579 Harrow Rd.
London W10 4RH, England

Salt-N-Pepa
c/o Hurby Azor
27-11 Humphrey St. E.
Queens, NY 11369

Salty Dog
c/o Geffen Records
9130 Sunset Blvd.
Los Angeles, CA 90069

Sam and Dave
c/o J. D. Brown
300 W. 55th St.
New York, NY 10019

Sample, Joe
8467 Beverly Blvd. (#100)
Los Angeles, CA 90048

Sanborn, David
c/o Patrick Rains
8752 Holloway Dr.
Los Angeles, CA 90069

Sanctuary
c/o Epic Records
51 W. 52nd St.
New York, NY 10019

Sandbloom, Gene
c/o MCA Records
70 Universal City Plaza
Universal City, CA 91608
A&R executive

Sanders, Pharoah
c/o Ted Kurland
173 Brighton Ave.
Boston, MA 02134

Sands, Tommy
c/o Gallup Ent.
9340 Queens Blvd.
Rego Park, NY 11374

Sang, Samantha
200 W. 51st St. (#1410)
New York, NY 10019

Santa Esmeralda
c/o Amusex
970 O'Brien Dr.
Menlo Park, CA 94025

Santana
P.O. Box 26671
San Francisco, CA 94126

Satellite, Billy
P.O. Box 2210
Novato, CA 94948

Satriani, Joe
P.O. Box 1994
San Francisco, CA 94101

Satriano, Sue
c/o EMI Music
1750 N. Vine St.
Hollywood, CA 90028
Corporate publicity executive

Satter, Jack
c/o EMI-Manhattan Records
1370 Ave. of the Americas
New York, NY 10019
Record company executive

Satterfield, Esther
1995 Broadway (#501)
New York, NY 10023

Savatage
c/o AMI
1776 Broadway
New York, NY 10019

Savoy Brown
c/o DMA
17650 W. Twelve Mile Rd.
Southfield, MI 48076

Sawyer Brown
c/o Jim Halsey Co.
24 Music Square W.
Nashville, TN 37203-3204

Saxon
P.O. Box 69
Wolverhampton WV6 9AQ,
England

Saxon, Sky
P.O. Box 1984
Kailua, HI 96734

Sayer, Leo (Gerard Sayer)
1801 Century Park E. (#1132)
Los Angeles, CA 90067

Saylor, Skip
506 N. Larchmont Blvd.
Los Angeles, CA 90004
Recording studio

Scaggs, Boz
(William Royce Scaggs)
c/o CBS Records
51 W. 52nd St.
New York, NY 10019

Scarlett and Black
c/o Summa
8507 Sunset Blvd.
W. Hollywood, CA 90069

Scarza, Vincent
145 E. 15th St.
New York, NY 10003
Music television director

Schanks, Nancy
c/o EMI-Manhattan Records
1370 Ave. of the Americas
New York, NY 10019

Schenkman, Richard
101 W. 12th St. (#21A)
New York, NY 10011
Music television director

Scheppke, Tom
c/o KISS
8023 Vantage Dr. (#1200)
San Antonio, TX 78230
Program director/disc jockey

Scher, John
c/o Monarch Ent.
17 N. Mountain Ave.
Montclair, NJ 07042
Rock concert promoter

Schifrin, Lalo
c/o Bennett Morgan
119 W. 57th St.
New York, NY 10019

Schilling, Peter
Abanda Musikunternehem
39 Zenetti St.
8000 Munich 2, West Germany

Schlamme, Thomas
1619 Broadway
New York, NY 10019
Music video director

Schlitz, Don
P.O. Box 120594
Nashville, TN 37212

Schmit, Timothy B.
80 Universal City Plaza (#400)
Universal City, CA 91608

Schneider, John
12031 Ventura Blvd. (#1)
Studio City, CA 91604

Schoolly D
c/o General Talent
1700 Broadway
New York, NY 10019

Schulman, Mark
c/o Atlantic Records
75 Rockefeller Plaza
New York, NY 10019
Record company executive

Schuur, Diane
9000 Sunset Blvd. (#1200)
Los Angeles, CA 90069

Schuyler, Knobloch, and Bickhardt
1101 17th Ave. S.
Nashville, TN 37212

Scorpions
P.O. Box 5220
3000 Hanover 1, West Germany
Fan club

Scott, Carl
c/o Warner Bros. Records
3300 Warner Blvd.
Burbank, CA 91510
A&R executive

Scott, Jef
1461 S. Sherbourne Dr.
Los Angeles, CA 90035

Scott, Jon
30 Hackamore Ln. (#18)
Bell Canyon, CA 91307
Radio contest promoter

Scott, Millie
156 Fifth Ave. (#623)
New York, NY 10010

Scott, Tom
9200 Sunset Blvd. (#823)
Los Angeles, CA 90069

Scott-Heron, Gil
P.O. Box 1417-838
Alexandria, VA 22313

Screamin' Sirens
6253 Hollywood Blvd. (#800)
Hollywood, CA 90028

ℓ The Screaming Blue Messiahs
c/o John Dummer
17 Crescent Way
London SE4 1QL, England

Screen Gems/EMI Music
6920 Sunset Blvd.
Hollywood, CA 90028
Music publisher

Scritti Politti
21 Atholl Crescent
Edinburgh EH3 8HQ, Scotland,
UK

Scruggs, Earl
P.O. Box 66
Madison, TN 37115

Sea Hags
P.O. Box 884341
San Francisco, CA 94188

Sea Level
119 W. 57th St. (#901)
New York, NY 10019

Seal, Kevin
c/o MTV
1775 Broadway
New York, NY 10019
Veejay

Seals, Dan
P.O. Box 1770
Hendersonville, TN 37077

The Searchers
1650 Broadway (#611)
New York, NY 10019

Sebastian, John
c/o David Bendett
2431 Briarcrest Rd.
Beverly Hills, CA 90210

Sedaka, Neil
330 W. 58th St. (#4A)
New York, NY 10019

Seduce
100 Universal City Plaza
(Bldg. 422)
Universal City, CA 91608

Seeger, Mike
c/o Folkways
632 Broadway
New York, NY 10012

Seeger, Pete
Duchess Junction (#431)
Beacon, NY 12508

Seely, Jeannie
38 Music Square E. (#300)
Nashville, TN 37203

Seger, Bob
567 Purdy St.
Birmingham, MI 48009

Seidenberg, Sidney
1414 Ave. of the Americas
New York, NY 10019
Personal manager

Seidman and Seidman
1200 Statler Towers
Buffalo, NY 14202
Business managers

Sembello, Michael
c/o Brian Avnet
3805 W. Magnolia Blvd.
Burbank, CA 91505

Sequal
c/o General Talent
1700 Broadway
New York, NY 10019

Serendipity Singers
P.O. Box 399
Lisle, IL 60532

Sesame Street
c/o Children's Television
Workshop
One Lincoln Plaza
New York, NY 10023

Setzer, Brian
4161 Fulton Ave.
Sherman Oaks, CA 91423

Severinsen, Doc (Carl)
c/o "The Tonight Show"
NBC-TV
3000 W. Alameda Ave.
Burbank, CA 91523

Seville, Taja
c/o Reprise Records
3300 Warner Blvd.
Burbank, CA 91510

Sexton, Charlie
10966 Le Conte Ave. (#A)
Los Angeles, CA 90024

Sha Na Na
P.O. Box 92326
Milwaukee, WI 53202

Shadowfax
11655 Genegal Rd.
Atascadero, CA 93922

Shadowland
c/o Geffen Records
9130 Sunset Blvd.
Los Angeles, CA 90069

Shaffer, Paul
c/o "The David Letterman Show"
NBC-TV
30 Rockefeller Plaza
New York, NY 10020

Shalamar
200 W. 51st St. (#1410)
New York, NY 10019

Shan, M.C.
c/o General Talent
1700 Broadway
New York, NY 10019

The Shangri-Las
168 Orchid Dr.
Pearl River, NY 10965

Shankar, Ravi
17 Warden Ct.
Gowalia Tank Rd.
Bombay 36, India

Shankman/DeBlasio
(Ron and Ned)
2434 Main St.
Santa Monica, CA 90405
Personal managers

Shannon
c/o Atlantic Records
75 Rockefeller Plaza
New York, NY 10019

Shannon, Scott
c/o Westwood One
9540 Washington Blvd.
Culver City, CA 90232
Disc jockey

Shargo, Becky
3815 W. Olive Ave. (#202)
Burbank, CA 91505
Film music supervisor

Sharkey, Feargal
c/o Cracks 90
66–68 George St.
London W1H 5RG, England

The Sharks
238 E. 58th St. (#22)
New York, NY 10022

Shaughnessy, Ed
c/o Willard Alexander
660 Madison Ave.
New York, NY 10021

Shaw, Greg
c/o Bomp Records
2702 San Fernando Rd.
Los Angeles, CA 90065
Record company executive

Shaw, Marlena
P.O. Box 82
Great Neck, NY 11021

Shaw, Sandie
c/o Negus-Fancey
66 Blenheim Crescent
London W11 1NZ, England

Shaw, Tommy
1790 Broadway (PH)
New York, NY 10019

Shaw, Woody
c/o Blue Note Records
1370 Ave. of the Americas
New York, NY 10019

Shear, Jules
P.O. Box 7451
New York, NY 10022

Shearing, George
P.O. Box 2120
Toluca Lake, CA 91602

Sheet Music Magazine
P.O. Box 933
Paramus, NJ 07653-0933

Sheila E. (Escavedo)
11355 W. Olympic Blvd. (#555)
Los Angeles, CA 90064

Shelley, Pete
c/o Frontier
1776 Broadway
New York, NY 10019

Shenandoah
c/o Entertainment Artists
819 18th Ave. S.
Nashville, TN 37203

Sheppard, T.G.
(Bill Browder)
c/o Scotti Bros.
2128 Pico Blvd.
Santa Monica, CA 90405

Sheriff
c/o Capitol Records
1750 N. Vine St.
Hollywood, CA 90028

Sherrick
c/o Warner Bros. Records
3300 Warner Blvd.
Burbank, CA 91510

Sherwood, Bob
c/o CBS Records
51 W. 52nd St.
New York, NY 10019
Record company executive

Shinehead (Carl Aiken)
325 Spring St. (#211)
New York, NY 10013

Shipley, Ellen
c/o Virgin Music
827 N. Hilldale Ave.
W. Hollywood, CA 90069
Songwriter

Shire, David
3815 W. Olive Ave. (#202)
Burbank, CA 91505
TV/film composer

The Shirelles
c/o Gallup Ent.
9340 Queens Blvd.
Rego Park, NY 11374

The Shirts
c/o Sphinx
2 Unity Pl., Westgate, Rotherham
South Yorks S60 1AR, England

Shocked, Michelle
c/o PolyGram Records
810 Seventh Ave.
New York, NY 10036

Shok Paris
25320 Clubside Dr. (#2)
N. Olmsted, OH 44070

The Shooters
c/o CBS Records
34 Music Square E.
Nashville, TN 37203

Shore, Dinah
(Frances Rose Shore)
10100 Santa Monica Blvd. (#1600)
Los Angeles, CA 90067

Short, Bobby
c/o Hotel Carlyle Cafe
35 E. 76th St.
New York, NY 10019

Shorter, Wayne
c/o Brighton Agency
9615 Brighton Way
Beverly Hills, CA 90201

Show Of Hands
100 Universal City Plaza
(Bldg. 422)
Universal City, CA 91608

Shriekback
c/o Word Service
235 Upper Richmond Rd.
London SW15 6SN, England

Shulman, Derek
c/o PolyGram Records
810 Seventh Ave.
New York, NY 10019
A&R executive

Shults, Lynn
c/o Capitol Records
1111 16th Ave. S.
Nashville, TN 37212
A&R executive

Siberry, Jane
P.O. Box 9388
Stanford, CA 94305

Siddons, Bill
1588 Crossroads of the World
Hollywood, CA 90028
Personal manager

Side Effect
c/o Hamilton
9022 Hamilton Pl.
Los Angeles, CA 90069

Sidran, Ben
2490 Channing Way (#406)
Berkeley, CA 94704

Siegel, Corky
1040 W. Granville (#222)
Chicago, IL 60660

Siegel, Dan
c/o TDA
1672 E. 23rd St.
Eugene, OR 97403

Sigerson, Davitt
8800 Sunset Blvd. (#401)
Los Angeles, CA 90069

Sigma Sound
1697 Broadway
New York, NY 10019
Recording studio

Sigue Sigue Sputnik
c/o EMI-Manhattan Records
1370 Ave. of the Americas
New York, NY 10019

Sikkas, Mike
c/o Arista Records
8370 Wilshire Blvd.
Los Angeles, CA 90211
A&R executive

Silas, Louill
c/o MCA Records
70 Universal City Plaza
Universal City, CA 91608
A&R executive

The Silencers
c/o Frontier
1776 Broadway
New York, NY 10019

Sills, Beverly
c/o New York City Opera
Lincoln Center
New York, NY 10023

Silver, Horace
c/o Bridge
106 Fort Greene Pl.
Brooklyn, NY 11217

Simmons, Aleese
P.O. Box 647
Orange, NJ 07051

Simmons, Gene
6363 Sunset Blvd. (#417)
Los Angeles, CA 90028

Simmons, Patrick
P.O. Box 7308
Carmel, CA 93923

Simmons, Russell
c/o Def Jam Records
298 Elizabeth St.
New York, NY 10012
Manager/record company
executive

Simon, Brad
122 E. 57th St.
New York, NY 10022
Personal manager

Simon, Carly
130 W. 57th St. (#12B)
New York, NY 10019

Simon, Fred
845 Via de la Paz (#365)
Pacific Palisades, CA 90272

Simon, Paul
1619 Broadway (#500)
New York, NY 10019

Simon F.
c/o Reprise Records
3300 Warner Blvd.
Burbank, CA 91510

Simone, Nina (Eunice Waymon)
1995 Broadway (#501)
New York, NY 10023

Simple Minds
63 Frederic St.
Edinburgh EH2 1LH, Scotland,
UK

Simply Red
36 Atwood Rd.
Didsbury, Manchester 20, England

Simpson, Donnie
c/o WKYS
4001 Nebraska Ave.
Washington, DC 20016
Program director/disc jockey

Sims, Joyce
c/o ICM
40 W. 57th St.
New York, NY 10019

Sinatra, Frank
1041 N. Formosa Ave.
Hollywood, CA 90046

Sing Out! Magazine
P.O. Box 5253
Bethlehem, PA 18105-5253
Folk music magazine

Singleton, Charlie
200 W. 51st St. (#1410)
New York, NY 10019

Singleton, Ernie
c/o Warner Bros. Records
3300 Warner Blvd.
Burbank, CA 91510
Record company executive

Siouxsie and the Banshees
The File
P.O. Box 763
London, England

Sister Carol
c/o Third World
200 Varick St.
New York, NY 10014

Sister Sledge
(Kathy, Debbie, Kim,
and Joni Sledge)
c/o Zane Mgmt.
1515 Market St.
Philadelphia, PA 19102

Sisters Of Mercy
19 All Saints Rd.
London W11, England

Skaggs, Ricky
P.O. Box 22419
Nashville, TN 37202

Skid Row
c/o Atlantic Records
75 Rockefeller Plaza
New York, NY 10019

Skin Deep
P.O. Box 69180
Los Angeles, CA 90069

Skinny Boys
c/o Jive Records
1348 Lexington Ave.
New York, NY 10128

• Skinny Puppy
1755 Robson St.
Vancouver, BC V6G 1C9, Canada

Skipworth & Turner
200 W. 51st St. (#1410)
New York, NY 10019

Skoro, Bob
c/o PolyGram Records
3800 Alameda Ave. (#1500)
Burbank, CA 91505
A&R executive

The Skwares
c/o Atlantic Records
75 Rockefeller Plaza
New York, NY 10019

Skyy
P.O. Box 846
New York, NY 10101

Slade
c/o ICM
40 W. 57th St.
New York, NY 10019

Slammin' Watusis
c/o Epic Records
1801 Century Park W.
Los Angeles, CA 90067

Slater, David
c/o Charles Dorris
110 30th Ave. N.
Nashville, TN 37203

Slave Raider
c/o Good Music
200 Third Ave. N.
Minneapolis, MN 55401

Slayer
c/o Def American Records
9157 Sunset Blvd.
Los Angeles, CA 90069

Sledge, Percy
P.O. Box 82
Great Neck, NY 11021

Sleepy La Beef
c/o John Penny
30 Guinan St.
Waltham, MA 02154

Slick, Earl
3 E. 54th St. (#1400)
New York, NY 10022

Slick, Grace
c/o RCA Records
6363 Sunset Blvd.
Los Angeles, CA 90028

Slick Rick
298 Elizabeth St.
New York, NY 10012

Sloane, Robin
c/o Elektra Records
9229 Sunset Blvd.
Los Angeles, CA 90069
Music video executive

The Sluggers
1700 Hayes St. (#301)
Nashville, TN 37203

Sly Fox
c/o Capitol Records
1750 N. Vine St.
Hollywood, CA 90028

Small, Jon
900 Broadway (#604)
New York, NY 10003
Music video director

The Richard Smallwood Singers
c/o Essex
1111 16th Ave. S.
Nashville, TN 37212

Smallwood, Rod
6625 Sunset Blvd.
Hollywood, CA 90028
Personal manager

Smash Hits
25 W. 39th St.
New York, NY 10018
Fan magazine

Smashed Gladys
c/o Elektra Records
75 Rockefeller Plaza
New York, NY 10019

Smiley Culture
c/o Artist Mgmt.
10 Inchmery Rd.
London SE6 2NE, England

Smith, Cal
P.O. Box 121089
Nashville, TN 37212

Smith, Connie
1300 Division St. (#103)
Nashville, TN 37203

Smith, Darden
c/o CBS Records
34 Music Square E.
Nashville, TN 37203

Smith, Jimmy
c/o Abby Hoffer
223½ E. 48th St.
New York, NY 10017

Smith, Joe
c/o Capitol Records
1750 N. Vine St.
Hollywood, CA 90028
Record company executive, author

Smith, Lonnie Liston
c/o Fontana
161 W. 54th St.
New York, NY 10019

Smith, Margo
38 Music Square (#300)
Nashville, TN 37203

Smith, Patti
c/o Arista Records
6 W. 57th St.
New York, NY 10019

Smith, Pete
360 Oxford St.
London W1, England
Personal manager

Smith, Rex
c/o Stephens Weiss
177 E. 75th St.
New York, NY 10021

Smith, Roger
c/o Elektra Records
9229 Sunset Blvd.
Los Angeles, CA 90069
Record company executive

Smith, Ron
7060 Hollywood Blvd. (#1215)
Los Angeles, CA 90028
Celebrity look-alikes

Smith, Russell
c/o CBS Records
34 Music Square E.
Nashville, TN 37203

Smith, Sammi
c/o Taylor
2401 12th Ave. S.
Nashville, TN 37204

Smith, Steve
P.O. Box 396
Beverly, MA 01915

The Smithereens
P.O. Box 1665
New York, NY 10009

The Smiths
c/o Frontier
1776 Broadway
New York, NY 10019

**The Smothers Brothers
(Tom and Dick)**
10100 Santa Monica Blvd. (#1600)
Los Angeles, CA 90067

Smyth, Patty
850 Seventh Ave. (#1105)
New York, NY 10019

Snider, Dee
P.O. Box 360
Merrick, NY 11561

Snow, Hank
P.O. Box 1084
Nashville, TN 37202

Snow, Mark
4146 Lankershim Blvd. (#300)
N. Hollywood, CA 91602
Film/TV composer

Snow, Phoebe (Laub)
c/o TWM Mgmt.
641 Lexington Ave.
New York, NY 10022

So
c/o EMI-Manhattan Records
1370 Ave. of the Americas
New York, NY 10019

Sobel, Karen
c/o Geffen Records
9130 Sunset Blvd.
Los Angeles, CA 90069
Music video executive

Social Distortion
P.O. Box 6246
Fullerton, CA 92634

**Society for the Preservation
& Encouragement of Barber Shop
Quartet Singing**
6315 3rd Ave.
Kenosha, WI 53140

Soft Cell
c/o Bizarre
17 Saint Anne's Ct.
London W1, England

Solti, Sir Georg
c/o Chicago Symphony Orchestra
220 S. Michigan Ave.
Chicago, IL 60604
Classical conductor

Somach, Denny
c/o Cinema Records
P.O. Box 775
Bryn Mawr, PA 19010
Record company executive

Somers, Suzanne (Mahoney)
8730 Sunset Blvd.
6th Floor
Los Angeles, CA 90069

Songwriter
6430 Sunset Blvd.
Los Angeles, CA 90028
Magazine

The Songwriters Guild of America
276 Fifth Ave. (#306)
New York, NY 10001

Songwriters' Hall of Fame
875 Third Ave.
New York, NY 10022

Sonic Youth
c/o Enigma Records
1750 E. Holly Ave.
El Segundo, CA 90245

Sonnier, Jo-El
1114 17th Ave. S. (#101)
Nashville, TN 37212

Sons of the Pioneers
12403 W. Green Mountain
Lakewood, CO 80228

Sony
1600 Queen Anne Rd.
Teaneck, NJ 07666
Audio equipment manufacturer

Sorrenti, Vince
P.O. Box 319, Cammeray
Sydney, NSW 2062, Australia

Soul Asylum
611 Broadway (#526)
New York, NY 10012

Sound City
15456 Cabrito Rd.
Van Nuys, CA 91406
Recording studio

South, Joe
P.O. Box 121557
Nashville, TN 37212

Southard, Scott
P.O. Box 396
Beverly, MA 01915
Booking agent

Souther, J.D.
P.O. Box 1333
Montclair, NJ 07042

Southern Pacific
c/o Jim Halsey Co.
24 Music Square W.
Nashville, TN 37203-3204

Southside Johnny (Lyon)
P.O. Box 405
Bogota, NJ 07603

Spandau Ballet
89 Great Portland St. (#7)
London W1, England

Spanjich, Scott
c/o Chrysalis Records
645 Madison Ave.
New York, NY 10022
Music video executive

Spanky and Our Gang
298 E. March St. (#7)
Santa Fe, NM 87501

Sparks
P.O. Box 1710
Beverly Hills, CA 91604

Spears, Billy Jo
P.O. Box 23470
Nashville, TN 37202

The Specials
c/o Kollectiv Mgmt.
132 Liverpool Rd.
London N1 1LA, England

Spector, Phil
P.O. Box 69529
Los Angeles, CA 90069
Record producer/songwriter

Spector, Ronnie
(Veronica Bennett)
218 W. 57th St. (#3A)
New York, NY 10019

Spence, Brian
c/o Kip Krones
Essex House
19–20 Poland St.
London W1V 3DD, England

Spence, Judson
c/o Atlantic Records
75 Rockefeller Plaza
New York, NY 10019

Spencer, Tracie
c/o Capitol Records
1750 N. Vine St.
Hollywood, CA 90028

Spheeris, Penelope
1737 N. Whitley (#500)
Los Angeles, CA 90028
Music film/video director

Sphere
240 W. 98th St. (#13A)
New York, NY 10025

Spicher, Buddy
Route #6 (#280-A)
Franklin, TN 37064

Spin
6 W. 18th St.
New York, NY 10011-4608
Fan magazine

Spinderella
c/o Chrysalis Records
645 Madison Ave.
New York, NY 10022

The Spinners
65 W. 55th St. (#6C)
New York, NY 10019

Spirit
17337 Ventura Blvd. (#300C)
Encino, CA 91316

Spookey
c/o CBS Records
51 W. 52nd St.
New York, NY 10019

Springfield, Bobby Lee
c/o Tangerine
1101 17th Ave. S.
Nashville, TN 37212

Springfield, Dusty
(Mary O'Brien)
130 W. 57th St. (#8B)
New York, NY 10019

Springfield, Rick
9200 Sunset Blvd. (PH 15)
Los Angeles, CA 90069

Springsteen, Bruce
136 E. 57th St. (#1202)
New York, NY 10022

Spyro Gyra
P.O. Box 7308
Carmel, CA 93921

Squeeze
40 Greenwich Market
London SE10, England

Squier, Billy
c/o Delote Mgmt.
850 Seventh Ave.
New York, NY 10019

The Stabilizers
P.O. Box 10905
Beverly Hills, CA 90213

Stacy Q
641 S. Palm (#D)
La Habra, CA 90631

Stafford, Jim
151 El Camino Dr.
Beverly Hills, CA 90212

Stairway to Heaven
P.O. Box 721
Rockville, MD 20851
Led Zeppelin tribute act

Staley, Karen
c/o MCA Records
1701 West End Ave.
Nashville, TN 37203

Staley, Lex
c/o WFYV
9090 Hogan Rd.
Jacksonville, FL 32216
Program director/disc jockey

Stamey, Chris
c/o Complete Circuit
17 Cadman Plaza W.
Brooklyn, NY 11201

Stampley, Joe
c/o Encore
2137 Zercher Rd.
San Antonio, TX 78209

Stan, Maurice
c/o Dick Scott
159 W. 53rd St.
New York, NY 10019

The Standells
5218 Almont St.
Los Angeles, CA 90032

Stanley, Chuck
298 Elizabeth St.
New York, NY 10012

Stanley, James Lee
P.O. Box 1556
Gainesville, FL 32602

Stanley, Ralph
P.O. Box 191
Floyd, VA 24012

The Staples
200 W. 57th St. (#901)
New York, NY 10019

Star Search
c/o Bob Banner Prods.
132 S. Rodeo Dr. (#402)
Beverly Hills, CA 90212
Television talent hunt

Stardust, Alvin
c/o Sounz
1 Brunswich Park Rd.
Wednesbury, W. Midlands,
England

Starpoint
P.O. Box 224
Crownsville, MD 21032

Starr, Brenda K.
65 W. 55th St. (#6C)
New York, NY 10019

Starr, Edwin
1680 N. Vine St. (#214)
Hollywood, CA 90028

Starr, Kay
c/o Purcell
964 Second Ave.
New York, NY 10022

Starr, Ringo
(Richard Starkey)
Tittenhurst Park
Ascot, Surrey, England

Starship
1319 Bridgeway
Sausalito, CA 94965-1992

Statler Brothers
P.O. Box 2703
Staunton, VA 24401

Statman, Anna
c/o Geffen Records
9130 Sunset Blvd.
Los Angeles, CA 90069
A&R executive

Status Quo
Hydon Grange
Hambledone, Surrey, England

Steady B
c/o Jive Records
1348 Lexington Ave.
New York, NY 10128

Stealin' Horses
c/o Arista Records
6 W. 57th St.
New York, NY 10019

Steals, Jean
c/o MCA Records
70 Universal City Plaza
Universal City, CA 91608

Steel Pulse
c/o Andy Bowen
42 Upper Dean St.
Digbeth, Birmingham 5, England

Steele, Tommy
c/o Talents
37 Hill St.
London W1X 8JY, England

Steeleye Span
c/o Allied
76 Tottenham Court Rd.
London W10 9PA, England

Stein, Ira (and Russel Walder)
c/o Windham Hill Records
247 High St.
Palo Alto, CA 94305

Stein, Jeff
6690 Whitley Terr.
Los Angeles, CA 90068
Music video director

Stein, Seymour
c/o Sire Records
75 Rockefeller Plaza
New York, NY 10019
Record company executive

Steinberg, Billy
c/o Manatt, Phelps
11355 W. Olympic Blvd.
Los Angeles, CA 90064
Songwriter

Steinberg, Richard
c/o Atlantic Records
75 Rockefeller Plaza
New York, NY 10019
A&R executive

Steinman, Jim
c/o DAS
83 Riverside Dr.
New York, NY 10024
Songwriter/record producer

Steps Ahead
1501 Broadway (#1506)
New York, NY 10036

Stern, Howard
c/o WXRK
600 Madison Ave.
New York, NY 10022
Disc jockey

Stern, Isaac
c/o ICM
40 W. 57th St.
New York, NY 10019

Stetsasonic
298 Elizabeth St.
New York, NY 10012

Stevens, Even
P.O. Box 140110
Nashville, TN 37214

Stevens, Ray
c/o Williams/Cimini
816 N. La Cienega Blvd.
Los Angeles, CA 90069

Stevens, Shadoe
9000 Sunset Blvd. (#1200)
Los Angeles, CA 90069
Disc jockey

Stevie B
141 Dunbar
Fords, NJ 08863

Stewart, Jermaine
c/o TBA International
575 Madison Ave.
New York, NY 10022

Stewart, Marty
c/o CBS Records
51 W. 52nd St.
New York, NY 10019

Stewart, Rod
9200 Sunset Blvd. (#415)
Los Angeles, CA 90069

Stigwood, Robert
118–120 Wardour St.
London, England
Record company executive

Stiletto Mgmt.
P.O. Box 69180
Los Angeles, CA 90069
Personal manager

Stills, Stephen
12077 Wilshire Blvd. (#745)
Los Angeles, CA 90025

Sting (Gordon Mathew Sumner)
250 E. 57th St. (#603)
New York, NY 10107

Stone, Cliffie
6255 Sunset Blvd. (#723)
Los Angeles, CA 90028
Music publishing executive

Stone, Mike
241 Central Park W. (#5A)
New York, NY 10024
Record producer

Stone, Rick
c/o A&M Records
595 Madison Ave.
New York, NY 10022
Record company executive

The Stoneman Family
c/o Taylor
2401 12th Ave. S.
Nashville, TN 37204

Stookey, Noel Paul
c/o Neworld
Route #175
South Blue Hill, ME 04615

Story, Liz
P.O. Box 9532
Madison, WI 53715

Stotter, Michael
c/o Capitol Records
1750 N. Vine St.
Hollywood, CA 90069
A&R executive

Strafe
c/o Paul Bloom
7 E. 14th St.
New York, NY 10012

Strait, George
c/o Erv Woolsey
1000 18th Ave. S.
Nashville, TN 37212

Stranger
P.O. Box 7877
College Park Station
Orlando, FL 32854

• **Strangeways**
c/o Bonaire
11 Harley St.
London W1, England

The Stranglers
c/o Fast Forward
110 W. 57th St.
New York, NY 10019

Straw, Syd
c/o Virgin Records
9247 Alden Dr.
Beverly Hills, CA 90210

▪ **Strawberry Alarm Clock**
c/o David Bendett
2431 Briarcrest Rd.
Beverly Hills, CA 90210

The Strawbs
P.O. Box 1333
Montclair, NJ 07042

Street Fare
1407 Webster St. (#213)
Oakland, CA 94612

Streisand, Barbra
1040 N. Las Palmas (Bldg. 17)
Los Angeles, CA 90038

Strings
407 San Anselmo Ave.
San Anselmo, CA 94960
Musicians' magazine

Stroud, James
c/o Universal Records
1701 West End Ave.
Nashville, TN 37203
A&R executive

Strunk, Jud
38 Music Square E. (#300)
Nashville, TN 37203

Stryken
P.O. Box 2107
Cedar Park, TX 78613

Stryper
P.O. Box 1045
Cypress, CA 90630

Stuart, Marty
P.O. Box 120308
Nashville, TN 37212

Studio Instrument Rental
6048 Sunset Blvd.
Los Angeles, CA 90028

Stump
c/o Chrysalis Records
645 Madison Ave.
New York, NY 10022

Style Council
c/o The Torch Society
45–53 Sinclair Rd.
London W14, England

The Stylistics
P.O. Box 82
Great Neck, NY 11021

Styne, Jule
237 W. 51st St.
New York, NY 10019
Songwriter

Styx
c/o A&M Records
1416 N. La Brea Ave.
Hollywood, CA 90028

Suave
c/o Capitol Records
1750 N. Vine St.
Hollywood, CA 90028

The Suburbs
c/o Levy Mgmt.
526 Nicollet Mall
Minneapolis, MN 55402

The Sugarcubes
c/o Elektra Records
9229 Sunset Blvd.
Los Angeles, CA 90069

Sugarman, Danny
449 S. Beverly Dr. (#102)
Beverly Hills, CA 90212
Doors expert/biographer, author

Suicidal Tendencies
c/o Frontier
1776 Broadway
New York, NY 10019

Sumac, Yma
1610 N. Vine St.
Los Angeles, CA 90028

Summer, Donna
(La Donna Andrea Gaines)
c/o Susan Munao
1224 N. Vine St.
Los Angeles, CA 90028

Summer, Henry Lee
7608 Teel Way
Indianapolis, IN 46256

Summers, Andy
c/o MCEG
11355 Olympic Blvd.
Los Angeles, CA 90064

The Sun and the Moon
P.O. Box 10, Middleton
Manchester M24 2AB, England

Sunset Sound
6650 Sunset Blvd.
Hollywood, CA 90028
Recording studio

Supertramp
3805 W. Magnolia Blvd.
Burbank, CA 91505

The Supremes
435 E. 79th St.
New York, NY 10021

Sure, Al B.
(Albert Brown)
c/o Warner Bros. Records
3300 Warner Blvd.
Burbank, CA 91510

Surf Punks
P.O. Box 815
Malibu, CA 90265

Surface
14332 Dickens St.
Sherman Oaks, CA 91423

Surratt, Hugh
c/o RCA Records
6363 Sunset Blvd.
Hollywood, CA 90028
Record company executive

Survivor
1046 Carol Dr.
Los Angeles, CA 90069

Sutherland, Joan
c/o Eric Semon
111 W. 57th St.
New York, NY 10019

Sutter, Kevin
c/o Chrysalis Records
645 Madison Ave.
New York, NY 10022
Record company executive

Sutton, Derek
c/o Stardust Ent.
2650 Glendower Ave.
Los Angeles, CA 90027
Personal manager

Swan, Billy
151 El Camino Dr.
Beverly Hills, CA 90212

Swayze, Patrick
8436 W. 3rd St. (#650)
Los Angeles, CA 90048

Sweat, Keith
P.O. Box 1002
Bronx, NY 10466-0305

Sweet
76 Tottenham Court Rd.
London W1P 9PA, England

Sweet, Matthew
c/o AGM
6412 Hollywood Blvd.
Hollywood, CA 90028

Sweet, Rachel
11726 San Vincente Blvd. (#300)
Los Angeles, CA 90049

Sweet Obsession
c/o Hush Prods.
231 W. 58th St.
New York, NY 10019

Sweet Sensations
141 Dunbar
Fords, NJ 08863

Sweet Tee
c/o Profile Records
740 Broadway
New York, NY 10003

Sweethearts of the Rodeo
38 Music Square E. (#300)
Nashville, TN 37203

Sweret, Richard
c/o Arista Records
6 W. 57th St.
New York, NY 10019
A&R executive

Swing Out Sister
c/o PolyGram Records
810 Seventh Ave.
New York, NY 10019

The Sylvers
1900 Ave. of the Stars (#1600)
Los Angeles, CA 90067

Sylvia (Allen)
P.O. Box 150912
Nashville, TN 37215

Sylvian, David
10100 Santa Monica Blvd. (#1600)
Los Angeles, CA 90067

Syreeta (Wright)
c/o Motown Records
6255 Sunset Blvd.
Los Angeles, CA 90028

The System
c/o AMI
1776 Broadway
New York, NY 10019

3 Times Dope
c/o Arista Records
6 W. 57th St.
New York, NY 10019

.38 Special
850 Seventh Ave. (#1105)
New York, NY 10019

220 Volt
c/o Epic Records
51 W. 52nd St.
New York, NY 10019

10,000 Maniacs
P.O. Box 642
Jamestown, NY 14701

TAMI Show
c/o Chrysalis Records
645 Madison Ave.
New York, NY 10022

TNT
11 Ketton Ave.
Norton Lees
Sheffield S8 8PA, England

TSOL
6253 Hollywood Blvd. (#800)
Hollywood, CA 90028

Ta Mara and the Seen
312 Washington Ave. N.
Minneapolis, MN 55401

Tabackin, Lew
38 W. 94th St.
New York, NY 10025

Take 6
c/o Reprise Records
75 Rockefeller Plaza
New York, NY 10019

Talbert, Hank
c/o Capitol Records
1750 N. Vine St.
Hollywood, CA 90028
Record company executive

Talk Talk
121A Revelstone N.
Wimbledon Pl.
London W15, England

Talkback
143 S. Cedros Ave.
Solana Beach, CA 92075

Talking Heads
c/o Overland
1775 Broadway
New York, NY 10019

Tamburro, Rich
c/o EMI-Manhattan Records
1370 Ave. of the Americas
New York, NY 10019
Record company executive

Tangerine Dream
P.O. Box 303340
1000 Berlin 30, West Germany

A Taste of Honey
c/o Denis Vaughan
Heathcoat House
19–20 Saville Row
London W1, England

Taupin, Bernie
8800 Sunset Blvd. (#401)
Los Angeles, CA 90069
Songwriter

Tavares
c/o Brian Panella
3820 Castlerock Rd.
Malibu, CA 90265

Tawatha
c/o E/P/A Records
51 W. 52nd St.
New York, NY 10019

Taxxi
P.O. Box 878
Sonoma, CA 95476

Taylor, Andy
9200 Sunset Blvd. (#415)
Los Angeles, CA 90069

Taylor, B.E.
P.O. Box 2070
Weirton, WV 26062

Taylor, Billy
500 Fifth Ave. (#2050)
New York, NY 10110

Taylor, Cecil
c/o Bridge
106 Fort Greene Pl.
Brooklyn, NY 11217

Taylor, Gary
c/o Virgin Records
30 W. 23rd St.
New York, NY 10010

Taylor, James
644 N. Doheny Dr.
Los Angeles, CA 90069

Taylor, Kate
P.O. Box 36
Chilmark, MA 02535

Taylor, Koko (Cora Walton)
P.O. Box 60234
Chicago, IL 60660

Taylor, Livingston
P.O. Box 16
Hillsboro, NH 03244

Taylor, Mick
150 Fifth Ave. (#1103)
New York, NY 10011

Taylor, Roger
Salterswell Farm
Moreton-In-The-Marsh
Gloucestershire, England

• Tears For Fears
50 New Bond St.
London W1, England

Tease
200 W. 51st St. (#1410)
New York, NY 10019

Teen Dream
P.O. Box 437
Excelsior, MN 55331

Teifeld, Jan
c/o Arista Records
8370 Wilshire Blvd.
Los Angeles, CA 90211
Record company executive

Teller, Al
c/o MCA Records
70 Universal City Plaza
Universal City, CA 91608
Record company executive

Tempchin, Jack
c/o Falk & Morrow
143 S. Cedros Ave.
Solana Beach, CA 92075
Songwriter

Tempest
326 N. Jackson
Oakland City, IN 47660

Temple, Julien
c/o Limelight
1724 Whitley Ave.
Los Angeles, CA 90028
Film/music video director

Templeman, Ted
c/o Warner Bros. Records
3300 Warner Blvd.
Burbank, CA 91510
Producer/A&R executive

●**The Temptations**
c/o Star Direction
605 N. Oakhurst Dr.
Beverly Hills, CA 90210

Ten Ten
c/o Wasted Talent
321 Fulham Rd.
London SW10 9QL, England

Tepper, Robert
South Park (#216)
U.S. Rt. 1
Walpole, MA 02081

Terry, Clark
c/o Willard Alexander
660 Madison Ave.
New York, NY 10021

Terry, Tony
152–18 Union Turnpike (#12R)
Flushing, NY 11367

Terry M
c/o Handle
1 Derby St., Mayfair
London W1Y 7HD, England

Tesla
P.O. Box 3070 Uptown
Hoboken, NJ 07030

Testament
P.O. Box 968
Old Bridge, NJ 08857

Textones
c/o Enigma Records
1750 E. Holly Ave.
El Segundo, CA 90245

Thackray, Jake
Winterfold House
46 Woodfield Rd., Kings Heath
Birmingham B13 9UJ, England

The The
10100 Santa Monica Blvd. (#1600)
Los Angeles, CA 90067

Thelonius Monster
11116 Aqua Vista St. (#39)
Studio City, CA 91602

Theodore, Donna
10100 Santa Monica Blvd. (#1600)
Los Angeles, CA 90067

Theresa
c/o RCA Records
1133 Ave. of the Americas
New York, NY 10036

Theroux, Gary
17 Piping Rock Dr.
Ossining, NY 10562
Pop record researcher

✦ **They Might Be Giants**
10100 Santa Monica Blvd. (#1600)
Los Angeles, CA 90067

Thielman, Jean "Toots"
c/o Abby Hoffer
223½ E. 48th St.
New York, NY 10017

Think Out Loud
c/o A&M Records
1416 N. La Brea Ave.
Hollywood, CA 90028

Third World
c/o Jah's Music
6 Dumfries Rd.
Kingston 10, Jamaica

This Mortal Coil
c/o Phil Carson
75 Rockefeller Plaza
New York, NY 10019

Thomas, B.J. (Billy Joe)
P.O. Box 120003
Arlington, TX 76012

Thomas, Irma
c/o Rounder Records
1 Camp St.
Cambridge, MA 02140

Thomas, Jay
c/o KPWR
6430 Sunset Blvd. (#418)
Los Angeles, CA 90028
Disc jockey

Thomas, Lillo
c/o Hush Prods.
231 W. 58th St.
New York, NY 10019

Thomas, Michael Tilson
24 W. 57th St.
New York, NY 10019
Classical conductor

Thomas, Philip
c/o Atlantic Records
75 Rockefeller Plaza
New York, NY 10019

Thomas, Vaughn
c/o Geffen Records
9130 Sunset Blvd.
Los Angeles, CA 90069
Record company executive

Thompson, Hank
1300 Division St. (#102)
Nashville, TN 37203

Thompson, Howard
c/o Elektra Records
75 Rockefeller Plaza
New York, NY 10019
A&R executive

Thompson, Linda
c/o CBS Records
34 Music Square E.
Nashville, TN 37203

Thompson, Richard
P.O. Box 7095
New York, NY 10116

The Thompson Twins
9 Eccleston St.
London SW1, England

Thorogood, George
P.O. Box 170
Kemblesville, PA 19347

Thrashing Doves
c/o Cheval Music
5 Dean St.
London W1T 5RN, England

Three Dog Night
151 El Camino Dr.
Beverly Hills, CA 90212

Three Man Island
c/o Chrysalis Records
645 Madison Ave.
New York, NY 10022

Thyret, Russ
c/o Warner Bros. Records
3300 Warner Blvd.
Burbank, CA 91510
Record company executive

Ticketron
142 W. 57th St.
New York, NY 10019
Ticket agency

Tierra
15445 Ventura Blvd. (#243)
Sherman Oaks, CA 91413

Tiffany (Darwish)
c/o George Tobin
11337 Burbank Blvd.
N. Hollywood, CA 91601

Tigertailz
c/o Combat Records
187-07 Henderson Ave.
Hollis, NY 11423

Tikaram, Tanita
c/o Reprise Records
3300 Warner Blvd.
Burbank, CA 91510

'Til Tuesday
c/o Symmetry
48 W. 75th St.
New York, NY 10023

Tillis, Mel
(Lonnie Melvin Tillis)
809 18th Ave. S.
Nashville, TN 37203-3218

Tillis, Pam
P.O. Box 121321
Nashville, TN 37203

Tillotson, Johnny
17530 Ventura Blvd. (#108)
Encino, CA 91316

● **Timbuk 3**
1046 Carol Dr.
Los Angeles, CA 90069

Times Two
c/o Reprise Records
3300 Warner Blvd.
Burbank, CA 91510

Timex Social Club
1442A Walnut St.
Berkeley, CA 94709

Tiny Tim (Herbert Khaury)
Hotel Olcott
27 W. 72nd St.
New York, NY 10023

Titelman, Russ
3 E. 54th St.
New York, NY 10022
Record producer

Tobey, Chris
c/o Chrysalis Records
645 Madison Ave.
New York, NY 10022
Record company executive

Tobin, George
11337 Burbank Blvd.
N. Hollywood, CA 91601
Producer/personal manager

Tobruk
c/o Simstar
30–43 Oxford St., Digbeth
Birmingham B5 5LI, England

Today
c/o Motown Records
6255 Sunset Blvd.
Los Angeles, CA 90028

The Tokens
P.O. Box 1987
Studio City, CA 91604

The Toll
c/o The Hushes
1035 W. Third Ave.
Columbus, OH 43212

Tolliver, Lynn
c/o WZAK
1729 Superior Ave. (#401)
Cleveland, OH 44114
Program director/disc jockey

Tom Tom Club
c/o Overland
1775 Broadway
New York, NY 10019

Tone Loc (Tony Smith)
c/o Island Records
14 E. 4th St.
New York, NY 10012

Tonio K. (Steve Krikorian)
c/o A&M Records
1416 N. La Brea Ave.
Hollywood, CA 90028

Tony, Toni, Tone
c/o PolyGram Records
810 Seventh Ave.
New York, NY 10019

Too Nice
c/o Arista Records
6 W. 57th St.
New York, NY 10019

**Toots and the Maytals
(Frederick "Toots" Hibbert)**
P.O. Box 82
Great Neck, NY 11021

Tori
c/o Atlantic Records
75 Rockefeller Plaza
New York, NY 10019

Torme, Mel (Melvin Howard)
10100 Santa Monica Blvd. (#1600)
Los Angeles, CA 90067

Torn, David
P.O. Box 396
Beverly, MA 01915

Toto
c/o CBS Records
1801 Century Park W.
Los Angeles, CA 90067

Toussaint, Allen
P.O. Box 19004
New Orleans, LA 70130
Record producer

Tower of Power
151 El Camino Dr.
Beverly Hills, CA 90212

Tower Records
2500 Del Monte, Bldg. C
W. Sacramento, CA 95691
Retail music chain

Towner, Ralph
c/o Ted Kurland
173 Brighton Ave.
Boston, MA 02134

Townshend, Peter
c/o Entertainment Corp.
565 Fifth Ave.
New York, NY 10017

T'Pau
c/o Frontier
1776 Broadway
New York, NY 10019

Trakin, Roy
c/o Hits
15477 Ventura Blvd. (#300)
Sherman Oaks, CA 91403
Music journalist

**Trans World Music
(also Vibrations, Peaches)**
38 Corporate Circle
Albany, NY 12203
Retail music chain

Transvision Vamp
c/o MCA Records
70 Universal City Plaza
Universal City, CA 91608

Trash
c/o Harry Maloney
18–19 Warwick St.
London W1R 5RB, England

Traut, Bill
845 Via de la Paz (#365)
Pacific Palisades, CA 90272
Personal manager

Travers, Mary
c/o Abby Hoffer
223½ E. 48th St.
New York, NY 10017

Travers, Pat
P.O. Box 7877
College Park Station
Orlando, FL 32854

Travis, Merle
Route #1 (#128)
Park Hill, OK 74451

Travis, Randy
P.O. Box 121712
Nashville, TN 37212

Travolta, John
c/o M.C.E.G.
11355 W. Olympic Blvd. (#500)
Los Angeles, CA 90064

Trbovich, Tom
20140 Pacific Coast Hwy.
Malibu, CA 90265
Music television director

Treat Her Right
c/o RCA Records
1133 Ave. of the Americas
New York, NY 10036

Tree International
8 Music Square W.
Nashville, TN 37203
Music publisher

The Treniers
7060 Hollywood Blvd. (#1212)
Hollywood, CA 90028

Trent, Buck
c/o Circuit Rider
123 Walton Ferry Rd.
Hendersonville, TN 37075

Triad Artists
10100 Santa Monica Blvd. (#1600)
Los Angeles, CA 90067
Booking agents

The Triffids
c/o Hot Records
326 Sixth St.
San Francisco, CA 94103

The Triplets
c/o Mega Mgmt.
71 W. 23rd St.
New York, NY 10010

Tritt, Travis
P.O. Box 120897
Nashville, TN 37212

Triumph
3611 Mavis Rd., Unit 3
Mississauga, ON LSC 1T7, Canada

Troop
c/o ICM
40 W. 57th St.
New York, NY 10019

Troubadour
9081 Santa Monica Blvd.
W. Hollywood, CA 90069
Nightclub

Trouble
c/o Def American Records
9157 Sunset Blvd.
Los Angeles, CA 90069

Trower, Robin
c/o Stardust
2650 Glendower Ave.
Los Angeles, CA 90027

Tubb, Justin
P.O. Box 500
Nashville, TN 37202

The Tubes
P.O. Box 894
San Francisco, CA 94101

Tuck and Patti
P.O. Box 9388
Palo Alto, CA 94305

Tucker, Tanya
2325 Crestmoor Dr. (#15245)
Nashville, TN 37215

Tuesday Blue
c/o EMI-Manhattan Records
1370 Ave. of the Americas
New York, NY 10019

Tuff
P.O. Box 3106
Hollywood, CA 90078

Tune, Tommy
c/o Marvin Shulman
890 Broadway
New York, NY 10003

Turner, Dennis
3500 W. Olive Ave. (#770)
Burbank, CA 91505
Personal manager

Turner, Earl, Jr.
c/o George Harness
1 Timberline Dr.
Springfield, IL 62707

Turner, Ike
1800 N. Highland Ave. (#411)
Hollywood, CA 90028

Turner, Joe Lynn
c/o Entertainment Services
212 Race St.
Philadelphia, PA 19106

Turner, Tina
(Annie Mae Bullock)
3575 Cahuenga Blvd. W. (#580)
Los Angeles, CA 90068

Turrentine, Stanley
c/o Blue Note Records
1370 Ave. of the Americas
New York, NY 10019

The Turtle Island String Quartet
c/o Windham Hill Records
247 High St.
Palo Alto, CA 94305

The Turtles
c/o David Fishof
1775 Broadway
New York, NY 10019

Tusken, Ray
c/o Capitol Records
1750 N. Vine St.
Hollywood, CA 90028
Record company executive

Tutone, Tommy
c/o ICM
40 W. 57th St.
New York, NY 10019

Twilley, Dwight
8306 Wilshire Blvd. (#196)
Beverly Hills, CA 90211

Twitty, Conway
(Harold Jenkins)
#1 Music Village Blvd.
Hendersonville, TN 37075

Tyler, Bonnie
17–19 Soho Square
London W1, England

Tyner, McCoy
c/o Abby Hoffer
223½ E. 48th St.
New York, NY 10017

Tyrant
18653 Ventura Blvd. (#311)
Tarzana, CA 91356

U2
4 Windmill Lane
Dublin 4, Ireland

UB40
c/o Warner Bros. Records
3300 Warner Blvd.
Burbank, CA 91510

UDO
c/o RCA Records
1133 Ave. of the Americas
New York, NY 10036

UFO
10 Sutherland
London W9 24Q, England

UTFO
c/o Steve Salem
217 Lafayette Ave.
Brooklyn, NY 11238

Uggams, Leslie
400 S. Beverly Dr. (#216)
Beverly Hills, CA 90212

Ultravox
c/o O'Donnell
9 Disraeli Rd.
London SW15, England

Uncanny X-Men
P.O. Box 221
Albert Park, VIC 3206, Australia

Uncle Sam
P.O. Box 67503
Rochester, NY 14617
Fan club

Underworld
c/o Warner Bros. Records
3300 Warner Blvd.
Burbank, CA 91510

Universal Recording
46 E. Walton
Chicago, IL 60611
Recording studio

The Untouchables
652 Angelus Pl.
Venice, CA 90291

Upchurch, Phil
c/o Wirtz
86 S. Sierra Madre Blvd.
Pasadena, CA 91107

Ure, Midge
Unit 32, Ransomes Docks
35–37 Parkgate Rd.
London SW11 4NP, England

Uriah Heep
c/o Miracle Agency
5 Dean St.
London W1V 5RN, England

Urso, Dave
c/o WTG Records
1801 Century Park W.
Los Angeles, CA 90067
Record company executive

Utopia
c/o Panacea
2705 Glendower Ave.
Los Angeles, CA 90027

VH-1 (Video Hits One)
1775 Broadway
New York, NY 10019
Music video network

Valdez, Daniel
11726 San Vicente Blvd. (#300)
Los Angeles, CA 90049

Vale, Jerry (Genaro Vitaliano)
c/o Willard Alexander
660 Madison Ave.
New York, NY 10021

Valentin, Dave
c/o DeLeon
4031 Panama Ct.
Piedmont, CA 94611

The Valentine Brothers
c/o Vision
2112 N. Cahuenga Blvd.
Los Angeles, CA 90068

Valli, Frankie
(Frank Castelluccio)
c/o Avnet Mgmt.
3805 W. Magnolia Blvd.
Burbank, CA 91505

Van Den Ende, Tony
155–157 Oxford St.
London W1R 1TB, England
Music video director

Van Halen
10100 Santa Monica Blvd. (#2460)
Los Angeles, CA 90067

Van Heusen, Jimmy
P.O. Box 44
Brant Lake, NY 12815
Songwriter

Van Matre, Lynn
c/o Chicago Tribune
435 N. Michigan Ave.
Chicago, IL 60611
Music critic

Van Ronk, Dave
c/o Folklore
1671 Appian Way
Santa Monica, CA 90401

Van Shelton, Ricky
c/o Campbell-Thompson
3039 Franklin Rd.
Nashville, TN 37204

Van Zandt, Steve
9200 Sunset Blvd. (#915)
Los Angeles, CA 90069

Van Zandt, Townes
c/o Keith Case
1016 16th Ave. S.
Nashville, TN 37212

Vance, Kenny
South Park (#216)
U.S. Rt. 1
Walpole, MA 02081

Vance, Ronny
c/o Geffen Music
9130 Sunset Blvd.
Los Angeles, CA 90069
Music publisher

Vandross, Luther
8271 Melrose Ave.
Los Angeles, CA 90046

Vangelis (Papathanassiou)
c/o Yanus Zographus
Nemo Studios
Hampden Gurney St.
London, England

Vanity
151 El Camino Dr.
Beverly Hills, CA 90212

Vannelli, Gino
c/o John Baruck
1046 Carol Dr.
Los Angeles, CA 90069

VanWarmer, Randy
P.O. Box 135
Bearsville, NY 12409

Variety
154 W. 46th St.
New York, NY 10036
Trade magazine

Variety Artists International
2980 Beverly Glen Circle (#302)
Los Angeles, CA 90077
Booking agent

Vartan, Sylvie
151 El Camino Dr.
Beverly Hills, CA 90212

Vaughan, Stevie Ray
P.O. Box Drawer T
Manor, TX 78653

Vaughn, Sarah
10100 Santa Monica Blvd. (#1600)
Los Angeles, CA 90067

Vee, Bobby
P.O. Box 41
Saulk Rapids, MN 56379

Vega, Suzanne
P.O. Box 4221
Grand Central Station
New York, NY 10163

The Vega Brothers
9255 Sunset Blvd. (#1115)
Los Angeles, CA 90069

Vela, Rosie
c/o Ford Model Agency
344 E. 59th St.
New York, NY 10022

Velore and Double O
c/o Virgin Records
9247 Alden Dr.
Beverly Hills, CA 90210

The Vels
c/o Symmetry Mgmt.
234 W. 56th St.
New York, NY 10019

The Venetians
P.O. Box 176
Potts Point
Sydney, NSW 2011, Australia

Vengeance
Bezuidenhoutseweg 106
2594 Az the Hague, Holland

Venom
c/o Frontier
1776 Broadway
New York, NY 10019

The Ventures
P.O. Box 1646
Burbank, CA 91507

Vera, Billy (and the Beaters)
8730 Sunset Blvd. (PH W)
Los Angeles, CA 90069

Verlaine, Tom
c/o Renegade
145 Oxford St.
London W1, England

Verona, Stephen
15301 Ventura Blvd. (#345)
Sherman Oaks, CA 91403
Music video pioneer

Vesta
c/o A&M Records
1416 N. La Brea Ave.
Hollywood, CA 90028

Vidal, Maria
1501 Broadway (#2300)
New York, NY 10036

View From The Hill
P.O. Box 337
London W5 4XG, England

Vigil
c/o Chrysalis Records
645 Madison Ave.
New York, NY 10022

The Village People
251 Park Ave. S.
New York, NY 10010

Vincent, Vinnie
c/o Chrysalis Records
645 Madison Ave.
New York, NY 10022

Vinton, Bobby
(Stanley Robert Vinton)
P.O. Box 906
Malibu, CA 90265-0906

The Violent Femmes
P.O. Box 1304
Burbank, CA 91507

Virgin Music
827 N. Hilldale Ave.
W. Hollywood, CA 90069
Music publisher

Virginia Wolf
10 Sutherland Ave.
London W9, England

Visions
c/o American Mgmt.
43 Foster Square
Pittsburgh, PA 15212

Vitamin Z
c/o Geffen Records
9130 Sunset Blvd.
Los Angeles, CA 90069

Vitous, Miroslav
c/o ECM Records
810 Seventh Ave.
New York, NY 10019

Vivid Prods.
1230 La Collina Dr.
Beverly Hills, CA 90210
Music video producers/directors

Vixen
2519 Carmen Crest Dr.
Los Angeles, CA 90068

The Vogues
P.O. Box 399
Lisle, IL 60532

Voice of the Beehive
c/o PolyGram Records
810 Seventh Ave.
New York, NY 10019

Voivod
18653 Ventura Blvd. (#311)
Tarzana, CA 91356

Vollenweider, Andreas
Sempacherstrasse 16
8032 Zurich, Switzerland

The Voltage Brothers
P.O. Box 11283
Richmond, VA 23230

Volunteer Lawyers for the Arts
1285 Ave. of the Americas
New York, NY 10019
Offers legal assistance

Vow Wow
c/o L.O.E.
159 Broadhurst Gardens
London NW6 3AU, England

Vukovic, Mio
c/o Geffen Records
9130 Sunset Blvd.
Los Angeles, CA 90069
A&R executive

W.A.S.P.
P.O. Box 1AP
London W1 L1P, England

Wa Wa Nee
c/o Epic Records
51 W. 52nd St.
New York, NY 10019

Wade, E.
6600 Beachview Dr. (#134)
Palos Verdes, CA 90274

Wagener, Michael
8033 Sunset Blvd. (#84)
Los Angeles, CA 90046
Record producer

Wagner, Jack
10100 Santa Monica Blvd. (#1600)
Los Angeles, CA 90067

The Wagoneers
8306 Appalachian Dr.
Austin, TX 78759

Wagoner, Porter
1522 Demonbreun St.
Nashville, TN 37203

Wailer, Bunny (also **The Wailers**)
(**Neville Livingston**)
c/o The Agency
370 City Road, Islington
London EC1V 2QA, England

Wainwright, Loudon, III
P.O. Box 210103
San Francisco, CA 94121

Waite, John
c/o ICM
40 W. 57th St.
New York, NY 10019

Waits, Tom
c/o Rothberg-Gerber Mgmt.
145 Central Park W.
New York, NY 10023

Wakeling, Dave
100 Universal City Plaza
(Bldg. 422)
Universal City, CA 91608

Wakeman, Rick
c/o Sun Artists
9 Hillgate St.
London W8, England

Walden, Narada Michael
P.O. Box 690
San Francisco, CA 94101

Waldman, Wendy
10100 Santa Monica Blvd. (#1600)
Los Angeles, CA 90067

Walk
c/o A&M Records
1416 N. La Brea Ave.
Hollywood, CA 90028

Walk the West
P.O. Box 150973
Nashville, TN 37215

Walker, Billy
P.O. Box 618
Hendersonville, TN 37075

Walker, Jerry Jeff
c/o North Light
1775 Broadway
New York, NY 10019

Walker, Junior
(Autry DeWalt, Jr.)
141 Dunbar Ave.
Fords, NJ 08863

Wallace, Bennie
P.O. Box 396
Beverly, MA 01915

Walrath, Jack
c/o Bridge
106 Fort Greene Pl.
Brooklyn, NY 11217

Walsh, Joe
9044 Melrose Ave. (#306)
Los Angeles, CA 90069

Walters, Norby
200 W. 51st St. (#1410)
New York, NY 10019
Booking agent/personal manager

Walton, Cedar
c/o DeLeon
4031 Panama Ct.
Piedmont, CA 94611

Wang Chung
c/o Geffen Records
9130 Sunset Blvd.
Los Angeles, CA 90069

Wansel, Dexter
1995 Broadway (#501)
New York, NY 10023

War
8306 Wilshire Blvd. (#789)
Los Angeles, CA 90048

Ward, Jacky
54 Music Square E. (#300)
Nashville, TN 37203

The Ward Brothers
c/o Johnathan Cooke
81 Harley House, Marylebone Rd.
London NW1 5HT, England

Wariner, Steve
P.O. Box 121684
Nashville, TN 37212

Warlock
c/o PolyGram Records
810 Seventh Ave.
New York, NY 10019

Warlord
18653 Ventura Blvd. (#311)
Tarzana, CA 91356

Warner-Chappell Music
9000 Sunset Blvd. (PH)
Los Angeles, CA 90069
Music publisher

Warnes, Jennifer
10100 Santa Monica Blvd. (#1600)
Los Angeles, CA 90067

Waronker, Lenny
c/o Warner Bros. Records
3300 Warner Blvd.
Burbank, CA 91510
Producer/record company
executive

Warrant
c/o CBS Records
1801 Century Park W.
Los Angeles, CA 90067

Warriorsoul
P.O. Box 3070 Uptown
Hoboken, NJ 07030

Warwick, Dionne
(Marie Dionne Warrick)
9200 Sunset Blvd. (#420)
Los Angeles, CA 90069

Was (Not Was)
8899 Beverly Blvd.
Los Angeles, CA 90048

Washington, A.D.
c/o MCA Records
70 Universal City Plaza
Universal City, CA 91608
Record company executive

Washington, Grover, Jr.
c/o Zane Mgmt.
1515 Market St.
Philadelphia, PA 19102

Wasted Talent
321 Fulham Rd.
London SW10 9QL, England
Booking agent

Watanabe, Sadao
648 N. Robertson Blvd.
Los Angeles, CA 90069

The Waterboys
3 Monmouth Pl.
London W2, England

Muddy Waters Museum
Carnegie Public Library
114 Delta
Clarksdale, MS 38614

Waters, Roger
c/o CBS Records
51 W. 52nd St.
New York, NY 10019

Watley, Jody
8439 Sunset Blvd. (#103)
Los Angeles, CA 90069

Watrous, Bill
c/o Willard Alexander
660 Madison Ave.
New York, NY 10021

Watson, Bobby
c/o Abby Hoffer
223½ E. 48th St.
New York, NY 10017-1538

Watson, Doc
c/o Manny Greenhill Mgmt.
1671 Appian Way
Santa Monica, CA 90401

Watson, Eric
20 Manchester Sq.
London W1A 1ES, England
Music video director

Watson, Gene
9507 Puritan Way
Rosharon, TX 77583

Watson, Johnny "Guitar"
c/o PDQ
1474 N. Kings Rd.
Los Angeles, CA 90069

Watts, Charlie
Halsdon House
Near Barnstable, Devon, England

Watts, Ernie
c/o Ted Kurland
173 Brighton Ave.
Boston, MA 02134

Waugh, Butch
c/o RCA Records
1133 Ave. of the Americas
New York, NY 10036
Record company executive

Wax, Steve
P.O. Box 69180
Los Angeles, CA 90069
Personal manager

Wax-UK
c/o RCA Records
1133 Ave. of the Americas
New York, NY 10036

Waybill, Fee
c/o Fitzgerald-Hartley
7250 Beverly Blvd.
Los Angeles, CA 90036

Waysted
c/o EMI Records
20 Manchester Square
London W1, England

Weather Girls
c/o Douglas Kibble
1414 Forest Ave.
Baldwin, NY 11510

Weather Report
8899 Beverly Blvd.
Los Angeles, CA 90048

Weaver, Dennis
c/o Nashville International
116 17th Ave. S.
Nashville, TN 37203

Webber, Andrew Lloyd
20 Greek St.
London W1V 5LF, England
Composer

Webber, Joel
c/o Island Records
14 E. 4th St.
New York, NY 10012
A&R executive

Weber, Eberhard
c/o Ted Kurland
173 Brighton Ave.
Boston, MA 02134

Wee Papa Girls
c/o RCA Records
1133 Ave. of the Americas
New York, NY 10036

Weidlin, Jane
644 N. Doheny Dr.
Los Angeles, CA 90069

Weil, Cynthia
3815 W. Olive Ave. (#202)
Burbank, CA 91505
Songwriter

Weinstein, Bobby
c/o BMI
320 W. 57th St.
New York, NY 10019
Songwriter

Weisner, Ron
9200 Sunset Blvd. (PH 15)
Los Angeles, CA 90069
Personal manager

Welch, Kevin
P.O. Box 120897
Nashville, TN 37212

Welk, Lawrence
1299 Ocean Ave. (#800)
Santa Monica, CA 90401

Weller, Freddy
2401 12th Ave. S.
Nashville, TN 37204

Wells, Junior (Amos Blackmore)
c/o American Famous
816 W. Evergreen
Chicago, IL 60622

Wells, Kitty (Muriel Deason Wright)
P.O. Box 809
Goodlettsville, TN 37072

Wells, Mary
1680 N. Vine St. (#214)
Hollywood, CA 90028

Wendy and Lisa
c/o Overland
1775 Broadway
New York, NY 10019

Wenner, Jann
c/o Rolling Stone
745 Fifth Ave.
New York, NY 10022
Magazine publisher

Wershow & Shapiro
9255 Sunset Blvd.
Los Angeles, CA 90069
Business managers

West, Dottie
(Dorothy Marie Marsh)
P.O. Box 120537
Nashville, TN 37212

West, Leslie (and Mountain)
8899 Beverly Blvd.
Los Angeles, CA 90048

West, Shelly
P.O. Box 158718
Nashville, TN 37215

West, Simon
52 Musard Rd.
London W6, England
Music video director

Weston, Jack
c/o RCA Records
30 Music Square W.
Nashville, TN 37203
Record company executive

Wet Wet Wet
c/o Pet Sounds
24 Gairbraid Ave.
Glasgow G20-IXX, Scotland, UK

Wet Willie
210 25th Ave. N. (#N-101)
Nashville, TN 37203

Whalley, Tom
c/o Capitol Records
1750 N. Vine St.
Hollywood, CA 90028
A&R executive

Whalum, Kirk
P.O. Box 182
Middle Village, NY 11379

What Is This
2519 Carmen Crest Dr.
Los Angeles, CA 90068

Wheeler, Billy Edd
P.O. Box 7
Swannonoa, NC 28778

When In Rome
c/o Virgin Records
Kensall House
533-579 Harrow Rd.
London W10 4RH, England

Wherehouse
19701 Hamilton Ave.
Torrance, CA 90502
Retail music chain

The Whispers
9229 Sunset Blvd. (#414)
Los Angeles, CA 90069

Whitburn, Joel
P.O. Box 200
Menomonee Falls, WI 53051
Pop record researcher

Whitcomb, Ian
P.O. Box 451
Altadena, CA 91001

White, Barry
2434 Main St. (#202)
Santa Monica, CA 90405

White, Dennis
c/o CEMA
1750 N. Vine St.
Hollywood, CA 90028
Record company executive

White, Josh
c/o Gersh
130 W. 42nd St.
New York, NY 10036

White, Karyn
c/o Warner Bros. Records
3300 Warner Blvd.
Burbank, CA 91510

White, Lenny
1995 Broadway (#501)
New York, NY 10023

White, Maurice
4303 W. Verdugo Ave.
Burbank, CA 91505

White, Michael
17337 Ventura Blvd. (#300C)
Encino, CA 91316

White, Sunny Joe
c/o WXKS
99 Revere Beach Pkwy.
Medford, MA 02155
Disc jockey

White, Tony Joe
35 Music Square E.
Nashville, TN 37203

White Lion
J.A.F. P.O. Box 1874
New York, NY 10116

The Whitehead Brothers
(Kenny and Johnny)
309 S. Broad St.
Philadelphia, PA 19017

The Whites
c/o Jim Halsey Co.
3225 S. Norwood
Tulsa, OK 74135

Whitesnake
15 Poulton Rd.
Wallasey, Cheshire, England

Whitfield, Barrence
25 Huntington Ave. (#420)
Boston, MA 02116

Whitley, Keith
c/o McFadden
818 18th Ave. S.
Nashville, TN 37203

**Slim Whitman Appreciation
Society**
1002 Thurber St.
Tucson, AZ 85705

Whittaker, Roger
50 Regents Park Rd.
Primrose Hill
London NW1, England

♪ **The Who**
112 Wardour
London W1V 3LD, England

Whodini
298 Elizabeth St.
New York, NY 10012

Wiedlin, Jane
c/o Summa
8507 Sunset Blvd.
W. Hollywood, CA 90069

Wilburn Bros.
217 E. Cedar St.
Goodlettsville, TN 37072

Wild Blue
c/o RB & Co.
504 W. Arlington Pl.
Chicago, IL 60614

The Wild Cards
1322 2nd St. (#2)
Santa Monica, CA 90401

Wild Cherry
28001 Chargrin Blvd. (#205)
Cleveland, OH 44122

Wild Seeds
6253 Hollywood Blvd. (#800)
Hollywood, CA 90028

Wilde, Danny
14755 Ventura Blvd. (#1-710)
Sherman Oaks, CA 91403

Wilde, Eugene
P.O. Box 11981
Philadelphia, PA 19145

Wilde, Kim
Big M House
1 Stevenage Rd., Knebworth
Hertfordshire, SG3 6AN, England

Wilder, Matthew
10100 Santa Monica Blvd. (#1600)
Los Angeles, CA 90067

Will and the Kill
8899 Beverly Blvd.
Los Angeles, CA 90048

Will To Power
c/o Epic Records
51 W. 52nd St.
New York, NY 10019

The William Morris Agency
151 El Camino Dr.
Beverly Hills, CA 90212
Booking agents

Williams, Andy
816 N. La Cienega Blvd.
Los Angeles, CA 90069

Williams, Beau
c/o Hush Productions
231 W. 58th St.
New York, NY 10019

Williams, Christopher
c/o Geffen Records
9130 Sunset Blvd.
Los Angeles, CA 90069

Williams, Deniece
c/o Alive Ent.
8271 Melrose Ave.
Los Angeles, CA 90046

Williams, Don
c/o Hallmark
15 Music Square W.
Nashville, TN 37203

Williams, Geoffrey
c/o Atlantic Records
75 Rockefeller Plaza
New York, NY 10019

**Williams, Hank, Jr. (Randall Hank
Williams, Jr.)**
P.O. Box 850
Paris, TN 38242

Williams, James "D-Train"
c/o CBS Records
51 W. 52nd St.
New York, NY 10019

Williams, Jason D.
c/o RCA Records
30 Music Square W.
Nashville, TN 37203

Williams, Joe
On The Bandstand, Box C
River Edge, NJ 07661

Williams, John
301 Massachusetts Ave.
Boston, MA 02115
Composer

Williams, Mark
c/o Virgin Records
9247 Alden Dr.
Beverly Hills, CA 90210
A&R executive

Williams, Mason
c/o D. Ross
3097 Floral Hill Rd.
Eugene, OR 97403

**Williams, Maurice (and the
Zodiacs)**
c/o Insight
2300 E. Independence Blvd.
Charlotte, NC 28205

Williams, Patrick
3815 W. Olive Ave. (#202)
Burbank, CA 91505
Film/TV composer

Williams, Paul
c/o Denny Bond
4570 Encino Ave.
Encino, CA 91316

Williams, Roger
c/o Americom
5150 Wilshire Blvd.
Los Angeles, CA 90036

Williams, Tony
P.O. Box 756
Fairfax, CA 94930

Williams, Vanessa
P.O. Box 40
Millwood, NY 10546

Williams, Vesta
5301 Mullen Ave.
Los Angeles, CA 90043

Williams, Wendy O.
P.O. Box 837
New York, NY 10013

Williamson, Robin
P.O. Box 27522
Los Angeles, CA 90027

Willis, Allee
c/o Unicity Music
90 Universal City Plaza
Universal City, CA 91608
Songwriter

Willis, Bruce
10100 Santa Monica Blvd. (#1600)
Los Angeles, CA 90067

Wills, David
c/o CBS Records
34 Music Square E.
Nashville, TN 37203

Wilson, Benny
P.O. Box 798
Lancaster, TX 75146

Wilson, Cassandra
c/o PolyGram Records
810 Seventh Ave.
New York, NY 10019

Wilson, Danny
c/o Virgin Records
Kensall House
533/579 Harrow Rd.
London W10 4RH, England

Wilson, Mary
9200 Sunset Blvd. (#1200)
Los Angeles, CA 90069

Wilson, Nancy
5455 Wilshire Blvd. (#1606)
Los Angeles, CA 90036

Wilson, Shanice
c/o A&M Records
1416 N. La Brea Ave.
Hollywood, CA 90028

Wilson, Teddy
c/o Edith Kiggen
50 E. 72nd St.
New York, NY 10021

The Winans
P.O. Box 1984
Thousand Oaks, CA 91360

Winbush, Angela
446 Liberty Rd.
Inglewood, NJ 07631

Winchester, Jesse
P.O. Box 7308
Carmel, CA 93921

Windplayer
14536 Roscoe Ave.
Panorama City, CA 91402
Musicians' magazine

Wingate, Dick
c/o PolyGram Records
810 Seventh Ave.
New York, NY 10019
A&R executive

Winger
c/o Atlantic Records
75 Rockefeller Plaza
New York, NY 10019

Winston, Cliff
c/o KJLH
3847 Crenshaw Blvd.
Los Angeles, CA 90008
Program director/disc jockey

Winston, George
c/o Windham Hill
P.O. Box 9388
Stanford, CA 94307

Winter, Johnny
3 E. 54th St. (#1400)
New York, NY 10022

Winter, Paul
2067 Broadway (PH B)
New York, NY 10023

Winterland Productions
100 Harrison St.
San Francisco, CA 94105
Manufacturers of t-shirts/posters

Winward, Rick
c/o Enigma Records
1750 E. Holly Ave.
El Segundo, CA 90245

Winwood, Steve
9200 Sunset Blvd. (PH 15)
Los Angeles, CA 90069

Wire Train
c/o Direct Mgmt.
945A N. La Cienega Blvd.
Los Angeles, CA 90069

Wiseman, Mac
c/o Robert Porter
1100 17th Ave. S.
Nashville, TN 37212

● **Wishbone Ash**
c/o John Sherry
65 E. 55th St.
New York, NY 10022

Witherspoon, Jimmy
c/o Abby Hoffer
223½ E. 48th St.
New York, NY 10017

Wittman, William
c/o RCA Records
1133 Ave. of the Americas
New York, NY 10036
A&R executive

Wolf, Peter
8800 Sunset Blvd. (#401)
Los Angeles, CA 90069

Wolfsbane
c/o Def American Records
9157 Sunset Blvd.
Los Angeles, CA 90069

Womack, Bobby
c/o Truth Records
2841 Firenze Pl.
Los Angeles, CA 90048

Womack & Womack
(Cecil and Linda)
1174 Longwood Ave.
Los Angeles, CA 90019

Womack, Steve
1990 Berry's Chapel Rd.
Franklin, TN 37064
Music television director

Wonder, Stevie
(Steveland Morris)
4616 Magnolia Blvd.
Burbank, CA 91505

The Wonderstuff
c/o Polydor Records
810 Seventh Ave.
New York, NY 10019

The Woodentops
c/o International Talent
200 W. 57th St.
New York, NY 10019

Woods, Phil
P.O. Box 278
Delaware Water Gap, PA 18327

Woodstock '69
P.O. Box 680
Stillwater, MN 55083
Memorabilia

Wooley, Sheb (Ben Colder)
c/o CRT
123 Walton Ferry Rd.
Hendersonville, TN 37075

Wopat, Tom
9255 Sunset Blvd. (#706)
Los Angeles, CA 90069

World At A Glance
c/o Island Records
14 E. 4th St.
New York, NY 10012

World Class Wreckin' Cru
21430 Strathern (#N/O)
Canoga Park, CA 91304

World Party
11355 W. Olympic Blvd. (#555)
Los Angeles, CA 90064

Worley, Paul
c/o Audio Media Recorders
808 19th Ave. S.
Nashville, TN 37203
Record producer

Wrathchild
1431 Duke St.
Alexandria, VA 22314

The Wrays
c/o Scott Dean
428 Hill St.
Reno, NV 89501

Wright, Gary
3 E. 54th St. (#1400)
New York, NY 10022

Wunsch, Roy
c/o CBS Records
34 Music Square E.
Nashville, TN 37203
Record company executive

Wylie, Pete
c/o International Talent
200 W. 57th St.
New York, NY 10019

Wyman, Bill
344 Kings Rd.
London SW3 5UR, England

Wynette, Tammy
(Wynette Pugh)
1222 16th Ave. S.
Nashville, TN 37203

Wyrostok, Steve
c/o WARM
3405 Piedmont Rd.
Atlanta, GA 30305
Radio station music director

X

X
10100 Santa Monica Blvd.
(#1600)
Los Angeles, CA 90067

XTC
c/o Geffen Records
9130 Sunset Blvd.
Los Angeles, CA 90069

Y & T
845 Via De La Paz (#365)
Pacific Palisades, CA 90272

Ya Ya
c/o Mr. I. Mouse
920 Dickson St.
Marina del Rey, CA 90292

Yamaha Music Corp.
6600 Orangethorpe Ave.
Buena Park, CA 90620
Instrument manufacturer

Yankovic, Frankie
251 E. 262nd St.
Euclid, OH 44132

Yankovic, Weird Al
c/o Imaginary Ent.
925 Westmount Dr.
Los Angeles, CA 90069

**Yarbrough and Peoples
(Calvin and Alisa)**
200 W. 51st St. (#1410)
New York, NY 10019

Yarbrough, Glenn
11514 Calvert St.
N. Hollywood, CA 91606

Yates, Lori Lee
c/o CBS Records
34 Music Square E.
Nashville, TN 37203

Year Zero
c/o Chrysalis Records
645 Madison Ave.
New York, NY 10022

Yellow Magic Orchestra
151 El Camino Dr.
Beverly Hills, CA 90212

Yellowjackets
9220 Sunset Blvd. (#320)
Los Angeles, CA 90069

Yes
c/o Atlantic Records
75 Rockefeller Plaza
New York, NY 10019

Yetnikoff, Walter
c/o CBS Records
51 W. 52nd St.
New York, NY 10019
Record company executive

Yoakum, Dwight
P.O. Box 4003
Beverly Hills, CA 90213

Young, Faron
c/o Tessier-Marsh
505 Canton Pass
Madison, TN 37115

Young, Jesse Colin
P.O. Box 569
Franklin, PA 16323

Young, Mighty Joe
c/o Cameron
822 Hillgrove Ave.
Western Springs, IL 60558

Young, Neil
c/o Lookout
506 Santa Monica Blvd.
Santa Monica, CA 90401

Young, Paul
P.O. Box 40
London WC2, England

Young, Steve
P.O. Box 121264
Nashville, TN 37212

♪ **Your Father's Mustache Banjo Band**
44 N. Central Ave.
Elmsford, NY 10523

Yukich, Jim
3620 Fredonia Dr. (#2)
Los Angeles, CA 90068
Music video director

Yuri
P.O. Box 69180
Los Angeles, CA 90069

ZOSO
1390 Market St. (#2623)
San Francisco, CA 94102
Led Zeppelin fan magazine

ZZ Top
P.O. Box 19744
Houston, TX 77024

Zack, Eddie
(also **Dotty and Richie**)
234 Potters Ave.
Warwick, RI 02886

Zadora, Pia
725 Fifth Ave.
New York, NY 10022

Zaentz, Saul
c/o Fantasy Records
Tenth & Parker Sts.
Berkeley, CA 94710
Record company executive

Zamfir, Gheorghe
89 Bd. Auguste Blanqui
Paris 75013, France

Zap, Steve
c/o Virgin Records
9247 Alden Dr.
Beverly Hills, CA 90210
Record company executive

Zapoleon, Guy
c/o KZZP
727 S. Extension Rd.
Mesa, AZ 85202
Radio station program director

Zappa, Frank
(also **Dweezil and Moon**)
P.O. Box 5265
N. Hollywood, CA 91616

Zappacosta
68 Water St. (#407)
Vancouver, BC V6B 1A4, Canada

Zawinul, Joe
c/o CBS Records
51 W. 52nd St.
New York, NY 10019

Zebra
c/o Freefall
40 Underhill Blvd.
Syosset, NY 11791

Zevon, Warren
c/o William Morris
1350 Ave. of the Americas
New York, NY 10019

Ziffren, Brittenham, and Branca
(**Ken, Skip, and John**)
2049 Century Park E.
Los Angeles, CA 90067
Attorneys

Zildjian
Longwater Dr.
Norwell, MA 02061
Cymbal manufacturer

Zimmerman, Don
c/o Capitol Records
1750 N. Vine St.
Hollywood, CA 90028
Record company executive

Z'Looke
P.O. Box 647
Orange, NJ 07051

Zoetrope
c/o Combat Records
187-07 Henderson Ave.
Hollis, NY 11423

The Zummos
P.O. Box 118
Hollywood, CA 90078

Zutaut, Tom
c/o Geffen Records
9130 Sunset Blvd.
Los Angeles, CA 90069
A&R executive

RECORD LABELS

A&M
1416 N. La Brea Ave.
Los Angeles, CA 90028

Also:
595 Madison Ave.
New York, NY 10022

Allegiance
7525 Fountain Ave.
Hollywood, CA 90046

Alligator
P.O. Box 60234
Chicago, IL 60660

Amherst
1800 Main St.
Buffalo, NY 14208

Angel
1750 N. Vine St.
Hollywood, CA 90028

Arhoolie
10341 San Pablo Ave.
El Cerrito, CA 94530

Arista
6 W. 57th St.
New York, NY 10019

Also:
8370 Wilshire Blvd.
Los Angeles, CA 90211

218 Harding Pl.
Nashville, TN 37205

ATCO
75 Rockefeller Plaza
New York, NY 10019

Atlantic
75 Rockefeller Plaza
New York, NY 10019

Also:
9229 Sunset Blvd. (#710)
Los Angeles, CA 90069

Beserkley
2054 University Ave.
Berkeley, CA 94704

Blue Note
1370 Ave. of the Americas
New York, NY 10019

CBS
51 W. 52nd St.
New York, NY 10019

Also:
1801 Century Park W.
Los Angeles, CA 90067

34 Music Square E.
Nashville, TN 37203

Capitol
1750 N. Vine St.
Hollywood, CA 90028

Also:
1370 Ave. of the Americas
New York, NY 10019

1111 16th Ave. S.
Nashville, TN 37212

Chrysalis
645 Madison Ave.
New York, NY 10022

Also:
9255 Sunset Blvd.
Los Angeles, CA 90069

Cinema
P.O. Box 775
Bryn Mawr, PA 19010

Compleat
21 Music Square E.
Nashville, TN 37203

Also:
810 Seventh Ave.
New York, NY 10019

Concord Jazz
2888 Willow Pass Rd.
Concord, CA 94522

Curb
111 N. Hollywood Way
Burbank, CA 91505

Def American
9157 Sunset Blvd.
Los Angeles, CA 90069

Def Jam
298 Elizabeth St.
New York, NY 10012

Elektra/Asylum/Nonesuch
75 Rockefeller Plaza
New York, NY 10019

Also:
9229 Sunset Blvd.
Los Angeles, CA 90069

1710 Grand Ave.
Nashville, TN 37212

EMI-Manhattan
1370 Ave. of the Americas
New York, NY 10019

Enigma
1750 E. Holly Ave.
El Segundo, CA 90245

Epic/Portrait/CBS Associated
51 W. 52nd St.
New York, NY 10019

Also:
1801 Century Park W.
Los Angeles, CA 90067

34 Music Square E.
Nashville, TN 37203

Fantasy
Tenth & Parker Sts.
Berkeley, CA 94710

Flying Fish
1304 W. Schubert Ave.
Chicago, IL 60614

Folkways
632 Broadway
New York, NY 10012

GRP
555 W. 57th St. (#1228)
New York, NY 10019

Geffen
9130 Sunset Blvd.
Los Angeles, CA 90069

Also:
75 Rockefeller Plaza
New York, NY 10019

I.R.S.
100 Universal City Plaza
(Bldg. 422)
Universal City, CA 91608

Also:
1755 Broadway
New York, NY 10019

Island
14 E. 4th St. (4th Floor)
New York, NY 10012

Also:
6525 Sunset Blvd. (2nd Floor)
Los Angeles, CA 90028

Jem
3619 Kennedy Rd.
South Plainfield, NJ 07080

Also:
18629 Topham St.
Reseda, CA 91335

Jive
Zomba House
1348 Lexington Ave.
New York, NY 10128

Kicking Mule
P.O. Box 158
Alderpoint, CA 95411

K-Tel
15535 Medina Rd.
Plymouth, MN 55447

London
c/o MCA Records
70 Universal City Plaza
Universal City, CA 91608

Also:
P.O. Box 2LB 15
St. George St.
London W1A 2LB, England

MCA
70 Universal City Plaza
Universal City, CA 91608

Also:
1755 Broadway
New York, NY 10019

1514 South St.
Nashville, TN 37212

MTM
21 Music Square E.
Nashville, TN 37203

Metal Blade
18653 Ventura Blvd. (#311)
Tarzana, CA 91356

Motown
6255 Sunset Blvd.
Los Angeles, CA 90028

Also:
157 W. 57th St. (#1400)
New York, NY 10019

Nettwerk
1755 Robson St.
Vancouver, BC V6G 1C9, Canada

Nonesuch
75 Rockefeller Plaza
New York, NY 10019

Olivia
4400 Market St.
Oakland, CA 94608

Pablo
451 N. Canon Dr.
Beverly Hills, CA 90201

Pasha
5615 Melrose Ave.
Los Angeles, CA 90038

Passport
3619E Kennedy Rd.
South Plainfield, NJ 07080

Philadelphia International
309 S. Broad St.
Philadelphia, PA 19017

Planet
5505 Melrose Ave.
Los Angeles, CA 90038

Polygram
810 Seventh Ave.
New York, NY 10019

Also:
3800 Alameda Ave. (#1500)
Burbank, CA 91505

10 Music Square S.
Nashville, TN 37203

Private Music
220 E. 23rd St.
New York, NY

Profile
740 Broadway
New York, NY 10003

Qwest
3300 Warner Blvd.
Burbank, CA 91510

RCA
1133 Ave. of the Americas
New York, NY 10036

Also:
6363 Sunset Blvd.
Los Angeles, CA 90028

30 Music Square W.
Nashville, TN 37203

Relativity/Combat
187-07 Henderson Ave.
Hollis, NY 11423

Reprise
3300 Warner Blvd.
Burbank, CA 91510

Also:
75 Rockefeller Plaza (20th Floor)
New York, NY 10019

Rhino
2225 Colorado Ave.
Santa Monica, CA 90404

Rooster Blues
102 S. Lemar Blvd.
Oxford, MS 38655

Rounder
1 Camp St.
Cambridge, MA 02140

Scotti Brothers
2114 Pico Blvd.
Santa Monica, CA 90405

Shanachie
Dalebrook Park
Hohokus, NJ 19144

Sire
75 Rockefeller Plaza
New York, NY 10019

Slash
P.O. Box 48888
Los Angeles, CA 90048

Solar
1635 N. Cahuenga Blvd.
Los Angeles, CA 90028

Tommy Boy
1747 First Ave.
New York, NY 10128

Virgin
Kensall House
533/579 Harrow Rd.
London W10 4RH, England

Also:
9247 Alden Dr.
Beverly Hills, CA 90210

30 W. 23rd St. (11th Floor)
New York, NY 10010

Warner Bros.
3300 Warner Blvd.
Burbank, CA 91510

Also:
75 Rockefeller Plaza (20th Floor)
New York, NY 10019

1815 Division St.
Nashville, TN 37212

Windham Hill
247 High St.
Palo Alto, CA 94305

Word
P.O. Box 1790
Waco, TX 76796

Also:
Northbridge Rd.
Berkhamster, Hertfordshire,
England

MUSIC BUSINESS GLOSSARY

A&R Director. Record company executive in charge of the Artists and Repertoire Department who deals with new artists and songs, and oversees coordinating the best material with a particular artist.

A/C. Adult contemporary.

ACM. Academy of Country Music.

Advance. Money paid to the songwriter or recording artist before regular royalty payments begin. Sometimes called "upfront" money, advances are deducted from royalties.

AFM. American Federation of Musicians. A union for musicians and arrangers.

AFTRA. American Federation of Television and Radio Artists.

AIMP. Association of Independent Music Publishers.

Airplay. The radio broadcast of a recording.

Aor. Album-oriented rock.

Arrangement. Adapting a composition for a performance or recording, with consideration for the melody, harmony, instrumentation, tempo, style, etc.

ASCAP. American Society of Composers, Authors, and Publishers. A performing rights organization.

A-side. Side one of a single, promoted by the record company to become a hit.

Assignment. Transfer of rights to a song from writer to publisher.

Audiovisual. Presentations using audio backup for visual material.

Bed. Prerecorded music used as background material in commercials.

Beta. ½ inch videocassette format.

BMA. Black Music Association.

BMI. Broadcast Music, Inc. A performing rights organization.

B-side. Side two, or flip side, of a single promoted by a record company. Sometimes the B-side contains the same song as the A-side so there will be no confusion as to which song should receive airplay.

Booking Agent. Solicits work and schedules performances for entertainers.

Business Manager. Person who handles financial aspects of artistic careers.

b/w. Backed with.

C&W. Country and Western.

CAPAC. Composers, Authors, and Publishers of Canada Ltd.

CARAS. Canadian Academy of Recording Arts and Sciences.

Catalog. The collected songs of one writer, or songs handled by one publisher.

CD. Compact Disc.

Chart. The written arrangement of a song.

Charts. Weekly trade magazines' lists of the bestselling records.

CHR. Contemporary Hit Radio.

CIRPA. Canadian Independent Record Producers Association.

CMRRA. Canadian Musical Reproduction Rights Association.

CMA. Country Music Association.

CMPA. Church Music Publishers Association.

Collaborator. Person who works with another in a creative situation.

Compact Disc. A small disc (about 4.7 inches in diameter) that is read by a laser beam in a CD player. On the disc, digitized music is stored as microscopic pits in an aluminum base.

Co-publish. Two or more parties own publishing rights to the same song.

Copyright. Legal protection given authors and composers for original work.

Cover Record. A new version of a previously recorded song.

CPM. Conference of Personal Managers.

CRIA. Canadian Recording Industry Association.

Crossover. A song that becomes popular in two or more musical styles (e.g., country and pop).

Cut. Any finished recording; a selection from an LP; or to record.

Demo. A recording of a song submitted as a demonstration of a writer's or artist's skills.

Disc. A record.

Distributor. Sole marketing agent of a record in a particular area.

Donut. Jingle with singing at the beginning and end and only instrumental background in the middle.

Engineer. A specially trained individual who operates all studio recording equipment.

Ep. Extended play record (usually 12 inch) containing more selections than a standard single, but fewer than standard LP.

Evergreen. Any song that remains popular year after year.

Exploit. To seek legitimate uses of a song for income.

Folio. A softcover collection of printed music prepared for sale.

GMA. Gospel Music Association.

Harry Fox Agency. Organization that collects mechanical royalties.

Hit. A song or record that achieves Top 40 status.

Hook. A memorable "catch" phrase or melody line which is repeated in a song.

IMU. International Music Union.

ips. Inches per second. A speed designation for tape recording.

IRC. International Reply Coupon, available at most post offices and necessary for the return of materials sent out of the country.

Jingle. Usually a short verse set to music, designed as a commercial message.

Label. Record company, or the "brand" name of the record it produces.

LASS. Los Angeles Songwriters Showcase.

Lead Sheet. Written version (melody, chord symbols and lyrics) of a song.

Leader. Plastic (non-recordable) section of a tape at the beginning and between songs for ease in selection.

Lp. Designation for long-playing record played at 33⅓ rpm or a cassette containing the same material as its album counterpart.

Lyric Sheet. A typed or written copy of a song's lyrics.

Market. A potential song or music buyer; also a demographic division of the record-buying public.

Master. Edited and mixed tape used in the production of records; a very high-quality recording; the best or original copy of a recording from which copies are made.

Mechanical Right. The right to profit from the physical reproduction of a song.

Mechanical Royalty. Money earned from record and tape sales.

MIEA. Music Industry Educators' Association.

Mix. To blend a multi-track recording into the desired balance of sound.

Mor. Middle of the road.

MS. Manuscript.

Music Jobber. A wholesale distributor of printed music.

Music Publisher. A company that evaluates songs for commercial potential, finds artists to record them, finds other uses such as TV or film for the songs, collects income generated by the songs, and protects copyrights from infringement.

NAIRD. National Association of Independent Record Distributors.

NARAS. National Academy of Recording Arts and Sciences.

NARM. National Association of Record Merchandisers.

NAS. National Academy of Songwriters, formerly Songwriters Resources and Services (SRS).

Needle-Drop. Use of a prerecorded cut from a stock house in an audiovisual soundtrack.

NMPA. National Music Publishers Association.

NSAI. Nashville Songwriters Association International.

One-Stop. A wholesale distributor of records (and sometimes videocassettes, blank tapes, and record accessories), representing several manufacturers to record stores, retailers, and jukebox operators.

Payola. Dishonest payment to a broadcaster in exchange for airplay.

Performing Rights. A specific copyright granted by U.S. copyright law to protect a composition from being publicly performed without the owner's permission.

Performing Rights Organization. An organization that collects income from the public performance of songs written by its members, and proportionally distributes this income to the individual copyright holder based on the number of performances of each song.

Personal Manager. A person who represents artists, in numerous and varying ways, to develop and enhance their careers. Personal managers may negotiate contracts, hire and dismiss other agencies and personnel relating to the artist's career, screen offers and consult with prospective employers, review possible material, help with artist promotion, and perform miscellaneous services.

Piracy. The unauthorized reproduction and sale of printed or recorded music.

Pitch. To attempt to sell a song by audition; the sales talk.

Playlist. List of songs that a radio station will play.

Plug. A favorable mention, broadcast, or performance of a song; to pitch a song.

Points. A negotiable percentage paid to producers and artists for records sold.

Press. To manufacture a record.

PROCAN. Performing Rights Organization of Canada Ltd.

Producer. Person who supervises every aspect of recording a song.

Product. Records, CD's, and tapes for sale.

Production Company. Company that specializes in producing jingle packages for advertising agencies. May also refer to companies that specialize in audiovisual programs.

Professional Manager. Member of a music publisher's staff who screens submitted material and tries to get the company's catalog of songs recorded.

Program Director. Radio station employee who screens records and develops a playlist of songs that the station will broadcast.

PRS. Performing Rights Society of England.

PSA. Public Service Announcement; a free broadcast "advertisement" for a non-profit service organization.

Public Domain. Any composition with an expired, lapsed, or invalid copyright.

Publish. To reproduce music in a saleable form and distribute to the public by sale or other transfer (e.g. rent, lease, or lend) of ownership.

Purchase License. Fee paid for music used from a stock music library.

Query. A letter of inquiry to a potential song buyer soliciting his interest.

R&B. Rhythm and Blues.

Rack Jobber. A wholesaler of records, tapes, and accessories to retailers and mass-merchandisers not primarily in the record business (e.g. department stores).

Rate. The percentage of royalty as specified by contract.

Release. Any record issued by a record company.

Residuals. In advertising or television, payments to singers and musicians for subsequent use of music.

Rhythm Machine. An electronic device that provides various tempos for use as background rhythm for other instruments or vocalists.

RIAA. Recording Industry Association of America.

Royalty. Percentage of money earned from the sale of records or use of a song.

SAE. Self-addressed envelope (with no postage attached).

SASE. Self-addressed, stamped envelope.

Scratch Track. Rough working tape demonstrating an idea for a commercial.

Self-Contained. A band or recording act that writes all their own material.

SESAC. A performing rights organization.

SFX. Sound effects.

Shop. To pitch songs to a number of companies or publishers.

Showcase. A presentation of new artists or songs.

Single. 45 rpm record with only one song per side. A 12 inch single refers to a long version of a song on a 12 inch disc, usually used for dance music.

Solicited. Songs or materials that have been requested.

Song Shark. Person who deals with songwriters deceptively for his own profit.

The Songwriters Guild of America. Organization for songwriters, formerly called AGAC.

Soundtrack. The audio portion, including music and narration, of a film, videotape, or audiovisual program.

Split Publishing. To divide publishing rights between two or more publishers.

Staff Writer. A salaried songwriter who writes exclusively for one publishing firm.

Standard. A song popular year after year; an evergreen.

Statutory Royalty Rate. The minimum payment for mechanical rights guaranteed by law that a record company must pay the songwriter and his publisher for each record or tape sold.

Stiff. The first recording of a song that fails commercially.

Subpublishing. Certain rights granted by a U.S. publisher to a foreign publisher in exchange for promoting the U.S. catalog in his territory.

Sweeten. To add new parts to existing recorded tracks to enhance the sound of a master recording.

Synchronization. Technique of timing a musical soundtrack to action on film or video.

Synchronization Rights. Rights to use a composition in time-relation to action on film or video.

Take. Either an attempt to record a vocal or instrumental part, or an acceptable recording of a performance.

Track. Divisions of a recording tape (e.g., 24-track tape) that can be individually recorded in the studio, then mixed into a finished master.

Trades. Publications that cover the music industry.

U/C. Urban Contemporary.

U-Matic. ¾ inch professional videocassette format.

Unsolicited. Songs or materials that were not requested and are not expected.

Veejay. Music-video program host.

VHS. ½ inch videocassette format.

Videocassette. Tape manufactured for video cassette recorder (VCR) that records and reproduces audiovisual programs.

Work. To pitch or shop a song.